HARLEY LOCO

HARLEY LOCO

Hard Living, Hair and Post-Punk,
From the Middle East to the Lower East Side

RAYYA ELIAS

BLOOMSBURY CIRCUS
LONDON · NEW DELHI · NEW YORK · SYDNEY

First published in Great Britain 2013

Copyright © 2013 by Rayya Elias
The moral right of the author has been asserted

Bloomsbury Circus is an imprint of Bloomsbury Publishing Plc
50 Bedford Square
London
WC1B 3DP

www.bloomsbury.com

Bloomsbury Publishing, London, New Delhi, New York and Sydney

A CIP catalogue record for this book is available from the British Library

ISBN 978 1 4088 3767 2

10 9 8 7 6 5 4 3 2 1

Typeset by Hewer Text UK Ltd, Edinburgh
Printed and bound in Great Britain by CPI Group (UK) Ltd, Croydon CR0 4YY

For my mom and dad, wish they could have been here to see me finish this.

"It doesn't matter whether you get knocked down, it matters whether you get back up."

—Vince Lombardi

INTRODUCTION

I FIRST MET Rayya Elias in early 2000, in the East Village—a neighborhood that utterly belonged to her, and in which I have always been a sort of a tourist. I lived in the West Village at the time, and the distinction seems important here. Manhattan is more evenly gentrified now than it used to be, but back in those days, "East Village" and "West Village" still meant something, and Rayya and I each respectively embodied those two vastly different "somethings." I was from Connecticut, ambitiously artsy, polite, and responsible, diligently working at becoming a writer (as I had been diligently working at everything throughout my life). The West Village was filled with people who finished their homework on time, and I was one of them. By day, I dressed like a salesclerk at Banana Republic. By night, you could find me going to bed at ten p.m., with the *Atlantic Monthly* tucked under my arm. I was married to a guy from Ohio, though the marriage wasn't going well, and I was becoming depressed. So that's where I was at.

1

Rayya, meanwhile, was a rough diamond—a black-clothed, raspy-voiced, tattooed dropout of a soul, and she owned a motorcycle, and she kept pit bulls, and she was gay, and she was of Middle Eastern descent, and she'd grown up in Detroit, and she fucking loved the NFL, and she'd been to prison, and she called everyone "dude" or "baby," and she was trying to clean up her life after years of heroin addiction and decades of an absolutely Byronic free fall into rock-and-roll abandon.

So admittedly, we were not the likeliest candidates in the world to become the heartachingly, soul-warmingly close friends we are today. If we had actually *been* dudes, it would be as if James Taylor and Keith Richards had met, connected, and immediately adored each other. (Only the "James Taylor" in this case had never struggled with substance-abuse problems—so we didn't even have *that* piece of life history in common.) Here's a better way to put it: If Rayya and I were a musical duo, you could call us Siouxsie and Garfunkel.

Nonetheless, love is love. And we loved each other from the first.

I met Rayya, I should say, because I needed a haircut, and she was hustling a living by running her own little hair studio at the time, right out of her walk-up. I had been sent to Rayya by my friend Jana (a girl far cooler than me—she lived right *between* the West and the East Village, symbolically enough). Jana was sick of my Art Garfunkel hair (I'm not kidding) and had suggested that I step up my game by visiting a woman she called "a true master of actual style."

So I crossed town, to Avenue C, climbed the stairs, and met my new, dearest friend—a Syrian lesbian, ex-junkie, ex-con, ex–street hustler, Detroit-tough, giant-hearted, rock-and-roll piece of work named Rayya Elias. I don't even remember how our conversation started. She was probably like, "Dude, what's up with your hair, baby?" And I probably immediately started talking about how sad and lost I was feeling in my marriage. And she fixed my hair and listened to my woes with real tenderness, and she gave the kind of no-bullshit advice you can only get from someone to whom *every hard thing on earth* has already happened. Twice. When I left, I was a little tiny bit cooler. And a tiny bit warmer, too.

The next time I went, I started listening to *her* stories. And here's the thing, which at this point should not surprise you: Her stories blew mine away. Rayya's life's journey had taken her from an elite Syrian background, through a head-spinning childhood immigration to Michigan, to the drug-rich streets of the Lower East Side, to a big record deal (which she botched), to the world of high-end London fashion (which she rocked), to a stint in prison on Rikers Island, to a park-bench-as-home in Tompkins Square Park. She'd experienced wealth, homelessness, brushes with fame, rehab (and more rehab), a million blown second chances, a dozen broken hearts, and one bloody-knuckled, ultimate spiritual redemption. She even died once in the process, and also probably had sex with your wife at some point, back in the eighties.

Through it all, Rayya had been trying to find her own voice— not the simplest feat, when English was her third language and alienation had been her only abiding familiarity. Yet she confessed to me that she had a yearning, now that she was sober, to share those flights and passages and transgressions, to put them into order, and with grace. She was writing songs again, for the first time in years. She was making a film about the darkest outer limits of her personal history. She was digging back into her family's old exoticism and studying her childhood displacement. After a few more visits, after a few more haircuts, I told her to just get serious and write a damn book.

Here's the book. And the book is terrific.

One of the best things about it is that Rayya doesn't write like anyone else. She didn't go to a fancy school. (Forgive her; she was busy with other affairs.) I don't believe she has studied the *Atlantic Monthly*. Her writing doesn't come out on the page feeling like it was squeezed from a standard-issue literary toothpaste tube. Instead, her stories are like tough little stray creatures, born in the lowest hollows of the dirtiest street corners, which then—as you watch, breath held—fight their way to rapture. My friend Jana was right: Rayya is a true master of actual style.

I was always going to love this book because I love its author with all my heart. But you will love this book, I must say, for the same reason.

It is my honor to introduce these pages—so gravelly, so straggly, so hopeful, bright, and true.

Just like the dude herself.

Elizabeth Gilbert
New Jersey, 2012

JUST FOR STARTERS

ANOTHER EVICTION—THIS TIME, unavoidable. Kim and I had known it was coming, but we still weren't ready to be thrown out of our home, no matter how much we deserved it.

We were pathetic. Tired, sick, numb, strung out. It was 1987 and we were living on Second Street between avenues A and B.

The marshall knocked on a bright, sunny morning. I cracked the door and begged him for a couple of hours so we could pack our stuff.

We had nowhere to go: no money, no car, no real friends. I hadn't spoken to my family in over a year, and after dad asked us to leave, my relationship with my parents was strained to say the least. It was different for Kim because she was still speaking with her mom, and yet we didn't feel we could call her during an eviction. These were dire circumstances; I had to think on my feet.

I had Kim start putting our things in big black garbage bags while I ran outside to see if I could find Gary to help us. Gary was a wealthy Polish guy who managed all the new construction sites on Avenue B. He was married and had a whole other life in Jersey that he didn't talk about when he was over getting high with Kim and me, after a long day of work. We'd been friends with Gary for about six months and hung out with him when he stayed in the city. Gary loved hookers, freebasing cocaine, and hanging out with us girls.

I walked over to the construction site, found Gary, and told him what was happening. He promised to help us on his lunch break, and said he would pull his truck around and put our things in it. He also said he would drive us out to a little New Jersey motel and put us up for a couple of days until we could figure out what to do.

I was so grateful for Gary's offer, but I was also afraid of being outside the city, without transportation or a way to cop drugs—even just for a couple of days. Frankly, I was more worried about that than about sleeping with all the other homeless people at Tompkins Square Park. Anyway, I knew I had to try to hustle up some money and score enough to keep us well for the time that we would be away.

I was thinking and pacing up and down Third Street, in front of the liquor store, to see if there was someone to work. It was past the morning shift, so none of my usual customers were around.

I lit a cigarette. As I took a drag, an older seedy man, who was skinny, tall, and looked homeless—with soiled baggy pants, a stained trench coat, and a head full of matted hair—shuffled up to me and asked me for a date. That was code, I knew, for his wanting to pay me for sex.

I'd never done that before—not that I hadn't been desperate enough to think about it, but I'd always been sure I'd never have to stoop so low. Now though, I looked him up and down. He looked basically harmless. "You couldn't afford this," I said cockily, motioning to my skinny waif of a body.

"I sure can," he growled, and he pulled out an absolutely enormous roll of twenty-dollar bills. I felt my eyes widen. This was more money than I'd ever seen in any one person's hand, let alone an elderly dude who looked like this. I swallowed. "You got a place?" I asked.

"Sure do, gorgeous." He smiled, and his mouth looked like a row of abandoned buildings in the projects.

I shuddered. "Let me get forty bucks so I can get straight first," I managed, and I held out my hand, knowing he'd give it up.

"You coming back right?" he demanded.

"Of course," I said, snottily. "But it will cost you."

"Oh, I plan on it. I know you want some of this change, baby." Smiling, he pulled a bottle, inside a brown paper bag, from his pocket, unscrewed the top, and took a long swig of something alcoholic and foul. He then slowly peeled two twenties off the top of the roll. "I'll wait right here for you," he said.

I snatched the two twenties and broke into a stride to get to the Dominican's bodega. The Dominican didn't have the best coke and dope around, but he sold both, and his store was conveniently located right around the corner.

I quickly copped and came back to find the old dude waiting and rocking while drinking his poison. "Knew you'd be back," he said. "I'm Frank."

"Ray," I said. "Let's go."

We started walking west, to Second Avenue. As I followed him, I tried to think of ways to get his money without servicing him. There was no fucking way I was gonna go down on that; even the thought of it made me dry heave. Normally I would've just taken the forty and split, but today I needed the rest of that money, so we'd have a cushion for a couple of days. The forty dollars had bought me only enough to get straight for a few hours.

"How much is this gonna cost me?" he said, as we walked.

"Two hundred, no kissing or fucking."

"What?" He stopped in his tracks and stared at me. "That's some golden pussy," he said, sounding annoyed.

"Hey, take it or leave it," I said. "You can always go down to Allen Street and get some used-up, old, diseased pussy. Anyway, you're the one flashin' the money . . . unless it ain't yours," I said, trying to sound threatening.

"Oh, it's mine, alright."

We started walking again, and I knew I had him. His ego wouldn't let him back out now.

We got to an old storefront that was once a locksmith on Second Avenue. There was a key lock sign partially hanging on top of the old accordion gate that Frank unlocked. He pushed the rusty gate to one side, then unlocked the heavy metal inside door. "C'mon in," he said, and he walked into the dingy, cavernous, concrete-floored place like it was a palace. There was a couch on one side and an old workbench on the other with all kinds of stuff—screws, vises clipped on dusty warped pieces of wood, glue, and cans of old paint—scattered all over it.

"Cash first," I said, pausing at the doorway.

He counted out ten twenty-dollar bills and slapped them into my hand like I'd just insulted him. I rolled them up and put them in my bra, then walked in. "This your place?" I asked, and I sat on the stool next to the workbench and started fixing myself a hit, so we could get the show on the road.

"The guy next door lets me stay here." He closed the gate, and then I heard the snap. He had padlocked us in.

Just then, I blasted off, a huge hit of speedball rushing through my veins. *I'll figure this out later,* I thought, closing my eyes.

When I opened them again a few minutes later, Frank was gone. I looked around, and as my eyes adjusted, I saw another door near the back of the room—no doubt a bathroom.

I got up and took a look at the gate to see exactly what I was dealing with. Sure enough, after I opened the metal door, I saw a padlock on the gate.

Frank came back into the room. "Where the fuck you think you're going?" he said, and then I saw: He was holding a shotgun.

Fear jolted through me. "What are you doing?" I cried out.

"Shut the door," he said, his voice low and calm.

I did as he said, completely terrified.

"I'm a Vietnam vet, you know," he crooned.

I nodded, trying to keep my cool. "Frank, put the gun down," I said. "You don't need it here."

"You gonna play nice?" He was advancing toward me.

"Of course." I nodded, trying to smile, though I was completely freaked out, my mind spinning out of control.

He motioned for me to sit on the dirty couch, so I did. To my relief, he went back to the bathroom and closed the door again. He was probably doing coke or speed.

I was beside myself. How would I ever get out of this? Maybe he didn't even want sex. Maybe he wanted to torture someone and kill them. This guy was a posttraumatic war dude who clearly didn't have ahold of himself.

The mystery door opened and Frank entered once again, this time with a handgun. "What the fuck, man?" I asked, and I started crying. "What's wrong with you?"

"Ain't nothin' wrong with me, bitch." He stood glaring at me, his eyes wide and filled with hate. "Pull your pants down," he said.

"Put the gun down," I responded, as calmly as I could.

"I said, pull your fucking pants down!" He edged closer, shaking the gun.

"Okay!" I yelled, losing it. I was trembling—my whole body vibrating with fear. "Relax!"

"Either you gonna give me head, or I'm gonna eat pussy," he said. "You decide."

I stood up, unzipped my pants, and started to work them down with my shaking hands, taking as much time as I could without completely pissing him off, and praying for a miracle to strike.

"Hurry up!" he snapped, moving even closer.

I pulled off my pants. Frank unzipped his own, then reached in his big baggy pocket, took out the wad of twenties, and stuffed them under the couch. He then sat on one end of the couch, patted it with his free hand (the other still held the gun), and told me to sit down and lie back. When I did, he pulled down my underwear and fell toward me.

I was high, but not high enough to check out of this nightmare. A hot vacuum clutched onto my lips and began to suck me dry. It was horrible and painful, but I was too scared to move or even flinch. I closed my eyes, trying to think about anything but this as he chomped on me as if I were a fried chicken wing at the local Chinese take-out joint. Finally, I couldn't take it anymore. "Ow!" I yelled, and I pulled away.

"Shut up and let me do my thing," he growled, tightening his grip on the gun. I lay back again and tried to drift into a nod, grateful at least for his missing teeth. After a moment, I felt the coolness of the metal of the gun slide down my leg as he finally lifted his mouth from me. I picked my head up to see what he was doing. Just as I had feared, he was slowly inserting the gun into me.

As sick as this sounds (and I know how sick it sounds), the coolness of the metal was a welcome relief after the gross heat of his mouth. I lay back again, praying he wouldn't pull the trigger. And then, somehow, there was a loud knock at the door. I jumped and opened my eyes.

Frank pulled out the gun, held it up to my face, and motioned for me to be quiet.

"Frank?" a man's voice said, from outside the gate. The knocking got louder. "Frank! You in there?"

Frank quickly stood up, holding the gun behind his back and looking at the door nervously, like a kid just caught by a parent. He then walked over to the metal door, unlocked it, and opened it. A huge, much younger black dude stood on the other side. He was dressed in a running suit and sported large-framed sunglasses and tons of bling—typical late-eighties rapper style.

"What's up, Joe?" Frank said, in a subservient voice.

"What's goin' on in here, Franko?" the kid asked. "What you doin'?"

"N-n-nothin' Joe," Frank stuttered. "Just tryin' to get a little pussy's all."

"Yo, unlock the gate and let me in."

Joe kept his eyes on me. I scrambled to get my underwear up, tears running down my face as I silently tried to let this guy know I was there against my will. I wasn't sure why he'd come, but he looked clean, and if Frank opened the door to let him in, maybe I could stage my escape.

Frank moved toward the door while trying to hide the gun, but Joe saw it. He didn't say anything until Frank had the keys in the padlock and popped it open. Then he said, "Yo Frank man, why don't you go and put that away, ain't no need for guns here."

Frank looked panic-stricken as he waived the gun around. "I'm gonna fuck this bitch, and you can fuck her when I'm done." He sounded almost terrified. "Okay, Joe?"

"Sure Frank. Just go put that away and we can do whatever you want when you get back," Joe said.

Frank nervously went through the mystery door again and shut it. I tried to look for my pants, but couldn't get past Joe's menacing glare.

"Joe," I pleaded, "will you let me go?"

"I can't do that," he said, stiff as hell.

"Please Joe! He's crazy! He was gonna kill me!" I started crying again, bordering on hysterics, but Joe stood his ground, unaffected.

"I saw him hide a ton of money," I said. "Please let me go and I'll tell you where it is."

He stood quietly for a moment; then we both heard some mumbling from Frank on the other side of the door. I had no idea what the hell Frank was doing in the other room, but whatever it was, I was grateful for the reprieve.

"Where's the money?" Joe said to me finally.

I reached under the couch and pulled out the wad of twenties.

What happened next was like a dance, in slow motion, perfectly choreographed: the timing and the steps were so brilliant that only a synchronized universal miracle could have made it happen. I reached out my hand to Joe, with the money in it; he reached for the money and stepped aside, leaving a small opening; I stepped out, into the beautiful sunlight. "Thank you," I whispered, and then I was gone, leaping across Second Avenue dodging traffic, wearing only my bra, T-shirt, and tighty whities. No shoes, socks, or pants, just the hard cool pavement hitting my bare feet as they scrambled for freedom.

I bolted through the neighborhood, car horns blaring at me, to a home that didn't exist anymore. Gary and Kim were waiting for me at our building, pacing in front of the loaded truck. When they saw me, the horrified look on their faces brought me back to the absurdity of my circumstance.

"What the fuck?" Gary said, catching me in full stride as I almost blew past them. He wrapped his arms around me, trying to cover me up.

"Baby, what happened? Are you okay?" Kim had run up, too, and was staring at me with shock and concern.

"I got two hundred dollars!" I screamed in total joy, my fists in the air.

Kim looked confused.

"Get her some pants," Gary said.

ONE

I WAS RAISED in an eight-room flat in Aleppo, Syria. Marble everywhere, and long hallways that led to different rooms with balconies overlooking manicured gardens. French doors opened from living rooms and parlors to family rooms. Our furniture was a mix of French empire–style antiques, deco, and mission, making our home extremely eclectic and cool. My father prided himself on having all the most modern kitchen and home appliances.

My first childhood memory is a story that has been told in my family so many times now that I can practically re-create the dialogue verbatim. Kids often got hurt while playing, and we were no exception. It was no one's fault; accidents happened and life went on. In hindsight though, I see that this created the basic map of my evolution. I always wanted to be the center of attention, no matter what. I jumped headfirst into situations without thinking because of the excitement and chaos of the moment. I've been the outsider, and felt different and separate from people for whom I have a general mistrust. I've been a prisoner, confined in my own skin, and wanting to break free no matter the cost. In addition, I've constantly searched for "the woman" who is going to champion me and love me through and through as my mom did here when I was helpless. I'd say this incident is very significant.

★

Jump! C'mon, jump," Fayez yelled with excitement.

It scared the crap out of me but sent a thrill quaking me to the marrow. "No!" I screamed with frightened laughter.

"I'll catch you, c'mon!"

"No, I'm scared."

"C'mon, I promise. Look. Jump Samer!"

Samer, who was six years old, jumped, and Fayez caught him. Samer screamed with delight and rolled off Fayez, then ran a victory lap around the living room. He slid down onto the floor and came to a quiet giggle when he realized he was being too rambunctious and that my mom could come in at any moment, find us horsing around, and scold us.

"C'mon Maya, you too!" Fayez yelled.

Maya, who was nine, jumped, and he caught her. She leaped off him like a gazelle, squawking with delight as she circled the vast room.

"C'mon, it's okay, I'll catch you, I promise!" Fayez said to me.

"JUMP!" He put his arms out like Jesus on the cross while lying on his back on the floor. He shook his hands wildly as if they were ready for me no matter what, and he smiled that smile that only my oldest brother had. A smile so beautiful, nothing else existed. I wanted to float toward him.

He was fourteen and I was two, the oldest and the youngest, the two that would always be synonymous as opposites.

I was so scared, standing on the edge of a red-velvet empire-style couch that seemed to be taller then everyone put together. Everything inside of me said, *no don't do it!*

"Come on," he urged. "Just jump, Rayya. I'll catch you, I promise."

Everything seemed to happen in slow motion until I finally jumped, trusting fully that his loving arms would be there to catch me. They weren't. He rolled over, laughing like crazy, leaving me to land on the hard marble floor. My leg caught part of his body as he turned, and it twisted in a sick and unnatural way. And then the slap of my landing, and the shock and confusion of having been abandoned by my brother, and then the pain, like a knife stabbing through my right thigh.

I lay there, in a wet puddle of tears and snot, crying and screaming, my cheek pressed against the cold floor.

The doctor didn't put a cast on my leg. (They didn't do that in 1962 in Syria, I guess.) Instead, for two months, I lay in a crib with metal octagon-shaped weights tied to each end of a rope, used for traction to hold my leg in place. At first I sat up only to eat and, occasionally, to watch life through the bars of my little cage. But after a while, I tried to entertain myself by teasing, making faces, and mimicking whoever was there to watch and take care of me. One time one of my aunties was there to babysit me, and she asked me if I liked her new brown shoes. I told her they were the color of baby diarrhea, which made her laugh and repeat the story to my mom and everyone who came over. I loved that, being the center

17

of attention. I didn't want them to forget about me as they moved about in their daily lives. I was like the pet in the crate that would do tricks for attention.

One of the first photos I saw of myself was when I was about four or five years old. It was at my brother's first communion party and I was singing for a table of archbishops and priests with a cookie in my hand. I remember the hymn that I sang in Aramaic; it was one that Te`Te, my father's mother, had taught me. In the photo I'm in my white knit hat, white kneesocks with pompoms dangling from each side, and the cutest little white knit dress with a cardigan over it. When I look at these pictures, I love myself, and I think I look perfect and adorable. These pictures spark memories of happiness and elation at all the attention I got for singing. I was the joy of my family and the talk of the town. Maybe that's when I got bitten by the performing bug. I remember the pride and love in my mom's face as she watched me sing that song. I would always long for that attention and approval from my family, although for many years I would do everything I could to make it seem the opposite.

I adored my dad and also was afraid of him, always having to be quiet and mindful when he was home, which wasn't often. He was a very serious man who worked hard in the fields of Tal Abiad, a northern farming region in Syria, and when he was home, on break, there were to be no disruptions. I'd heard stories about my dad being out on the land for months with his men, and I remember seeing him once when he got back from his usual three-month stint and tried to surprise my mom. He was bearded and filthy and smelled like dirt; he looked like an Arabic Grizzly Adams. I remember my mother—who, having been raised with six sisters, was tidy and organized and used to living in a high-class, affluent household—yelling at him to get out of the house and go to the hotel she'd booked for him before he scared the family. She wanted him to get cleaned up and groomed and shaved before he came home so she could see the dapper man she had fallen in love with and married. (My father hadn't always been a farmer.) He teased her and chased her around the house and they laughed together, and then he left and did as she asked. Later, they would go out with friends and family and eat, dance, and romance together for the night. Then he would come home and spend time with us. He always brought us little gifts and delicious and exotic treats, like chocolates and candies from Europe. When he was home, my family felt whole. We would gather around to listen to tales of his workers and their families.

★

Both sets of my grandparents were Christians living in Turkey in the late 1800s. My mother's family moved to Aleppo just before the Armenian and Christian genocide started in Turkey in 1915. My grandfather Kayser, on my mother's side, was a silk merchant and extremely wealthy. I've heard stories that when they moved from Turkey they used a caravan of horses and buggies and had so many barrels filled with gold coins that guards were hired to accompany them all the way to Aleppo. Most people, including my dad's family, traveled the 450 miles on foot.

My father, Zachary Elias, was born in the Mardin province of Turkey in 1920. He was the first and only child (Te`Te married my grandfather, who was a widow with two kids from his previous marriage). My father's family left during the Armenian genocide in 1921. They were Syrian Orthodox and were afraid for their lives because the New Turks had taken over the region and were slaughtering Armenians and Christians alike. With many other families migrating to Syria, my grandparents took my father (when he was a little over a year old), his brother (who was eleven), and his older sister (thirteen) and joined the walking migration.

It took them almost a month to get to Damascus. My uncle Ghattas, my father's older brother, told me the stories when he was ninety-five years old. My dad, a mama's boy, was very spoiled, and on that trip—unlike most of the children, who were passed around depending on the needs of their parents—he was glued to his mother's side, whining if anyone tried to watch him until he was put back into her arms. At one point, my dad cried for so long in the middle of the night that my grandfather put him outside of the barn where they encamped for the night, in the rain (like a bad dog, my uncle said), so the rest of the families could sleep and recuperate from their long travels. My grandmother wept knowing he was cold, wet, and afraid out in the dark by himself, but she was forbidden to bring him back inside or to sleep outside with him. My grandfather stood his ground for the good of the whole community, claiming it would toughen up my father, and he was left outside until sunrise. Eventually he cried himself to sleep, while my grandmother's heart broke. I believe this event had a lot to do with my dad's rigid and stern character for years to come.

I learned lessons from him that took me a lifetime to put into practice. "Sometimes we have to be thrown into the water to learn how to swim." He told me this as he threw my first puppy (Boy) into the lake while I screamed bloody murder. "Pain makes you stronger, and nothing is too great for us to achieve, not even for a little mongrel." I believed him when I saw Boy's head come up and he swam back to me like a champ. I *was* my father's daughter—I *am* my father's daughter, and I have slung myself headfirst into many things, needing to belong. I learned from a very young age that life was chaotic, but if I could hold my breath long enough (even while kicking and screaming), and come up for air once in a while, then I would have the chance to fight for what I wanted or needed.

Most of the young men in Syria had to serve in the army when they turned eighteen, and my father enlisted and went to France during the Second World War. He was there for one year and then became the official Syrian procurement agent. At nineteen, he was responsible for all the grain that came from the fields of Syria to be sent to Europe to feed the Allied troops, which meant that a lot of money was flowing through his hands. He was a born hustler, one of our parallel traits.

My father got very ambitious or greedy; I prefer to think ambitious. He basically extorted millions of French francs from the government and set himself up really well. I don't know exactly how, because no one in my family talks much about it; unfortunately, they like to leave these things out of my dad's story. My oldest brother finally spilled a bit of it after my dad passed away. Apparently, my dad was sent to a French prison and could have spent many years behind bars, but a French general and a captain in the French army by the name of Sinclair advocated on his behalf. They liked my father; he was a real charmer. He could look you in the eye, tell you a story, and at the same time snag the pants off of you, and you wouldn't know you were missing them until he was gone and a cold breeze hit you in the ass. So they got him out of jail and sent him packing, back to Syria, never to be in charge of their grain supply, or the army's money, again.

My dad was also a renowned playboy, drinker, and gambler at that time; he earned a lot of respect and street credibility for ripping off the French, because the Syrians hated the French mandate governing their country. He was infamous within his group of wise guys and well known among the rich and cultured. Dad spoke many languages: Arabic, French, Aramaic, Turkish, German, Portuguese, and later English. He was obviously good with numbers and knew a thing or two about importing and exporting.

Zachary Elias was a tall, dark-haired, good-looking, dapper ladies' man. With the money that he'd "earned," he bought land in Syria that he farmed himself (since he now knew there was good money to be made in trading grain). When he was twenty-five years old, Zachary Elias thought that maybe he should get married and settle down.

The Kayser family was a very well-respected and well-known family. Like the Elias family, the Kaysers were Christians and belonged to the Syrian Orthodox Church. They also had come from Mardin, Turkey, during the genocide and settled in Aleppo. The Kaysers had eight children: seven daughters and one son, who was like their little king. They were known to have the most cultured, beautiful, and educated girls in Aleppo.

My uncle Ghattas knew the family well and wanted Zachary to marry one of the girls, Alice, who was a few years younger than Zachary. She was a schoolteacher at the Syrian Orthodox private school in Aleppo, and he had seen her a few times walking with her older sisters as he sat in the cafés with his boys in the afternoon, playing poker or carousing. She had smiled and flirted with him, and indeed she was a beauty. Ghattas told his brother Zachary that he would have to temper his ways because the girl's mother was not going to be seduced by his handsome face and charming manners. Basically, she was a tough nut to crack and protective as hell when it came to her kids.

Zachary was intrigued by this family and knew in his heart that he'd never met a woman he couldn't charm. He went to have coffee at the Kayser residence one afternoon, so he could ask my grandmother Rose Kayser if she would consider letting him court her fifth daughter, Alice. The day that they met is another story that I love. It has been re-created, through family lore, with dialogue, so many times now that I know it by heart. Rose invited Zachary into the proper sitting room, where only formal guests were received. She sat on the red-velvet sofa and my father sat in a chair, feeling scrutinized from head to toe, yet very sure of himself in his best suit, made to order by a famous Armenian tailor.

My grandmother was curious but perplexed about this man. Why was he so popular and talked about? Yes he was handsome, but she couldn't find the substance that was important to her; she saw only pride and arrogance. Rose Kayser had married a smart, successful, and pious family man who was widowed with four daughters. He went to church every Sunday and believed in art, culture, education, and honest hard work. This young boy, by contrast, seemed scandalous, egocentric, a playboy to whom she could never entrust her daughter's future. The stories had filtered through the community, not that he was a bad man, actually everyone who knew Zachary and spoke about him said that his heart was gold, but that he was different; an adventure-seeking entrepreneur who threw caution to the wind and enjoyed life. Rose was also familiar with his family. His mother was very well respected and so was his older brother, whom she knew pretty well.

My father cleared his throat and sat up straight. The maid, Alia, brought the Turkish coffee into the parlor with some small pastries. As a gift for my grandmother, my father, of course, had brought a box of French chocolates, which he set on the table.

"So Zachary, why are you here?" she said. "What are your intentions?"

"Mrs. Kayser, I have only the best intentions at heart." He flashed a wide smile. "I am here because I am interested in . . . "

Before he could finish, someone barged into the parlor—a girl of about fifteen who was being chased by a younger boy: Alice's younger sister and brother.

"Come back here!" Joseph shouted, pulling on her dress. "You can't go in there, Josephine."

"Who says?" the girl snapped, but she screeched to a halt as she saw her mother and Zachary sitting in the parlor with serious expressions on their faces. Zachary, intrigued by this young girl and her rebellious spirit, sprung to his feet and took a slight bow. Their eyes met and she stopped cold in her tracks.

24

Her mother felt it, saw it, and wanted no part of it. She tried to quickly hurry Josephine out of the parlor, but not before Zachary Elias said, "And may I ask who this fine young man is?"

"I'm Joseph, and this is my sister Josephine," the boy announced.

"Well, hello, Joseph," said my father. "I am Zachary Elias."

Zachary held his hand out and shook little Joseph's hand. Then, with a deeper bow and a warm smile, he held out his hand and raised his eyes to see Josephine, her loosely finger-waved light brown hair tossed around her fair, delicate features. Josephine's skin gleamed with a light perspiration, and when she looked up at him and smiled, her eyes, almond-shaped and a magnificent brown, sparkled like they were backlit. She put her hand in his and curtsied.

"Hello, Mr. Elias," she said, looking directly at him.

"Please, call me Zachary."

My grandmother cleared her throat and threw a look that the kids knew only too well. They scampered out of the parlor so fast that Zachary wondered if they were a figment of his imagination, until Joseph came back quickly and said, "Mr. Elias, I mean Zachary, is it true that you served in France in the army and that you are friends with great generals and captains?"

"Yes Joseph, this is a fact." Zachary nodded humbly.

"Joseph!" Rose Kayser said, and he dashed out of the room again. She turned to my father. "Now, Zachary Elias, what is it that you want?"

My father sat down and couldn't find the words to express his thoughts, so he was silent. He was confused and perplexed at what he felt. Everything he'd come to ask was jumbled in his head, and all he could see was Josephine's sparkling eyes and radiant smile, like the sun and the moon and the stars all wrapped up into one.

As stern as she was, Rose Kayser couldn't help but feel this man's confusion and the admiration and light that came into his face after meeting her Josephine. Quickly, as if to snap him back to reality, she said, "Ghattas said you wanted to talk about courting Alice. And the only reason you are here is because Alice wanted me to give you a chance."

"Ah yes, why I'm here," my father said. "May I ask how old your son is?"

The smile on my grandmother's face when she spoke about Joseph was indulgent and animated. "Joseph is thirteen, and Josephine is too young for you, Zachary."

"Then I will just have to wait until she is ready, now that I've seen her and met her," my father said. "I can't ask for anything else."

In the following months, flowers and chocolates came on a regular basis—not for Josephine or Alice, but for Rose Kayser, with notes praising her excellent and honorable lifestyle, impeccable household, well-raised children, and cultured background. He sent imported scotch and the best hand-rolled Cuban cigars to Mr. Kayser, and gifts for Joseph that came from Europe: little soldiers made out of porcelain, and tokens from the French military that he thought would interest a young boy. Zachary Elias became a household word in the Kayser family, even though he was not allowed to come calling. The kids were all infatuated with him, my grandfather was intrigued yet skeptical, and my grandmother was as much amused as she was disgusted by his charming ways and mannerisms. He had found a way to get under her skin.

Alice was soon engaged to a clothing merchant named Chafik, and the engagement party was to be a splendid affair, with invitations to more than 150 people. My father was invited not only because of his close friendship with Chafik, but also because of his status and his family. My uncle Ghattas was a respected official working for the Syrian/French immigration department. He, too, was invited, along with his wife, and they came all the way from Damascus—about two hundred miles from Aleppo.

It was at this event that my uncle saw the attraction between Zachary and this fabulous young woman he couldn't stop talking about, Josephine Kayser. Zachary's eyes followed her around the room as though she were the only person present. She wore a hand-beaded dress that made her soft white complexion appear ethereal, and red lipstick that made her look adult and glamorous. He had heard that she was born with a dislocated hip and had a slight limp, and that's why Rose was so protective of her, but he could see nothing but perfection when he looked at Josephine. He barely ate anything during the party, and stuck to one glass of champagne because he didn't want his drinking to get out of hand as it sometimes did. He instead stood gallantly aside and watched as Josephine danced with Joseph, then her father.

My father had begged my uncle to speak to Rose on his behalf, and after seeing how smitten my father was, Ghattas pulled him aside and asked if he was truly prepared for the task at hand. My father assured him he was. He had been around the block quite a few times, but, he told Ghattas, he had never felt this way about anyone. There was a spark of limitless potential that he felt when he looked into Josephine's eyes—a glow that mirrored himself and made him feel he could become a better man with her at his side. He could endure anything asked of him, he told his brother, as long as there was a chance he could be with this young, bright-eyed woman.

So Ghattas went to work, both at the party and during the rest of his stay in Aleppo, to persuade Rose Kayser to consider my father a worthy suitor for her young daughter. Between toasting the newly engaged couple and dancing with his own wife, Ghattas told Rose how, since he'd known of the Kayser family, he'd always hoped one of the sisters could become a part of his own family. He told her Zachary was a wonderful man; that he had lost his way for a short while but was serious and good now, and that the love and security and responsibility of a wonderful woman would change his brother's life into something so admirable that she could not imagine. He said he'd never seen his brother so smitten with someone as he was with Josephine, and that Zachary would do anything, taking any and all direction from Rose, if she would only give him the hope of one day being married to her daughter.

At the end of the evening, after all the guests had gone and only my father, his brother, and his brother's wife remained, Rose Kayser walked up to Zachary Elias. "If you stop drinking, gambling, and womanizing until year end, then you may start to court her," she said. "She will not marry until she is at least seventeen, and I expect that the drinking, gambling, and woman-izing will be in your past and not her future. Zachary Elias, you can thank your brother for successfully pleading your case and setting such a good example on your behalf. Please don't make us both regret this."

Zachary bowed deeply and kissed Rose Kayser's hand, which made her both uncomfortable and light-headed. Then he went out and drank a fifth of scotch, staying out all night celebrating with his boys.

The next day, he started his quest for the hand of Josephine Kayser. He quit drinking, which was quite a feat, as my father had a real drinking problem at that time. People didn't often use the word *alcoholic* then, but if they had, Zachary Elias would surely have been called one. But Zachary also believed in sheer will, strength, and hard work, and that if you wanted something badly enough, nothing would hold you back. He began attending the Syrian Orthodox Church, in Aleppo, every Sunday when he wasn't away farming his land. He knew this would score points, since the Kaysers played an integral part in the church community. (Joining the church also made his mother and brother very happy, as they'd always tried to push him into becoming more devout.)

Zachary fulfilled all of his promises and began courting Josephine within a year, but never without Joseph in tow. On walks and dates to the park, Zachary would give Joseph money to go and find an item that my dad knew would take time and effort. Joseph, never wanting to disappoint, would go on a "mission" and find the item, then come back, only to be sent off on another mission. My father was the perfect gentleman and cherished the little time alone that he had with Josephine, whether he was sitting on a park bench holding her hand and listening to her enthusiastic views on life, or watching her as she got lost listening to a movement of a piano concerto. He was in love.

Josephine loved art and music, and wanted to travel the world. She dreamed about Europe and America and hoped that one day she could see *Swan Lake* performed in Moscow. She thought about having children who would be well educated and highly cultured. She loved Syria, but knew there was more opportunity elsewhere for her future family than had been available to her. She felt that women should have the same chances men do, in business and art. Josephine was also an expert marksman (or woman). My father, during the courtship, took her and Joseph out on day trips to hunt birds. She would dress in khaki pants and shirt, sporting riding boots, sunglasses, and her signature red lipstick, and carrying a shotgun over her shoulder. (I saw one of her pictures from the mid-forties and just about died, she looked so hot.)

My parents were married in 1947, just after my mother turned seventeen. It was a storybook wedding, with all the postwar glamour. I have my father's custom-made wool gabardine tuxedo hanging in my closet to this day. My parents look so happy, care-free, and in love in the wedding photos that my sister has framed on her mantel. The fruits of my father's labor paid off once and for all, and the appreciation these two lovebirds had for each other was evident. Even Rose Kayser was convinced that she'd made the right choice for her daughter. The smile on her face in the wedding photos was one of pride at a job well done.

TWO

TE`TE, MY FATHER'S mom, moved in with us when I was five. No one really knew how old she was. Te`Te was a tall, strong, and prideful woman. She wore, always, a long black dress (still in mourning for her husband, who had passed away some thirty years earlier), and twisted her waist-length silver hair into a tight, neat bun every morning after brushing it for half an hour. This was the woman who had walked from Turkey to Syria in the early 1920s with three children in tow to avoid being massacred by the New Turks.

Soon after my grandparents settled in Damascus, my grandfather died, leaving Te`Te with nothing. She took jobs cleaning people's homes and put three children through private school, two of them her husband's from his first marriage. She was true and loving and very hardworking, a fierce woman with her pride as her strength protecting her pack. By the time she came to live with us she had become a bit ornery, but she still had a wonderful sense of humor. Te`Te was the Fred Sanford of my household, a good and loving ogre who pretended to hate everything. Her joy and delight were us kids and the occasional cigarette or glass of red wine.

My brother Fayez gave her, as he did all of us, a run for her money—in her case, literally. A teenager by this time, Fayez was a hooligan and the light of her eye.

"Te`Te, give me a cigarette," he would say to her at least a few times a week.

"You know I don't smoke. It is not proper," she would answer with her sly smirk.

"Okay, then give me some money," he'd insist.

"Oy yoy yoy! I don't have any money!" she'd holler in Aramaic.

"I know where you're hiding your money, and if you don't give me some, I'll take all of it."

She would curse and pray at the same time, in Aramaic, under her breath, but loud enough so God could hear that she was speaking to Him in his own language, which was the only way she thought he would listen. Then she'd run to her favorite hiding place to grab her goods and hide them elsewhere. Fayez would sneak up on her and catch her in the act, then blackmail her, saying he'd tell my dad that she was smoking, or flirting with the gardener . . . whatever it took to get what he wanted from her. (It was true about the gardener; she laughed with him while he picked our fruit, and then he'd hoist the fruit basket, tied to a rope, up to our balcony for her, with cigarettes, fruit, and other little gifts.) It was a cat-and-mouse game that Te`Te bitched and complained about, but clearly loved every minute of.

We had a neighbor who lived in our building. Audette, who was a divorcée; in Syria in the early 1960s this wasn't the norm nor was it looked upon in a positive light. My mom and Audette were good friends, so Audette was at our house quite a bit. Te`Te thought Audette set a bad example for my mother, and had no problem letting her know exactly how she felt, under her breath but audibly, and sometimes even to her face.

"EFFFF, leave her be, she talks too much and smokes too much and stays too long and she is an ugly woman," Te`Te would snort. But the truth was, my grandmother had a soft spot for Audette and really cared about her. I remember walking into the house one afternoon and finding my Te`Te comforting Audette about something. The kindness I saw in her eyes toward our neighbor shocked me. But as soon as I walked in, the game started all over again, both of them playing willingly. "Go home Audette, quit wasting my time," Te`Te said.

Audette quickly got up and brushed away the sadness. "Oh shut up, you old bat, I was just waiting for Josephine."

"Wait in your own house," my grandmother said, and with a quiet acknowledgment she waved Audette off.

I became extremely close to my Te`Te while she lived with us, and she helped me care for the pets that my father brought home for us. My dad would bring home baby lambs or rabbits and would ask me to feed them and take real good care of them, and I did. Then at the next celebration, holiday, birthday, or anything of that sort, I would see my beloved pet hanging from the tree in the courtyard of our building being slaughtered for the occasion. I would scream bloody murder and cry, and Te`Te would always console me by repeating sayings in Aramaic to me that translated into, "Someone has to love and care for them while they're here."

Or, "death is a part of life." But sometimes if I'd gotten particularly close to one of the baby lambs, she would just hold me and shield my eyes and mutter that she was sorry, and allow me to sob all over her black robe of a dress, until the buttons that ran down the front had made little marks on my face. She would then wash my face, clean the snot off her dress, pinch my cheeks, and kiss me before sending me off to the celebration.

I learned how to speak Aramaic from Te`Te (the language she loved most). She could speak both Turkish and Arabic as well, but when it came down to it, she thought Aramaic was the language of God and all the saints. I also learned how to speak French in school. I had been placed in a kindergarten class at the early age of four, and my auntie Alice (my mom's sister), who was the school principal, always put me in the first row of the class, as I was the youngest and tiniest. I had quite a mouth on me and never learned how to edit my thoughts and opinions, and I constantly got in trouble with the teachers for being outspoken. I was always getting smacked with the ruler in the palm of the hand, or made an example of by having to stick a piece of gum on the end of my nose (when I'd get caught chewing it) and stand facing the corner with a book on my head until the bell rang. Still, I loved school, and got some notoriety there for being both so young and such a rebel.

My favorite period was of course recess—it was the best opportunity to act up. I remember the way the kids responded to my devilish behavior, and how ecstatic that made me. They laughed at me and looked up to me and wanted to hang out with me, which made me act out even more.

There was one particular swing that all the kids ran to immediately when the recess bell rang. It was a double-benched swing, where two kids sat on either side of the bench facing each other and put their feet on the middle wooden bars, which were the footrest. The swing would move back and forth with four screaming kids on it, and it was a blast. I was always told, along with everyone else, to keep my feet on the footrest and not let them dangle out. I didn't think this little detail was as crucial as the warnings it had come with. So one day, when I was six, I climbed onto the swing with two boys and another girl. The teacher pushed the swing until the four of us could use gravity to lift it higher and higher. She had again warned us to keep our feet on the footrest, but I ignored her; it felt so good to let my feet dangle and wiggle and kick outside of the swing in my little white tights—plus, my friends were laughing at the pure naughtiness of it. I was laughing, too, because being naughty felt so good and thrilling. And then it happened: As we ascended, my leg got caught on the bar support of the back of the swing. The swing came back down, and my leg snapped in two places.

Again, they didn't give me a cast, but used weights and traction to set the broken bones. It was near the end of the school year, and once more—just as when I was two—I was stuck at home in my bed, weights attached to a rope chain that dangled over the side and held my leg down and still. It was the worst event and, soon, summer of my childhood in Syria. The school year ended, and my family went off on vacation to the islands without me. I hadn't really believed they wouldn't take me until the final minutes, when my mother lovingly kissed me and, weeping, said good-bye.

And then they were gone, to a summer of riding my dad's thoroughbred Arabian horses and frolicking in the sea, while I woke up every morning with my Te`Te in our house in the city: hot, miserable, and full of resentment that they'd left me behind.

Te`Te did her best with me—she tried to keep me entertained. She read to me, and told me stories of her childhood, and how she'd broken her jaw as a little girl, which is why she could never eat solid food. It was hard to believe that she was ever a child because she seemed so old. She cooked all of my favorite foods and would bring out her favorite candy, which was always wrapped in a little black silk pouch. She took such care in unwrapping these orange candies that I'd practically be drooling while waiting for her to hand one to me. I would quickly pop it into my mouth and wait for the fizzle, and then squeal in delight, as my mouth would come alive with flavor. I would then watch as she put one in her mouth and wait until it foamed out of her lips while she chuckled in naughtiness, then would quickly clear her throat and recompose herself, as if I'd forced her to do something improper that would be our secret. Once in a while she even called up to Auntie Audette to come visit, and would bitch out loud because she knew it would make me laugh. I appreciated everything my Te`Te did, but it couldn't make up for the anger I felt, and when my family came back that summer, I had turned from a fun-loving kid into a brooding, deep thinker, reading everything I could get my hands on (my favorite being *Le Petit Prince*), and experiencing life from an observational and critical perspective. They brought me back presents, but I wanted nothing to do with any of them. I was jealous, especially of the doll my sister was playing with, which was as big as she was, and could "walk." It was beautiful and blond with huge blue eyes that opened and closed. The first chance I got, I used my thumbs and my rage to poke its eyes out into little black holes. I wanted to ruin her perfection a little bit. Being bad was what *I* did best. Growing up, I always knew I couldn't be the "best of the best"; my brothers and sister claimed those positions because they were such high achievers. I think at a very young age I decided to become "the best of the worst," which seemed to attract even more attention.

★

The following year I got the two firsts of my life: we got snow in Aleppo—something I'd never seen before. We all went down to our courtyard to revel in the light, fluffy flakes. The kids in our building all raced out, and I remember running around and screaming with joy at this phenomenon. Even Phatima, the Turkish maid who lived with the people downstairs, got to come out. She was in her teens and basically treated like their slave, I think because they took her in when she was abandoned as a child. Perhaps in response, she'd always been mean and nasty to us, calling out obscenities from her window when she saw us. But when her remarks became religious slurs, as we were Christian and she was a Kurdish Muslim, I experienced for the first time the religious tension mounting in Syria.

Until Phatima called us dirty, filthy Christians and spit at my sister, I had never noticed any vicious outward bias between the two religions. Both Muslim and Christian families lived in our building and neighborhood, and we all respected one another and our differences. The older Muslim man who lived in our complex with his family had many wives and children, the wives varying in age. He was always kind to us, as were the wives, and he was extremely respectful of my mom and Te`Te, asking about my dad and the crops and constantly wishing him well. He and his family visibly prayed much more than we did, and the wives' hair was covered, but to me, that was just part of normal Syrian living. Once, I had asked my mom why there were so many ladies over there and why Fahad (one of the kids) called more than one of them mom, and she'd said that this was their custom and that the father liked to have many children and one lady couldn't take care of so many. That made sense to me, probably because it made sense to my mom, and I'd never questioned it. But then Phatima rose like a vampire and beat up my sister, calling her a *Christian* as if that meant she was a dirty whore.

When Maya came in that day, crying and battered, my mother and my grandmother were up in arms, but they didn't know how to deal with it. My father wasn't around, of course, so my brothers decided they would take care of this peasant. Our courtyard was like a basketball court, built with huge pieces of beautiful limestone. It was in the belly of three buildings and was extremely safe for us to play and ride our bicycles in, because we were protected from street traffic and strangers coming in and out. There were ledges built into the limestone that we could sit or play on, and once a year, the neighbors with whom Phatima lived spread their fresh hot red peppers on one of the ledges to dry so they could be made into cayenne. It was Phatima's job to lay them out, press, and turn them until they were ready to be ground and packed.

The night after she tortured my sister, my brothers hid and waited in the courtyard. I hid behind the stairwell, not knowing what was going on but realizing it was something big. When Phatima came out to collect the peppers, my brothers ran up, grabbed one of them, and rubbed it in her face. "This is what you get, you dirty Kurd!" Fayez yelled.

"This'll teach you to beat Maya up and call her names," Samer followed with a screech, his voice cracking. Phatima screamed and cried and ran in the house.

I was mortified at what I'd witnessed. It was scary to see my brothers so venomous toward our neighbor, even if she was the hated Phatima. The next day she came up to our home with her foster father and apologized for calling us names, her face completely swollen from the hot pepper. Her father swore it would never happen again and that she would get a beating that she would never forget. But my mother asked him to please spare her, as my brothers obviously had already made her pay enough. I was glad she said that, and I still am. I didn't understand back then why religious difference had to be a bad thing, mean and hateful and extreme. In many ways, I still don't. Nonetheless, I would soon see much more of this way of thinking and the enormous damage it could do.

Soon after all that, there began to be a frantic buzz in the air at home. I didn't know what was happening, because no one ever talked openly about anything, but I slowly deduced that we had to move. It started when I overheard my dad tell my mother that his land was going to be taken. I didn't know exactly what that meant, but I could tell it wasn't good. There was an uncomfortable tension that hung like a dark cloud over us, constantly threatening. The radio was on all the time, Te`Te hushing us if we were too loud. *Nationalization, new policies, regime,* and *class* were words I heard constantly and didn't understand, words that seemed to make my family distraught.

The tide was changing in Syria, and religion and politics were front and center. During the 1960s, the Ba'ath Party (which was Sunni Muslim) came into power. The government took over most major businesses, land, banks, and agriculture, and began to address class differences. All of this, they said was for the purpose of economic development.

My mother talked about moving to Beirut. She had three sisters who lived there, and the educational system was of the highest caliber in the Middle East. I had been there once to visit, and it was like a fantastical lush paradise, with cliffs overlooking the ocean and mountains less than an hour away from the city. Also, I loved my cousins who lived in Beirut; they were all around my age and so much fun to be with. I remember dreaming and praying that we would move to Beirut. But my father wanted out of the whole Middle East and the religious mess it was becoming. He had only one place on his mind and that was the United States. I heard him say that America would never be plagued by religious wars because they had separation of church and state, cherished their freedom, and put all their efforts into capitalist endeavors. They had no time to worry about religion.

Mom's only brother, my uncle Joseph, lived in the United States, having moved there following his successful stint of sweetly chaperoning my parents. He'd served in the U.S. Army and recently had been divorced from an American woman who was an alcoholic. (That was the first time I'd ever heard that term, and it was used like a bad swear word.) Soon enough, Joseph and my parents started the paperwork, and we prepared for the biggest change of our lives. We would move to Michigan, where my uncle lived with his two boys, and where there was the largest Arabic community in the United States, with the hope that all of us kids would get an excellent education and a chance at a life my dad knew was now impossible in Syria.

My parents planned every detail of the move: what to take, what to sell or give away, and which family relics were so indispensable that they would have to be shipped no matter the cost. Auntie Audette would come over for coffee and help my mom organize things while my father was away. When he returned, I would hear my parents whispering about my Te`te and whether she could make the move with her deteriorating health, or if it would be better for my uncle Ghattas to take her back to live with him in Damascus. I could tell by the way my father looked at his mother how torn he was about having to make these decisions, especially since Ghattas was also preparing for a move to Brazil with his family.

I remember the agony on my father's face one night as he talked to my mother in the kitchen about our future. (I was eavesdropping, curled up in a corner just beyond the door.) He was distraught and in tears, and it was the first time I'd ever seen my father show deep emotion. He'd always seemed like a monument of a man, but this night he was small and ashamed and uncertain. He laid his head in my mother's lap and said, "Josephine, what do I do? She's too old to travel with us, and we can't wait any longer to leave."

"We will wait as long as we have to, Zachary," my mother replied. "She is your mother."

I sat in the dark and cried quietly, so hard that my head hurt as much as my heart. I loved my Te`Te and couldn't imagine life without her. My mom soothed my dad and held his head and stroked his hair. This was a sight I'd never imagined, an extremely tender moment between my mom and dad, and I remember the love and sympathy I felt for them.

About a week later, at dinnertime, I went to get my grandmother up from her nap so she could come in and eat. "Wake up Te`Te," I said. "Dinner is ready."

I nudged her, but she didn't wake up; she lay peacefully in her dark room on top of her perfectly made bed, wearing her usual long black dress, her hair perfectly coifed. She looked like she was posing for death, like someone laid out in a movie, and I couldn't help feeling that she had *chosen* to leave, in order to spare my father from having to make such a hard decision. Even so, I didn't think it was possible that I'd never see her again; I kept thinking she'd wake up. People came to visit, to see her in her bedroom, and I waited in the kitchen, expecting her to come out and yell at Auntie Audette to go the hell back home. Eventually, my mom sat me down and told me not to be scared, that Te`Te would be with the angels now and would be happy. I wasn't scared, I told her; just sad, because I knew I'd never see my Te`Te again, and she was my best friend growing up.

With Te`Te gone, there was nothing to stop us from leaving, and suddenly getting ready to go was exciting and chaotic. My parents were secretive and seemed scared, frantic, and suspicious of everything and everyone. They smuggled Fayez out of the country months before we left, because he was turning eighteen and would have to serve in the army. My uncle Ghattas worked for immigration, and somehow got him out on a student visa to go and live with my uncle Joseph in Detroit. Everyone hovered over us like rock stars ready to embark on a world tour. I was seven when we finally left Aleppo and went to Beirut for one week before embarking on the flight that would take us to Detroit, Michigan, the promised land.

THREE

THOUGH THE SEVERAL physical traumas of my childhood in Syria resulted in some emotional alienation from my family, for the most part, we all did okay. Our surroundings were familiar and more or less consistent. And of course, Muslim and Christian conflicts aside, we all fit in culturally; after all, we'd grown up there.

I followed my parents around wide-eyed and watched my brother Samer, then only twelve years old, carry huge suitcases, pulling and tugging them onto the scales for international flights. I kept asking my sister where we were going and why, because I still didn't *really* get it. She was like a little recording: "To America, for a better life."

A better life? In one way, this would prove to be true. My dad's foresight about the political situation and the war turned out to be right on the money; he got us out before his two boys had to join the army and before the government took his land and reallocated it, and we all got the excellent educations that would help secure our futures.

But there were other ways that the move made our lives anything but better, at least from my point of view. And that day, when my sister kept mentioning "a better life," I couldn't help thinking, *If that's true, then why does no one seem happy?* The tortured look on my mother's face when we were climbing the metal stairs to board the plane, as she turned to see her family gathered on the tarmac waving, and smiling with tears streaming down their faces, was the same look I had seen when she left me behind for that summer at the beach: the look of pain and longing. Unfortunately, they were feelings I'd come to know myself again and again in the United States.

★

Detroit, Michigan, was a different story completely in 1967. It was a battle zone of its own, with racial riots (known also as the Twelfth Street riots) that had taken place and run rampant through the city. The "Tac Squads," which were elite, white, four-man units, frequently stopped youths driving or walking through predominantly black neighborhoods and verbally degraded them by calling them "boy" or "nigger." One Tac Squad tried to raid an after-hours bar known as the Blind Pig (located at Twelfth Street and Clairmount Avenue) because of a civil disturbance. In the early morning hours of Sunday, July 23, 1967, when they broke down the doors, they found more people than they could handle. They called for backup and then aggressively arrested everyone. The eighty-two people in the bar were having a party for their buddies, two Vietnam vets who were celebrating coming home. The rest of the neighborhood was confused and angry and started looting and burning down stores on the northwest side of Detroit. The violence spread and crossed over to the east side where whole neighborhoods were burning, and within forty-eight hours the National Guard was mobilized. On the fourth day of the city being burned down, the Eighty-second Airborne came in as well, and police and the military tried to regain control of the city. At the end, after five days of rioting, forty-three people lay dead, hundreds were injured, and over seven thousand people were arrested. Local militant leaders were emerging and preaching self-determination and separatism for black people, arguing that whites were unwilling to share the power. The fighting wasn't about religion, but racial discrimination was certainly just as potent an issue.

We rented a house out in a suburb called Royal Oak, where we were supposedly safe from all that. Our house, a two-story with white aluminum siding and a very small yard across the street from Dondero Park (where I thought squirrels were snakes, as I'd never seen a squirrel), was tiny; the rooms were so puny we lived practically on top of each other. Everything inside it was strange to us: the carpeting was that gold textured stuff that only could be found in cheap prefabricated houses in the sixties, and the whole house was badly wallpapered. It was so dingy and cramped in comparison to the home that we came from, the marble palace of Syria.

My parents' bedroom, the kitchen, and the only bathroom in the house were on the ground floor. Maya, Samer, and I slept in the moldy attic, which we converted into a bedroom dorm, with bunk beds. Every day, I remembered how my parents had talked, before we left Syria, about how America was the Promised Land. I had expected it to be extraordinary. I had dreamed of big rooms with windows that overlooked rich green gardens, and that we'd live even more grandly than we had before. Instead, this house was dark and cramped, everything seemed to be half broken, the grass in the front was yellow and patchy at best, and I knew right away I didn't want to be there.

I hadn't started school yet and I couldn't speak English; none of us could. Still, since I had loved school in Syria and been a good student, I couldn't wait to get registered, and to start meeting American kids and learning new things and this new language.

On this particular night, my dad had just gotten home and it was already dark. It got dark here so early, and it was cold for late October. We ate our dinner of layered eggplant, rice, and beef, which my mom had spent some time cooking, and then settled in to watch TV, to try to study things we didn't know about America and to help us learn English.

The doorbell rang, which was unusual since no one here seemed to know we existed. My father was hesitant at first, but when it rang again, he got up from his gold corduroy La-Z-Boy chair and answered the door, all of us piled behind him to see who it was. As he pulled the heavy wooden door open, we all gasped: Through the screen stood a gaggle of short, ugly monsters. "Wri wru wreet! Wri wru wreet!" they yelled.

I was terrified. I'd never seen anything quite like them. Worse, when I looked down the sidewalk, there were more coming, and there were also big ones waiting at the end of the sidewalk. They were shouting things at us and holding things up to the rusted screen door and yelling. "WRI WRU WREET! WRI WRU WREET! WRI WRU WREET!"

My father yelled back and shook the door like someone trying to loosen a fly off the screen. He yelled things first in Arabic and then in French, and then he slammed the big wooden door closed. Horrified, we yelled over each other trying to come up with an explanation as the doorbell rang again.

This time my father, with a grand heroic gesture, told us to all stay back and sit still, that he would take care of this. We huddled together around his chair while he went to the door and opened it, this time not all the way. Again they were all there, seeming even angrier this time; they waved and flailed their arms, hands outstretched and carrying bags of something.

My father, who was six foot one, stood up tall and yelled, "I NO SPEAK ENGLISH! WHAT, YOU GO!"

They all laughed at the big yelling man in his pajama bottoms, and then their own yelling continued. "WRI WRU WREET! WRI WRU WREET!"

My dad shook the screen door again, trying to scare them off, but the more he shook the more of them came, until they filled our entire small porch. My dad closed the door and locked it, then quickly moved my brother, my sister, my mom, and me into their bedroom in the back of the house. The doorbell continued to ring; every time we heard the *ding-dong*, anxiety hit the pit of my stomach. My father told us not to worry, that he wouldn't let the little devils get us no matter what, but I had never seen him look so confused and, frankly, afraid.

We sat on our parents' bed, huddled together, for what seemed like hours. The doorbell rang thirty-two times, I counted each one, and that didn't include the periods they pounded angrily on the door when no one answered it. I was in my mother's arms with the lights out; my dad stood guard at the door. I could see the whites of my father's eyes as they widened and squinted, trying to listen to the noises and voices of the monsters.

Then, as quickly as the storm of these monsters came, it stopped. Now it was perfectly, uncomfortably silent. My father still wouldn't let us out of the bedroom; he didn't want to take any chances. So we stayed frozen in our positions, my brother Samer on the floor, my sister and I with our mom in the bed. Finally, we all fell asleep except for my dad, who stayed on guard patrol in the living room all night.

In the morning, I'd never been so happy to see daylight, and I know the rest of my family felt the same way. My dad gingerly opened the big wooden front door, and I saw the damage from the night before. There were broken eggs covering the porch floor, and drippings dried and stuck to the rusted screen door. Toilet paper was unraveled all over the bushes and wrapped around the branches of the big tree in our front yard. The windows were soaped up with words that I only later discovered the meaning of. We were shaken and afraid to go outside. My father stepped out to see if any of the other houses were attacked, but ours was the only one.

My uncle Joseph came in that evening. We were all dreading sundown again, and were already huddled in the kitchen, helping my mom make dinner. He walked in through the front door laughing in disbelief at the sight of the house. "What happened here?" he asked.

We all started talking and telling our tales of the night before, urging him to hurry up and close the door before the monsters came and got him.

When we finally finished, he laughed so hard we thought he'd pass out. We were all stunned watching him, and I was getting really mad at him. When he finally caught his breath, he said, "Oh my god, I'm so sorry. I forgot to tell you about Halloween! They were just kids dressed up in costumes!"

"But Uncle Joseph, they were screaming things at us that we didn't understand, scary things! WRI WRU WREET! WRI WRU WREET! And they kept pushing things into the door! They were really mad and scary," I said.

He let out a huge belly laugh. "They were saying 'trick or treat,' honey. They wanted you to fill their bags with candy!"

I relaxed a little. We all did. Although I must say I was very confused, *it's just a silly American custom*, I told myself, *maybe even something I'll get to do myself someday*. But I couldn't help thinking that, even if the trick-or-treaters were doing something normal or participating in a tradition, our house was the only one egged and toilet papered. And those words soaped on the windows—*weirdo* and *fucktards* and *camel jockey*—weren't at all "normal." We were different from these people. They knew it, and now I did, too.

★

I watched my father, who had been treated like a king in Syria, give up his and our prestigious life and become just another number in a new country that was cold and callous. I watched as my mother wept for my dad because he was now a janitor, washing windows for a local furniture store until he could speak enough English to land an accounting job. My mother, for her part, became

51

a seamstress, mending the rips and tears of other people's lives as she let mine fall to the wayside.

My existence had started to become painful. I didn't fit into this new life—that was obvious. But I also became increasingly alienated from my family and my former culture. As I said earlier, my family had picked Detroit partly because it had the largest Arabic community in the United States. They had no intention of Americanizing, only of utilizing America for what it could give them while still maintaining as much of the Syrian culture as they could. So they entertained within the community, attended the Syrian Orthodox Church, and blended right in with the other immigrants. My sister who was fifteen years old loved doing everything with my parents and fit in perfectly with their community, just as she had in Syria. And my brothers were allowed to have outside friends and socialize separately from the family because they were boys. We moved into our new house, which was across town in Warren, Michigan (where all the car factories were located). Fayez moved back in with us; my parents wanted him back home. My dad paid thirty-five thousand dollars for a corner lot with a 1970s tri-level brick house on it from money he had brought with him from Syria. I loved this new place, as Maya and I shared a bedroom, and Samer had his own. There was also a finished basement that Fayez got to live in with his own private entrance and bathroom. We had a large front yard and backyard with lush green grass, a sunroom, a driveway, and a two-car garage. Things seemed to be settling in quite nicely for everyone.

In contrast, I had not acclimated so well to my family's world when I was small, partly because I was still so young, and partly because, due to my broken legs, I was often housebound with my Te`Te. Even in Syria I had frequently felt like the outsider; now, with so many choices like chess clubs, dances, and other after-school activities, I found it even harder to buy into my family's ideals and community. Yet I hadn't created a new world that worked for me, either. I was lost and confused, in emotional and cultural limbo. I didn't trust either world enough to fully engage, so I isolated myself and lived in my head, and that became my safe place. I became secretive about everything, not telling my family what was going on in school for fear of being ridiculed because I knew they wouldn't understand. They were very proud of who we were. But I wasn't.

I felt like a new breed or species that was dropped off in the center ring of a circus with expectations from the ringmaster to perform, yet with no idea about how to do so. At eight years old, with dark skin, dark hair, and dark brown eyes, I spoke no English and had a haircut—courtesy of my uncle, who buzzed my head with the clippers he used to cut his boys' hair—that made me look like a potato with bangs. The food I brought to school in a brown paper bag contained typical Syrian fare—fried lambbrains on a pita, or a sandwich of sliced lamb tongue cooked in vinegar. Yet I desperately wanted to blend in, because I loved the way this new world looked: It was colorful and active and felt so unrestricted in comparison to what was at home. My parents were so worried about money and our future that they had no time for casual activity. They spoke in hushed tones and both seemed to be tired and weary, and when I came home from school excited about things that I'd learned, they were usually dismissed or frowned upon as being silly; at any rate, never as good as the things they'd learned in Syria. Not surprisingly, I started separating the two worlds, and keeping secrets from both.

*

My mother's world—and my sister's—was a combination of the Arab community in Detroit and the fantasy world of the TV soap opera *All My Children*, which they watched when they could, without fail. They were riveted to the plots in the absurdly unrealistic town of Pine Valley—and, of course, falling in love with every man on the show—and gauged their style and fashion from the soap. After each episode, and even in between the Tide, Pampers, and baby wipes commercials, they excitedly discussed not only whether the twins were from two different fathers, or if the child begotten of rape and given away was the one stalking the town, but also the outfits that Erica Kane/Susan Lucci had sported that week. Then they bought or made themselves similar clothes. In fact, my family looked more like the people on *All My Children* than anyone I knew. My mom and sister dressed to the nines and entertained people from the Arabic community, and from our church. There were doctors who would come calling to date my sister, the children of friends from Lebanon or Syria who now lived in the United States. I, on the other hand, had no interest in looking like my family or the soaps. I was perfectly happy in a pair of jeans and a sweatshirt, watching football with my dad on Sundays or Monday night. I loved the NFL and so did my dad. "Football has the same principle as life, Binti," he would say. "It matters who you surround yourself with, and if everyone is working together, for one purpose, then you will have success." My mom and sister never understood the draw, but for me, the conversations that I couldn't directly have with my father, I got triangularly through the game of football. The lessons were precious, and the game was fierce, even if I didn't understand much English.

I pretended to hate *All My Children* even while being completely addicted to it. I would tell my mother I was watching only because it was a great way to learn English, which became my excuse to join her and my sister in viewing the most retarded, unrealistic portrayal of an entire culture I could ever imagine. Because of my rebellious nature, any time I heard my mom and sister trash a storyline, I paid more attention, and soon I found myself advocating for the drug addicts and the first daytime television lesbian love affair. I felt so much more connected to the characters who were shunned and judged and pushed out of society, persecuted for things they didn't know how to change or resolve, than to the "beautiful" ones everyone loved.

Still, it was a great way to bond with my sister and mother on the snowy days when school was cancelled. My mother would say, "Come sit, *habibty*, and watch *All My Children* with me; let's see what there is to learn today." I would mutter horrible critiques during every vignette in order to show my lack of support for the characters and for the show itself, but would still curl up on the couch, reveling in the comfort of my mother's attention and the ridiculous story lines. Many years later, in September of 2011, Maya and I were completely bummed out when we heard the show was being cancelled. It was a consistent connection that we'd had since we were kids. We watched the finale together, remembering mom, and the moments of calm from our past.

At school, between my lunches, my haircut, and my lack of English, I was a perfect target for the bullies. My clothes didn't help, either. My mom, who took pride in how she dressed her girls, sewed our clothes; she took the patterns from French *Vogue* and made them look like they'd come off the racks of Saks Fifth Avenue. Mom was so excited when she'd finish an outfit for me; she couldn't wait for me to wear it to school. Having seen what the other kids wore (jeans and sweatshirts), I was completely mortified to wear her fancy outfits, but I also didn't want to hurt her feelings—plus, I really did like some of them. One time she sewed me a leopard tunic, buying black tights, a black turtleneck, and black patent-leather Mary Janes to go with it. In retrospect, it probably would've been better suited for a late 1970s punk-rock show than for my school, but I loved it, right down to the shoes, and she was so proud of the outfit that when she got me ready that morning, she smiled so big the whole world seemed to shine.

"Look at you, *habibty*, you look like you stepped out of the magazine!" she said, beaming at me.

"Thanks, Momma," I replied. And she was right; I did look like I came straight out of the French *Vogue*. My sister and brothers also complimented the lovely job my mom had done. I left for school that day optimistic that everyone would appreciate my outfit as much as my family had.

But as soon as the Bracco sisters saw me walking to school that morning, they started following and taunting me. "She thinks it's Halloween," one of them said.

The Bracco sisters, who lived on the block just behind us, looked like Laurel and Hardy. Nancy Bracco, the big, fat white trash flunky who everyone feared, was two years older than the rest of us, but still in fourth grade. She wore her brother's hand-me-down flannels and always looked greasy, dirty, and mean. Nancy's sister, Lori Bracco, was a tall, skinny wallflower who might have been attractive if she'd ever groomed herself. She had long, stringy dirty-blond hair and big blue eyes. She followed Nancy around doing whatever was asked of her. (I think she was afraid of Nancy, too. Lori would later go on to become the high school slut.) Their brothers were known drug addicts and criminals, one of them was in jail for assault, so no one argued or fucked with these chicks; we just took their abuse year after year. The Bracco sisters would become my nemeses and cause much of my misery throughout my school years.

But that day, still a naive eight-year-old with no idea what they were saying (I thought surely they were complimenting my great outfit), I shot them a big smile. *"Merci beaucoup,"* I said.

"Mercy what?" Nancy said. "You want mercy?"

Finally, I realized that what she'd said to me was anything but a compliment. I turned quickly and picked up my pace, realizing that these were not friendly faces. They tormented me all the way to school, where they got everyone else to jump on the bandwagon. They made fun of my sweet outfit and mocked everything from my shoes to my hair. Needless to say, I never wore that beautiful tunic or those pretty shoes again.

The kids hated me and I didn't know why. I had been popular in Syria, and I wanted to fit in here, too—to laugh and have fun.

For years I tried to get on everyone's good side, but instead I became their bitch and doormat. Once in a while, to amuse themselves, they would take me in like the lambs my father used to bring home for me to feed before the slaughter. They would give me just enough attention to make me think that they finally really liked me, and then start abusing me again. Still, I fell for it every time. I had such a need to be accepted by this group of people that I would do anything, literally, to fit in.

But the teasing continued. If it wasn't one thing, it was another. I did what I could to comfort myself, which quickly became eating nonstop: I stuffed down candy, chocolate, McDonald's, Burger King, Hardee's, and cafeteria food, soon turning from a skinny little Syrian girl into a chubby American fast-food junkie. This made my mother angry and upset, but that was okay with me: At least she was paying attention. Still, I'll never forget the look of disappointment on her face when the saleslady at Sears pointed us toward the husky section for blue jeans.

"What is husky?" my mom asked.

"Overweight," the saleslady whispered, as if it were a horrible thing. I was ashamed and could feel my face turning red at the failure of being who I was in my body.

To make it worse, my mom discovered Weight Watchers and took me there to help me lose weight. There were huge, obese older women in a dank room bitching about being fat, while talking about eating constantly, and after reluctantly going a few times, I refused to return. I didn't want to be a member of a self-deprecating "old lady's" club centered around food and self-hatred; I had plenty of that on my own. Now, when I look at pictures of myself back then, I think, *I wasn't even fat. I was normal.* But I wasn't a cute girl like my sister (who I found nauseatingly girly, not to mention a complete kiss-ass to my mom). In fact, I wanted no part of "cute": I wanted to be a tough guy, to show people that I was the toughest chick out there and if they could dish it out, I could handle it.

Conveniently, my two boy cousins, who were my age, lived with us, and soon I began to take on all of their masculine traits, which I found much more comforting. I could hide under the loose-fitting clothes, and my uncle would buzz cut my hair along with his boys' so I didn't have to worry about doing anything with it. I was a fighter, a survivor; I could hang in with the best of them, and beat them at their own game.

I sat at the mirror for countless hours trying to lose my accent and sound "American," and it worked; to this day, I'm still the only one in my family who doesn't have an accent. I stopped speaking French and Arabic in public; at home, when spoken to, I always answered in English—even if just to be antagonistic and rebellious.

I wanted to bury every part of me that was different and embrace everything that would help me to fit into this new life, this cold and cruel American blue-collar existence. And I did. I buried the little girl in pigtails who, in my family passport picture, has her hand so gently lying on her mother's shoulder; the girl who once sang ever so proudly for the archbishops and the patriarch.

Instead, I became angry and hateful toward my family. I wanted nothing to do with them and their traditional foods, dress, and parties. I hated my parents and blamed them for my not having any friends. And I rejected the Syrian Orthodox Church, which I felt was a joke, now that I saw how organized religion was ripping my homeland to shreds.

Soon enough, I'd rejected so much that there was a void inside me. I became hard and began to turn to more than just food to fill that void, and to shield myself from the pain around me.

FOUR

"CHECK OUT THE backseat—it's missing," my cousin David said as he squeezed in next to me in the front of the red Corvair, sandwiching me between him and my father. It was freezing out, but the warmth of his breath so close to my ear made me barely notice the weather. "What's the shag carpeting for?" he asked my dad, as he shot me a smile and inched even closer to me.

"Deliveries," Dad answered, absently. "We are doing dry-cleaning deliveries now." By "we" he meant himself and my uncle Joseph, with whom he owned a dry cleaners. After the stint as a janitor when we'd first arrived in the United States and then a year working in the billing department of a local car-parts manufacturing company, my father, seeing the success of the cleaners my mother worked for at the time, had bought his own. His too was somewhat successful, though sometimes the work seemed to drive him into the ground.

I swung around to look, and saw a steel garment rod stretched across the back of the car. As I turned back, my chest brushed against David's arm, and a rush of excitement penetrated me.

David, one of my uncle Joseph's sons, was thirteen, two years older than me. He had light hair and fair skin with big, beautiful grayish blue eyes. He was smart, sweet, witty—and totally cool; unlike me, he'd been born and raised in America. He also happened to be living in my house at the time, as he'd come along with my uncle, who'd divorced his alcoholic wife, who lived in Dallas, won custody of his two boys, and headed for Detroit.

The car tore off.

"Dad, you can't see anything!" I yelled, momentarily forgetting about David, because the windshield was so fogged I was sure we would crash. There was a lone spot getting blasted by the defroster, but otherwise, the window was opaque with ice.

"I see enough," my father responded, breathing heavily, as he always did in the car—perhaps because he was concentrating so hard he could do nothing else.

I craned my neck over my shoulder to make sure we weren't about to get killed on our way to school. David pulled me back next to him, squeezing the back of my arm, and again I got that rush.

"Always cold," Dad muttered. "Damned ice." The car fishtailed as we swerved around a corner, and then another corner as we got on the main road. I brushed against my cousin again, and this time I felt him purposely touch my breast. It felt so good it made me light-headed—especially with my dad sitting on the other side of me. I loved the danger and thrill of acting out in front of him while he didn't have a clue.

It's not like David and I hadn't touched each other before. That past New Year's Eve—almost a year earlier, just after Uncle Joseph, David, and Tom (David's younger brother who was my age) had moved in—our parents went out and left the three of us home alone. We drank shots of vodka and watched Three-Dog Night on the *Dick Clark Show*, while showing each other our privates. Tom was content with just looking, but not David. I had thought David was stupid when he asked me to squeeze and touch his "pooky," but I did it anyway, because I saw that he liked it. All the girls at school had crushes on him, and the fact that he liked me elevated my status from an F to a D . . . so why not, I'd figured. The touching had continued all year, and by the time I was turning twelve—I was getting off on it, too.

Dad shifted gears, and the car raced down Eight-mile Road, the dividing line between downtown Detroit and the suburbs. He was clueless about what was happening between David and me right next to him in the car. In fact, he was clueless about pretty much everything happening in my life. His only concerns were the necessities: keeping food on the table, gas in the cars, and the mortgage and bills paid. Today—as usual—he was driving fast and wild, muttering that he was late for work and bitching that we had missed the bus. He was also making sure no one passed him on the road, even if they didn't mean to. He was one of those drivers who thought that everyone was out to race and beat him, so he drove aggressively everywhere. We got a kick out of watching him curse at the other drivers while they were completely oblivious to him.

"It's coming up, Dad," I said. "You need to get into the right lane."

"I know where I am," he retorted, swerving over. His brakes screeched as he pulled up to our junior high school.

But when he turned to me to say good-bye, all his gruffness melted away.

"Bye-bye Rayoochty. I love you, Binti." He said this so softly I wondered if the gentleness of his voice and kindness in his eyes, for that moment alone, would melt the frost and warm the car as completely as it did my heart.

"Bye, Daddy," I said, smiling at him.

"Thanks for the ride, Uncle Zach," David said, slamming the door. We backed away from the car, and I watched as my poor, stressed-out dad drove off into the wild winter wonderland.

★

Because of David and Tom, school was no longer the nightmare it had been for me; if I wasn't exactly accepted there, at least I wasn't made fun of all the time. The three of us hung out regularly. We stole cigarettes from the local drugstore, and smoked pot (which they'd bought from kids at school) out in the field next to our house, looking at *Playboy* magazines that David had stolen from his dad's stash. I fucking loved the thrill of being on the edge, of doing something that was not only illegal, but also mind altering. I couldn't wait to go out in the field and burn a joint so I could escape. That first rush was awesome and made me feel weightless and free. Then I'd get the munchies and eat a whole bunch of garbage—Funyuns, cheese puffs, PayDays, and chocolate—and that was another escape. What could be better?

But the fun stopped abruptly on Christmas Eve of that year. While my family was getting ready for dinner and everyone was milling about, another cousin, also close to my age, who I'd had some sexual exploration with, arrived. He came up to my brother's bedroom where I was watching *A Christmas Carol*. While Scrooge looked at his past, present, and future, this cousin and I fooled around on the bed. We never kissed, but were grinding on each other and getting far more carried away than ever before. My mother walked in while he was tea bagging and titty fucking my breasts. He was sitting on top of me, rubbing his balls on my chest while his cock went in and out between my boobs. The abrupt entrance and exposure made him quickly jump off and pull up his zipper.

I can still see the unforgettable red robe she was wearing, the huge rollers that sagged in her fine hair . . . and the look of horror in her eyes. I still remember the fear and shame I felt in the pit of my stomach when she looked first at him, then at me. "Rayya," she said, finally, when she was able to talk. "Come with me."

I sat up, pulled down my shirt, and followed her into my bedroom. I was scared shitless.

"Are you okay?" she asked, her face so white I could hardly see her features.

"Yes." I answered, looking down at the floor unable to meet her gaze.

"Has this happened before?" she asked, but I knew she didn't want to hear the answer I was about to give.

"Yeah, but not really," I replied hesitantly. "We've never done *that* before."

"What else has he done to you?" she asked, her voice weakening as she reached for my hand.

"He hasn't done anything *to* me Mom, sometimes I hold his thing really tight and move my hand up and down," I said, starting to cry because I was so ashamed.

"And that's all?" she asked. "Nothing else?"

"Yes I swear," I replied. "You're not gonna tell Dad are you?"

"No," Mom said. "As long as you're sure you're okay and nothing else happened." But she looked very distraught as I tried to reassure her that I was okay.

I was so naive, I still had no idea what the "else" was; I knew what we were doing was sneaky, but didn't really know why, as no one had ever explained it to me.

My uncle Joseph got his own apartment shortly after that, and he and the boys moved out and into a new school district. My mom wasn't taking any chances with *any* of the cousins. And that was the end of my first decent year of school; I was once again left alone to fend for myself. As for my mom and me, we never talked about that night again, but after that, I was always conscious of her watchful eye whenever Tom, David, and that other cousin were around.

The good news was that my English was getting better and better, and I was learning to camouflage myself so well that instead of standing out as a weirdo or freak, I could just disappear. In that way, I navigated through junior high. I had to look and dress like the cool kids, appease the bullies, and sneak out once in a while so I could become a bit more social and find some new friends.

I was working at my father's cleaners by then. But one day after school—amazingly, on a day when I didn't have to work—I was invited to the Bracco sisters' house after school. I was ecstatic; much as I still despised them, they were part of the cool crowd, and the invitation meant that they considered me to be cool, too. So I told my mom I was studying at the library, and Abby and I went together. Abby was my only friend, though I could never count on her to be on my side because she was popular with everyone.

When we got to the Bracco sisters' house, everyone was in the backyard already hanging out. There were a couple of cute guys there who were a year or two older and handing out pills.

"What is that?" I asked.

"Mescaline," said Nancy, the fat Bracco. She held one out for me.

"What does it do?" I asked Abby.

"I don't know," said Abby. "I think it's supposed to make you crazy and laugh a lot."

"Everyone took one," Nancy said. "*Take* it!"

So I took it, of course, like a good, abiding, I'll-do-whatever-it-takes-to-fit-in-so-please-like-me teenager. Soon enough, everyone was running around the backyard and jumping off the picnic table, yelling and screaming. I, however, felt completely normal. Soon, everyone started asking me if I felt anything. "No," I said, telling the truth.

But then the paranoia kicked in. I wasn't like them. I would never be cool. What was wrong with me? I waited a bit longer, and still didn't feel anything. I was the only person sitting on the grass, not moving around or giggling, and I felt self-conscious and stupid.

What the hell, I thought, and I got up and started jumping off the picnic table, yelling and laughing, even though I still felt absolutely normal. I couldn't believe there was so much hype and paranoia around taking mescaline, if this is what it did (or *didn't* do), but at least now I was having fun and letting loose, and I was glad to have bonded with everyone over it, glad to be having fun, finally.

The next day, feeling like I'd finally connected with people—especially the bullies—I was excited to go to school. But as I passed the railroad tracks where the burnouts and druggies hung out and smoked cigarettes before school, a sea of people parted for me with sneers and jokes. "Ah ha, you fuckin' dumb ass," someone yelled out from the crowd.

"Freak!" someone else yelled.

"She got high on aspirin!" yelled a third.

I looked for Abby—my only hope for a friendly face. She was standing, straight-faced, with the bullies who were smiling and pointing at me.

★

The joke had been on me: to see if I would lie and run around like a stupid fool and act crazy just to try to fit in.

"It was mescaline." It came out *muscaleen*; my accent botched the word because I was upset.

Everyone laughed and imitated me.

"You're too much of a pussy to take real mescaline," the fat Bracco sister said.

They knew exactly how to play me and push my buttons. I'd show them who was a pussy. I was so upset it was like someone punched me in the gut and left me with no breath or voice to argue. What's sad is that I didn't realize then—and not for a long time—how obvious it was that I didn't need drugs to have a good time.

I took the dollar Mom had given me for lunch that day and walked over to the dude I knew was the drug dealer. "A hit of purple mescaline, please," I said. He handed it to me, and I swallowed it dry, right in front of everyone.

Oh boy, did I feel the difference. I laughed so hard during math and English, I practically peed in my pants. In chemistry lab, I watched the flames of a Bunsen burner turn unimaginable colors. By the time I got to Mr. Sage's humanities class I was peaking. But rather than get me into trouble, he just laughed. He was an old hippy who knew that most kids were experimenting with psychedelics. He taught me so many things about art and music, but most of all, that day, he taught me how to relax and breathe. "Turn down the noise in your head and just experience," he said. "Use your senses, your right brain." His cool-cat voice washed over me.

All day, I bragged to everyone about how high I was. In return, all eyes were on me to see if I'd lose my cool or step out of line. I guess there were bets that I would freak out before the day ended and wind up either busted or in the hospital on a perm-a-trip. But none of those things happened; I just had a really good time, though by the end of the day I was exhausted and ready for the ride to end. After work at my dad's cleaners (until seven), I came home and went to bed, not eating dinner or doing any of my homework.

The next day at school was a different experience than I'd ever had there. For the first time I had earned street credibility—not because of my cool cousin, but because of what I had done. I was christened into the club of psychos and constantly asked how I was able to handle classes on my first trip without freaking out. I loved the attention, the instant status; I was finally tough and cool in people's eyes. I'd also found something that allowed me to check out of my body and go on a journey of the mind without having to think about my reality, or my body. That something was mescaline.

After that, I used my lunch money every day to buy hallucinogenic drugs—mescaline or acid—that I'd drop in the morning. Abby and I would walk to the tracks and buy the flavor of the day: acid, mescaline, and sometimes THC. After school, she worked at the cleaners with me, so we spent quite a lot of time together and became close, especially since I was now kind of cool. The Bracco sisters had lost credibility when they'd bet that I'd freak out that day. I had won that battle because of my will to survive and my toughness, which would become my modus operandi for the rest of my life.

Still, that day didn't solve all my problems. For a long time around then, I had had my eye on one of those cool 1970s saddle-colored leather jackets with wide lapels and a belt that was attached on both sides. It was very expensive and I knew we couldn't afford it, so I offered my mother a couple of my paychecks to help pay for it and asked her to please consider how

great it would look on me. A week before my fourteenth birthday, we went to Hudson's to try it on again, and it was gone. I
was so bummed out I almost cried, but I consoled myself by
saying we couldn't afford it anyway.

But on my birthday I opened the present my mom had wrapped,
and there in the box was the leather jacket. I don't think I'd ever
felt such a surge of love and gratitude for my mom as I did on that
day. I wore the jacket to school the next day and didn't take it off
once. Everyone complimented me and asked where I'd gotten it,
even the really cool fashion chicks. Hudson's was a big deal then
and I was so proud that my jacket came from there.

On the bus home, I was basking in the aroma of new leather
and the glory of spring when I smelled a wretched burning and
heard laughing behind me. I turned around. The left side of my
leather belt was on fire. I quickly beat it with my hand and put it
out while everyone laughed; at the end, it looked like a charred
piece of jerky, the tip of it crisp and hard. Then I saw the Bracco
sisters laughing, and I realized what had happened: Lori Bracco
had lit one side of my belt with her cigarette lighter. I couldn't
hold back this time. Without saying a word, I punched that bitch
in the face as hard as I could.

The bus driver stopped the bus and threw us off, and then I got
the shit beat out of me by the bully sisters. But it was worth it,
because I'd given Lori Bracco a bloody nose she'd remember for
the rest of her life.

When I got home, I was shut down and quiet and wanted to
quickly wash up and hide my jacket. My mom happened to be
home that afternoon and saw the state I was in. "What happened

to you?!" she asked, her mouth dropping, and her arms reaching out for me.

That was too much. I began to sob, and I didn't stop for over an hour. I cried for myself, for my jacket, and for how disappointed Mom must've been to see it ruined after she'd spent so much hard-earned money on it. I cried for everything, while Mom held me and rocked me and told me not to worry. Then she took the leather jacket, grabbed her sewing scissors, and disappeared into her sewing room. When she emerged, she was holding the leather jacket like a prized possession with its reconstructed belt.

"See *habibty*? No matter what happens in life, we can take a new shape and be better." She smiled and held the jacket up as if it were a work of art, hiding how deeply saddened she was by my experience. She'd have been even sadder if she'd had any sense of the reality of my life.

By the end of eighth grade, I was getting high on a daily basis and was known as one of the hardest, toughest drug users in junior high. My favorite bands were Pink Floyd, Led Zeppelin, the Rolling Stones, Jethro Tull, and Yes. This was music I could get lost in and disappear into—a spiritual journey that only rock and roll and psychedelics together could form. I had finally found a language that was universal—a connection to my peers, which broke down all the culture barriers that had before stood in the way. It meant everything to me to have this common ground. I snuck out whenever possible after my parents went to sleep, and crept back in after I'd gotten fucked up with everyone. I knew every creak in the stairs, and how to avoid the squeak from the sunroom door opening, and every quiet step it took to get to the downstairs bathroom, where I'd hide my pajamas so I could put them back on later and sneak back to my bed.

My parents could see that something had shifted within me, that something had died behind my eyes; they just didn't know what it was. So in 1974, after we'd become U.S. citizens, they decided that I should go back to Syria and visit for the summer. I would stay with my grandmother Rose Kayser who lived with my auntie Alice and her husband Chafik. I would spend a couple of weeks visiting family in Aleppo, and then go to Damascus to see my dad's side of the family. Finally I would get to go to Beirut and spend the last few weeks with my cousins (who were the coolest out of everyone) on the beach and in the mountains.

Of course, I didn't want to go. I was fourteen years old and hated everything Syrian; also, I had no interest in leaving the crew of hardcore burnout "friends" I'd finally accumulated. I'd gained credibility, and didn't want to lose any momentum. But they gave me no choice. Off I went for the summer, fighting it with every breath I had.

I was miserable in Syria for the first two weeks, but then as I unwound, I really enjoyed it. I reconnected with my Sito' (my grandmother Rose on my mom's side), my cousins in Damascus, and went to Beirut and spent some time by the sea. It was a bit scary sometimes, because at night, we would hear bombs exploding in the distance, and my cousins would be talking about the war that was starting and what they would do if it reached the city. I didn't really think it was that serious, because they moved through their daily lives and never allowed it to distract them.

One night, one of my older guy cousins picked us up in his Fiat and drove us to a disco club in the mountains. My first thought was that maybe I'd find some drugs, as I was boasting that I'd done them before. My cousins were a bit freaked out and said they thought I was lying. But when I found some hash and smoked it in front of them, not really asking for their approval, they were shocked and said they believed me.

Nothing had changed when I got back. The mean girls were still mean; Abby was still on the fence, one day my best friend, the next day siding against me. And I was still taking all the crap. So I dove right back into the drugs I'd been doing, getting high on acid and mescaline all the time, and loving it. I was no longer smart in school; my grades had dropped, but I really didn't care. I called in for myself when I skipped school, which was all the time. I mimicked my mom's voice and accent, telling the school secretary that "my daughter Rayya" was sick with a cold or the flu, and she believed me. For once, the accent I had fought so hard to lose worked in my favor.

FIVE

KURT WAS THE hottie in high school who all my friends wanted to fuck. He had shaggy, sandy colored hair, hazel eyes, and really cute crooked teeth, kind of like David Bowie's back in the day, before he got his veneers (which to me look like a row of perfect, white, refrigerators lined up next to each other at the appliance store). He also was becoming my good friend, maybe partly because I wasn't interested in him in that way. Instead, I had a crush on his friend's older brother Jim, who looked like Elton John. (I was in love with Elton John.) Jim was interested in two things: drinking, and having sex with whomever he could.

I spent the last two years of high school chasing Jim and trying to get him to notice me. But he only wanted me when he was drunk or high, and even then, not all the time. I didn't really care that I was usually the last resort. I would wait around until the end of the night, and if he hadn't gone off with whatever blonde bimbo was around (one of them almost always managed to leave with him), I'd make my move to try to get him to make out with me, flirting suggestively or rubbing up against him, and sometimes, the fact that I was the last one standing next to him at the end of the night was enough for him to leave with me. I was still pretty innocent sexually; I knew some people were having sex, but I was afraid of it, and the only girls I knew who were fucking were considered sluts—not something I needed to add to my repertoire of already bad reputations. Anyway, on the nights I snagged Jim, we'd go off into a dark corner and make out, and when it got heated, he'd feel me up, playing with my boobs a bit. Then, near the end of the night of Kurt's graduation party, our big "affair" finally happened.

By then, everyone else had hooked up except the two of us. Seeing my chance, I took Jim by the hand and led him out to my 1968 Le Mans that I shared with my brother. In the car, we made out for a while—our usual—and pretty soon things started to get hot and heavy. But then he unzipped his pants and pushed my head down for a blow job. The Moody Blues's "Tuesday Afternoon" was playing on the eight track, and I tried to think about the lyrics rather than the fact that I had someone's cock—even Jim's—in my mouth. But it didn't work. I gagged, stopped, tried again, gagged again, and finally pulled away for good, almost throwing up in his lap. He was pretty drunk—we both were—but not too drunk to be pissed that I couldn't follow through. He gave me a look of total disgust, then pulled up his pants, got out of the car, and stormed off. We never kissed and barely spoke again.

Still, I had Kurt, my good friend whom I partied and hung out and drove around and laughed my ass off with. I wasn't thinking about college or studies or anything that my parents constantly nagged me about. In my mind, I was lucky to even be graduating. I begged and pleaded with my father to allow me to go on my senior class trip, and for weeks he didn't budge. I convinced my mom to fight on my behalf and promised her that I would be an absolute angel if only I could go to Daytona Beach with my school. After all it would be chaperoned so what harm could be done? She succeeded and my dad caved.

For our senior class trip to Daytona Beach, like good budding addicts, we celebrated with drugs. Kurt and I bought a gram of cocaine. Neither of us had ever done coke, and the thought of this glamorous drug was exciting, intriguing, and dangerous. We plotted how we would do it, the ritual of it drew me in.

The white powder was pretty, sparkly with a pink glow, and contained a few little rocks that glistened when they rolled away from the pile. But all in all, I wasn't impressed; it looked like a heaping tablespoon of fine sugar with lumps; not nearly worth the hundred bucks we'd paid for it.

"Do we have to do little bits at a time?" I asked, because that's what I'd heard, but Kurt just shrugged and made the pile into four big lines, each weighing about a quarter of a gram. Neither of us knew what the hell we were doing; if we had, we'd have made the gram last all night.

"Do you want to go first?" he pulled out a twenty-dollar bill and rolled it up into a tight little tube.

"No, I don't know what I'm doing. You go first."

Obediently, Kurt bent over the mirror, put the bill up to one of his nostrils, and pushed the other nostril closed with the index finger of his free hand. Then he snorted while running the tube over the line of coke; it disappeared, like a dust ball sucked up by a vacuum cleaner. His face was red as he came up, and his left eye was tearing. "Whoa!" he said, and quickly sat down, holding his chin up and closing his eyes.

It was my turn. Nervous and excited, I took the bill out of his hand and did exactly what I'd seen him do. I inhaled hard to make sure I got every bit of it.

This was the first of my romantic relationships that started (and ended) with drugs—different people, different drugs, but always the same outcome. The sensation of escape and release (into someone else) became inextricable for me at some point, and it probably started with Kurt, who was to become my companion for the next six years.

After soaking in the aftermath of the second line, I wanted to move. I needed to leave the confines of the room. "Let's go dance somewhere, I want to move to some music," I said.

Kurt had planned a walk on the beach, so I left him and walked to the nearest beach club, where I let loose like I'd never done before. For the next two hours, I swirled on the dance floor, alone, not giving a shit about anything. I had never felt so happy and unrestricted; my body seemed weightless and moved every which way I wanted it to, and I had absolutely no inhibitions.

When I'd finally had enough dancing, I went up to the bar and ordered a Harvey Wallbanger and drank it right there while I flirted with the drummer of the band, who was on break. He wanted me to meet him after he got off work. I told him I would, but I didn't mean it; I just wanted to say yes to everything at that moment. But after a while, at the bar, the coke started to wear off, and I felt the heaviness in the air again. The humidity was intense, and what was balmy and lovely just a little while earlier felt thick, sticky, and dirty now. I walked back to the hotel slowly, had another beer, and lay in bed going over the night frame by frame. I was exhausted and content.

The next day I was fried; I hadn't slept well and kept waking up to drink water. When I finally got out of bed, my legs were sore and felt like they did when I was in traction. Everything was blurry and badly lit, and all I wanted to do was to eat a greasy burger and fries and fall back into bed. But I got up and dragged myself to the beach with a couple of girls from my class, hoping I'd be able to rest in the sun for a bit. After I'd been there about an hour, I heard a car engine nearby, and opened my eyes to see Kurt's convertible rental Jeep inches from my head; he'd driven right up to me on the sand. "Hey Ray, you wanna go have some lunch?" he asked.

★

After graduation, Kurt formally asked me out on a date. We were hanging out in the parking lot of a local park one night playing night Frisbee. When I was ready to leave, early as usual, he offered to drive me home because my friends weren't ready to go yet. Kurt pulled up to my house and leaned in unusually close.

"I wanna take you out Ray."

"Cool, is there a party coming up or something?" I answered, feeling a little bit awkward, as he'd never looked at me that way before.

"No, I mean on a date," he said. "Would you go out on a real date with me?"

"I'd love to Kurt, but I can't, my family doesn't allow dating."

"Hmmm . . ." he calmly answered leaning back slowly, "maybe they need to meet me."

I was shocked, and wasn't sure what a real date meant, except that maybe he wanted to have sex with me. I was nervous about it, but I wanted to go. I liked him as a friend, of course, and had always thought he was hot, and the thought that he liked me in that way made me like him even more.

I had always lied to my parents about everything, including school events like roller-skating parties or dances. I had to, as they basically did not allow any social activity that was outside of their circle of friends. So I would tell them I was at the library, or at my friend Abby's house studying, and even then it was sometimes a fight to get them to let me go out at all.

And it got even worse after one particular night. My mom had come to pick me up at the public library when it closed, at nine, but I had been hanging out in my friend's van with Abby and lost track of time. When we finally pulled back into the library parking lot—me jumping frantically out of the sliding door of the airbrushed van called the Dragon Wagon—my mom had been waiting there for a half hour. I'd never seen her so upset with me—especially when three of the guys leaned out the window to yell and wave good-bye and Abby ran back to the window to give the guy she was dating a huge kiss.

"Bye baby," he yelled after her as she sauntered to my mom's car.

"Later Ray Ray!" The other two waved as the van took off.

I knew I was in trouble, and begged my mom not to tell my dad, but that night, not a chance. She told him the minute we got home, and for the first time ever, he slapped me across the face— just once, and honestly, I can say that it hurt him more than it hurt me. I was pissed, but I barely felt anything because I was high. He, in contrast, was sick over it for weeks.

After that I was pretty much forbidden to go anywhere. That's when Kurt asked me out, and as much as I wanted to go, I told him that dating was impossible. But he was determined, and he started coming over every other day or so to try and hang out. I'd shuffle him off when my parents were home, but he said again that he wanted to stay and meet them.

Finally, I introduced him as a friend from school who'd stopped by to say hello. My father was polite enough to shake Kurt's hand, but all the while giving me a look of death. I couldn't help being a little amused as Kurt bore the brunt of it with my dad, who yelled in a thundering voice, in Arabic. "*Ma bissir tjibbi subienne al beit!*" You're not allowed to bring boys home! My mom was more tolerant though, and actually said hello to Kurt in English. Then she turned to my dad, gave him a glaring look, and said, "*Mahlesh Zachary, ma ishbo shi hal wallad.*" It's okay Zachary, this kid doesn't look so bad.

Kurt remained undaunted, and his determination fueled my rebellion toward my family: I was so tired of having to constantly lie or fight with them, and I wanted to see what I was missing in life. So I decided that if my dad didn't scare Kurt off, he was a keeper. He was so understanding, and so patient . . . different from anyone I'd ever been friends with. He wanted to hear about the intricacies of my family, and he really wanted them to like him. Finally, after he'd come around for a good two months, my mom surrendered, and let me go out on a date with him.

I was eighteen by then, and had graduated from high school; this was my first real date. It was late in the summer, and Kurt took me downtown to the waterfront festival in Detroit to listen to live music. It was unbearably hot and muggy that night and after having a couple of cold beers, he asked me where I wanted to eat.

"Big Boys!" I replied quicker than I should have, but I was craving one of those famous burgers.

"Really?" He smiled, reached out, and took my hand.

I was uncomfortable, and not because he held my hand, but because he was smiling and looking directly into my eyes. I felt like he was mocking me, so I quickly let go of his hand and barked. "Yeah why, is that a problem?"

"Not at all toughie, I love the food at Big Boys, I just thought you'd want something fancier." He sweetly took my hand again, but I was uncertain and didn't give it up. Anyone who had ever smiled at me that way before had usually tricked me into believing they were sincere, then shit on me afterward. I didn't trust Kurt enough to believe that he wasn't secretly laughing at me.

"C'mon" he said, "Big Boys it is!" He clutched my arm and started walking me toward the car.

At the restaurant, we sat in a tacky booth opposite each other. I was nervous because I had heard that when you're out with someone who's paying for dinner, you're supposed to wait till they order, then order something less expensive than they did. I wanted the hamburger platter, it was my favorite thing there, and I was hungry. Kurt ordered the Big Boy platter, then looked at me to see what I wanted.

"I'll have the same," I said.

He smiled that same way that had made me so uncomfortable just a bit earlier.

"What is so funny?" I said with a hard edge.

"I love a girl who eats like I do!" he responded, and his eyes were so sincere that I knew he wasn't joking or making fun of me. I knew I really liked this guy. He was interested in me, and not just because he wanted sex or to get high and drink with someone; but he was actually attracted to me.

In my entire life, I'd never felt desired. His attention made me feel special and sexy, and I loved it. He seemed to appreciate everything about me that other people had made fun of my whole life. He loved my big boobs and the few extra pounds that I carried. And I loved those butterflies in my stomach when I thought about him touching me.

Still, I made him wait for months before I had sex with him. I needed to make sure that he wasn't playing me. It was hard for me to trust that after we had sex, he wouldn't leave me the way he had other girls. I didn't want to end up on that list of casualties. I was also a little scared to have full-blown sex because I was made to believe that sex was a bad thing unless you were married. I knew this wasn't true, but deep down, I wanted to be in love with Kurt before I gave myself to him on that level.

I did try to give him head in the meantime, but, as I had with Jim, I got dry heaves. Unlike Jim, though, Kurt was patient and compassionate, and never made me feel bad about it.

I finally lost my virginity to Kurt on my uncle Joseph's living-room floor. It was my cousin's birthday party, so I had a good reason to spend the night there, and none of the adults were around. We did it after everyone passed out. I bled all over the tan carpeting and spent the early hours trying to clean the stains before anyone woke up and saw them. Having sex for the first time was the most painful experience I'd ever endured, including my two broken legs; it was a searing, tearing pain that moved through me and kept burning my insides for hours. It was a violent invasion of my body and I hated it.

Kurt, on the other hand, couldn't wait to do it again.

He told me it would get better, and he was right; after the first few times, it didn't hurt anymore. In fact, it actually felt good for the first few minutes until I was numb, and then it became dull and boring. I would lie back and wait for Kurt to have a good old rodeo of a time, and then I would throw him off like a dirty blanket. I never got what the big deal was, why people talked about sex as if it was some earth-shattering experience. I never had an orgasm with Kurt; I didn't even know that I was supposed to. And I hated the mess he made on my stomach when he pulled out and came, and the dirty sock he used to wipe it up.

"Why do you have to do that?" I finally asked him, after the third or fourth time.

"So you don't get pregnant," he said, looking surprised and yet so tender.

"I thought we were supposed to use a rubber for that," I said, a little annoyed, but sweetly enough, hoping he would get the message and spare me this gross aftermath from then on.

He finally bought a pack of condoms. But on New Year's day, parked by the gravel pits, we fucked in my Le Mans, and the rubber broke. When I missed my period a few weeks later, I was terrified that my parents would find out, and afraid to tell anyone about it. I went to a local clinic and peed in a cup, only to find out a couple of days later that I was pregnant. There was no discussion with Kurt about this, I knew what I had to do, and he didn't try to talk me out of it. We were both on the same page. Kurt took me to the local abortion clinic and paid the hundred and fifty dollars, and they gave me a Valium, told me to relax, and put a vacuum cleaner–like tube inside of me. I wasn't at all sad, in fact it was one of the easiest decisions I'd ever made. I was totally stressed out having to coordinate the procedure between taking off work from the dry cleaners and lying to my parents, but mostly I was relieved that I didn't have to face the shame I would've been made to feel from my family for having sex before marriage.

If I didn't enjoy sex with Kurt before I got pregnant, after my abortion, it was even worse; for one thing, I was neurotic about getting pregnant again. I went on the pill, and made him use a condom anyway. But I kept doing it. The good little Syrian girl who still lived inside of me reminded me that I had made him wait for six months before having sex with him, so now I needed to reward him for his patience. But also, I wanted to hold on to him: because he was a hot commodity, and because my parents were actually getting used to having him around. They had finally made peace with my dating someone, and the fact that he sucked up to them didn't hurt his chances of being welcomed into the family. Kurt knew how to make himself indispensable. He started helping my dad with everything, and soon he was working for him at the dry cleaners, too.

I had enjoyed Kurt much more when my parents didn't want him around; now, I hated how ingratiating he had become toward them. I knew that in their eyes, because he wasn't Syrian, he would never be good enough for me, but I also knew that my parents wanted me to marry—the sooner the better—to settle me down. They really liked Kurt, and were utilizing him, taking advantage of his kindness, for their own purposes, even if he was American— and I hated him for not realizing that. The more comfortable he got within the confines of my family, the more I lost passion and respect for him. Our relationship turned stale. Kurt became subservient to me as well, and I became distant and uncompromising. Finally, in what I can only think of as a desperate attempt to save us, Kurt asked me to marry him. When my mom tried convincing me that Kurt was a great guy, I knew something had to change.

SIX

BUT NOTHING DID change, really. Kurt continued to hang around, and I continued to treat him alternately like an annoying little brother and the good friend/boyfriend he was and would continue to be for many years to come. He and I went to small clubs like Paychecks or Lillis in Detroit all the time, to listen to music, see great bands, dance, and party with friends. We were getting into punk-a-billy, a new genre that blended 1950s rock-a-billy with punk rock. The guys looked like a blend of Elvis and Johnny Rotten, and the girls tried to look like fifties pinups. I never fit either category, and had to find a happy medium, so mostly, I looked like a gay rock-a-billy boy.

One night while I was drunk and hanging out in the bathroom of a club, a kid walked in, pulled out a pair of clippers that he'd nicked from home, and asked me to give him a Mohawk. I thought it was a strange request—I didn't know the first thing about cutting hair—but I was drunk enough to play along, so I plugged them in and went to work. When I'd finished, I stepped back to observe. Lo and behold, I'd birthed my first kick-ass Mohawk at the age of twenty.

I was so thrilled about my newfound talent, that just before I got my associate's degree from college, I quit and signed up for beauty school. Kurt and I had enrolled at Macomb County Community College together, right out of high school, but I hated it. I couldn't really concentrate on biology or algebra anyway, nor was I very good at them, and though I had taken a couple of piano and performance classes—two things I generally liked—I hated the material they made us play, and it was hard for me to read music, since I'd only ever played by ear. I enjoyed my psychology and social science courses—I loved to observe people and their behavior—but Kurt and I skipped most of our classes anyway and hung out in the parking lot, in his van, snorting cocaine and playing cards. Sometimes, we got so toasted we'd forget to go to work at dad's cleaners.

But most of the time, thankfully, we remembered, and with the money I made there, I enrolled in the Sybil Beauty School. It was the cheap, not-so-cool school for hair in Detroit, and was the opposite of glamorous. The teachers were old and so were the clients: seventy-something ladies waiting for a three-dollar haircut, which included a shampoo and blow-dry, and for an extra fifty cents they could get a blue, pink, or purple rinse. These were ladies who got their hair done once every week—or two—and then waited to see how long the hairdo would last. The higher you teased and sprayed their hair, the better they liked it. I remember one woman who came in and told me her hairdo had lasted an entire month. Gross! That's when it was time to get the disinfectant, plug your nose, and put on the rubber gloves in order to shampoo them. It was great for the students because we didn't have to feel bad if we messed up their hair; basically, they'd signed up for it.

Rosie was a rough-and-tumble, old-school Italian lady who we nicknamed the Hawk because she was in charge of everything including the dispensary. She seemed to have eyes everywhere and always knew what was going on at all times. Rosie had a disdain for fashionable, thin, and pretty girls. She was four foot nine on a tall day and always had a cigarette hanging out of her mouth; you could find her by following the cloud of smoke that floated around her. Brooks, my beauty school gay boyfriend, was hustling part time to pay for school. He also had a sugar daddy, an older married man, who paid for an apartment around the corner from the school. Brooks looked like a Ken doll, always perfectly tanned, usually dressed in a pressed suit and tie, or a sweater combo. He had dirty blond hair that was parted on the side and brushed back to create a duck tail at the nape of his head, never a hair out of place. He was sarcastic and hilarious, and we hit if off right away.

I didn't care if Sybil's was old school; I just wanted a license to cut hair. I knew I was good at it. Like music, doing hair came easily to me; I felt the natural flow and went with it. I was excited for maybe the first time in my life about being good at something that I enjoyed, something that was creative and alternative. When I worked on my mannequins at school I'd always receive praise from the teachers about the unique flavor of my cuts.

"You're a natural artist," Miss Virginia, one of the instructors would always say.

It felt natural when I had scissors in my hand, and used them like an eraser to take away all the unneeded hair and leave the exact shape that I wanted to create. It was effortless for me, and soon I had people from the clubs coming over to my house for avant-garde haircuts that I would create especially for them. Kurt, I'm afraid, got the brunt of some of my "experiments gone wrong," sporting a few bad cuts while I worked out the details to bring out the best in facial features.

One night Kurt and I decided to go out to a large dance club we'd heard about called Clutch Cargos. Everyone had been raving that it was the best new wave club, and we wanted to see what it was all about. I danced in a corner with Kurt to the song "Don't You Want Me," by The Human League, trying to mimic the new wave and punk rock kids who looked comfortable in their pirate-looking, new romantic threads—ruffled and billowy oversized white shirts, belted at the hips. Some with small vests, massive amounts of dangling beads and bracelets, wearing really cool tights and pointy boots—sweating up the dance floor. I was still in my punk-a-billy phase, not used to how slick these people were, and trying out this new style of music and dance. It was so interesting to me; the music was strong, electronic, and edgy, yet still so melodic. I'd been into rock and roll my whole life and then, just a year earlier, had fallen in love with punk, and then punk-a-billy. But this new wave music was different. Everyone at the club looked so icy and cool, and androgynous; I was confused and excited, and felt like I was on the set of a Fellini movie. That's when I saw Sofia for the first time. She was cool and detached as though she were the only person on the dance floor. Her hair was sensational, bleached to a stunning white blond and cut with precision and perfection—an asymmetric, razor-sharp swing-line bob that fell just below her left ear and brushed her right shoulder as she moved her head to the beat. She looked like one of those northern Italian models: blue eyes, skin that seemed naturally tanned, features exquisite and delicate. Her hair swooshed across her face while she danced, making her appear even more mysterious. She resembled Deborah Harry, the lead singer of Blondie—the hottest chick in the punk rock/new wave world at that time.

Now, at the beauty school two weeks later, the door to the classroom opened and Rosie, who gave the tour of the school to the not-yet-signed-up students, stood in the doorway. You could tell by her scrunched-up face—a look she usually reserved for a smelly permanent wave—that she didn't like the girl she was introducing. When she said the girl's name: "This is Sophia Gross-a-Nelly, guys," she growled, with her gnarly smoker's voice.

"That's Grasselini," a confident voice corrected from behind her, and then Sophia Grasselini walked into the room, and I thought I would die and sing a thousand songs to the angels. *It was her!* The Debbie Harry clone from the club!

Sophia scanned the room, then gave me a nod of recognition and a short smile, which I quickly acknowledged.

"Wow," Brooks smiled, then made a purring sound. "She's a hot kitty!"

"Yeah," I replied, trying to be cool.

"You think she's gonna sign up?" Brooks elbowed me.

"I hope so," I said.

"Pick up your jaw honey, you look simple," Brooks added while shooting me a smirk.

I quickly snapped to and started working on my redheaded mannequin, unfortunately shredding her hair into a raggedy shag.

A few weeks later, when they introduced the new class, I checked the room to see if Sophia had enrolled. Sure enough, there she was, wearing an off-the-shoulder, black-and-white striped T-shirt, black pants, and red pumps. What's more, all the guys were talking about the hot new chick with the great haircut. I kept my mouth shut, but I stepped up my game, coming to school every day dressed like I was going out to a club. I didn't know why I was so excited about this girl, but Brooks did; he knew right away that I had my first girl crush, and he pestered me constantly, saying, "Are you *sure* you're straight, Rayya?"

"Of course!" I answered, again and again, and I believed myself; I had no idea why I felt such a pull toward Sophia. But I made sure we became friends, approaching her to say hello and mentioning seeing her at the club. Since most of the people at Sybil's wouldn't be caught dead at a punk rock/new wave club, we bonded instantly.

Pretty soon, I made myself available to her at every turn. She was a couple of years older than me, and because she was popular in the punk/new wave underground music scene, when I was introduced through her, I was welcomed with open arms. Her friends were wild, exotic artists and musicians. They were gay, straight, and bisexual eccentrics whom I loved immediately. What's more, I—who'd never really fit in anywhere before—was absorbed by this crowd and scene quickly and seamlessly. I looked forward to dressing crazy, sometimes even wearing my dad's blue paisley pajama bottoms rolled up and belted, combined with large thrift-store tweed jackets, scarves, and bangles. I went to Sophia's hairdresser, Barry, and got my own version of an asymmetric short haircut that I could flick into my face to cover one of my eyes, which made me look cool and sultry.

We were going out to the clubs, dancing and mingling with the bands that were performing. The music was fresh and upbeat and I wanted to be a part of it. I made Kurt, who'd never cared much for that scene, come with me to the parties and shows. I dressed him up and gave him some really cool haircuts, as I was getting really good: spiky with really short bangs so he looked like a singer in a punk band, I sometimes even colored his hair red or black (people said he looked like Joe Strummer from The Clash). He complained at first that guys were hitting on him, but he got used to it fast and soon he actually appreciated the attention he got from everyone.

★

I had always felt like I was special, or unusual—an artist, maybe a musician—because I had a hunger for a completely different kind of life than the one I'd been raised in, and a longing to fill some cavernous hole of need inside me. Now, though I'd barely played music before (there was the singing as a child and the half dozen piano lessons, the few music classes in college), I started dreaming that I could be in one of those bands on stage. The music scene had been mostly punk rock, which was guitar driven, loud, antifashion and style, very rebellious music without melody, just raw energy. The Sex Pistols were well known for not being able to play their instruments, yet they moved us to oblivion with their antiestablishment rants and anthems. Iggy Pop and the Stooges, the Ramones, and The Clash were some of the other bands that ruled that genre. But electronic new wave was making a big push and I loved it because it was melody driven, with syncopated droned bass lines, and keyboard parts that were layered and textured. I loved being able to hear the crisp vocals, sing along, and dance to the beats. I went to Bookies, the City Club, Clutch Cargos, and St. Andrews Hall, and saw bands like Ministry, Bauhaus, U2, Duran Duran, Flock of Seagulls, and Orchestral Manoeuvres in the Dark. These new bands looked more like the people I hung out with. They had bleached and dyed hair that was either teased up or cut into various asymmetrical shapes, and they wore loads of makeup. The boys were very effeminate and weren't afraid to flaunt their feminine-styled clothing, with billowy shirts, fringed vests, and lots of jewelry. Bands like Blondie, Siouxsie and the Banshees, the B-52s, Patti Smith, and Nina Hagen featured gorgeous, strong, and unapologetic female vocalists. Just as music had influenced fashion in the previous decades—the fifties, sixties, and seventies—this was the 1980s, my time, and I was enamored with both the music and the look. They allowed me to escape; with no rules or boundaries, I could express myself and be part of an underground culture that accepted my newfound ambivalence toward being "normal," and make cross-gendered sexuality look cool. Instinctively, I got it. Everything about this genre spoke to me, and it was the first time and place in society that I felt cool and accepted by gentle, intelligent, creative, and like-minded people. There was no judgment like there had been in high school with "friends" who just tolerated me. These people were actually drawn to me, and were interested in who I was and what I was doing. I'd found my clan, my own pack of wolves.

I rented an electric piano and started teaching myself how to play. I listened to records over and over and practiced until I nailed the songs. My favorite tunes to emulate were "Enola Gay," by OMD and "The Low Spark of High Heeled Boys," by Traffic.

Soon I got tired of mimicking the songs and playing alone. A couple of Kurt's friends from high school were getting together and playing covers by the Stones and Crosby, Stills, Nash, and Young in their basements. Kurt, as always supportive of me, asked if I could join in, and they said yes. I wasn't very good, but they didn't care because they had no aspirations of becoming anything other than a basement cover band, smoking pot, and trying to figure out how to play "Heart of Gold." It was fun for a little while, but since I practiced extremely hard while still living with my parents, I soon found that each time we got together, I played much better than I had the time before. And after a while I felt that I needed to step up our game.

So I started inviting my basement band over to jam when my parents had dinner parties. I'd lure them with the promise of great food (my mom was an amazing cook), and in turn, my mom's Arabic friends got a form of live entertainment. It was a wonderful exchange for everyone. My mom would spend days in the kitchen preparing stuffed eggplant, grape leaves, kibbe (ground lamb and bulgur), ouzi (lamb over rice with toasted almonds), and all kinds of wonderful side dishes, sometimes with help from my sister, who had married a sweet guy, a doctor, and lived nearby. At the shows, we had a list of songs that we would play over and over in the sunroom, and my mom's friends would pop by once or twice during the evening and interact with us, making requests for songs in Arabic that we had no idea how to play. I loved the attention we got and the look on my parents' faces when their friends clapped for us to play another song. They lit up and were so proud of me, and that made me so happy; it had been so many years, I thought, since they'd felt that way about me.

At one of our practices, I suggested that we try and write our own songs. The boys thought I was nuts, and shortly thereafter they stopped inviting me to play. I know they didn't like a chick coming in and taking over the rehearsals; it was their little dudes' club and they wanted to keep it that way, and I think I intimidated them with the notion that we could actually become something more serious.

Mostly, though, I just wanted to play. I loved the feeling of being transported by a melody I was creating, and of being in the midst of the sound and energy of a song. I wanted to learn how to keep a beat and rhythm, so I started using my mom's pots and pans as drums, pounding dents into them in the process. Finally, fed up, she gave me fifty dollars so I could buy a used drum kit. It was a red Slingerland—snare, base, high hat, and tom-toms. I set it up in the sunroom. Soon I'd taught myself to play to Aerosmith's entire *Dream On* album.

I saved more money, still working at my dad's dry cleaners part time, and by experimenting on club kids for twenty dollars a haircut in my parent's basement.

I was really good at creating new looks for people. Once I got the scissors going, I entered a zone where I was completely at ease, where everything flowed like water through my hands. I had a confidence that I'd never had anywhere else. My new friends and clients loved what I created for them and would boast about my talents, which made me more popular at the clubs.

I bought an old Rickenbacker bass and amp, which I set up in my rehearsal space in the sunroom. My mom and dad thought it was crazy, but they liked the fact that I was passionate about something, and that I was doing it at home. I returned my rental piano and bought my first synthesizer, a Moog, and a Roland drum machine, which I loved because I could get electronic string or drum sounds and wasn't limited to just piano. These instruments produced a layered sound, eliminating the need for other musicians to play with me. My music was like a blue light with fog—it was moody and thought provoking, yet always had a great hook. First I'd create a beat on the drum machine, then I'd link that to a keyboard bass line that would continue to pulse so you couldn't help but move to it. I would then play a keyboard melody on top of the pulsating beat and sing the lyrics I'd written. I didn't completely understand how I was making this music, but somehow, when I closed my eyes and laid my fingers on the keys, I was able to translate my feelings into sound: I could write my deepest thoughts, put them to a melody, and make something beautiful. It gave me a freedom I'd never felt before, and music became my best friend, my greatest escape, my therapy, and my most beloved inspiration. It didn't matter to me whether it had "correct form," or if I played with two fingers or ten to create the sound that I was looking for. I projected the melody that was uniquely my own. The music that came out of me was beautiful experimental expression: electronic sounding, emotionally fueled, and different from anything I'd ever heard. I'm sure that my Syrian heritage (as much as I tried to deny it) had something to do with the sound I was creating, because my melodies were chromatic and Middle Eastern. Yet they still maintained the electronic sound of the eighties.

I was determined to one day play at the clubs that I loved. So I went on a search for talented, like-minded people and talked to different musicians about starting a band. First there was a photographer named Jim, who I met at Clutch Cargos, who only wanted to play hard-core punk. Since I was mostly a keyboard player, and hard-core punk rock, which is guitar based, wasn't geared to using keyboards, that didn't work out so well.

After Jim, there was Jarred, who was very talented but also very depressed. He brought over a beautiful, gay Cuban boy named Roger, who was a singer. When Jarred took charge and named the band Gone Morose, I knew it was time to shift again.

Roger and I were mostly on the same page. We rehearsed together and, together, named our band Kill Pig (which didn't last very long). I wrote the songs, programmed and sequenced all the bass lines, drum machines, and keyboards, and played behind a wall of synthetic sound, and Roger sang. Well—he whined and screamed most of the time. We had a blast together and sounded good with a handful of songs that I'd written, but we knew we needed more: another dimension and some fire to take us out of the typical, wimpy, new romantic sound of the 1980s. I wanted to add guts to the music, to make it more dangerous.

One night Roger called me and asked me to come out to meet this guy. "He's one of the coolest drummers ever," he said. "His name is Kory Clarke."

My mouth dropped. I knew Kory; he was a popular punk-rock kid, a few years younger than me, who played a mean set of drums. He usually hung out outside of Bookies, the ultimate punk-rock club in Detroit, because he wasn't old enough to get in; he'd sit outside with his drumsticks and drum on the sidewalk. I had always loved his energy; he was tough, loud, wiry, and absolutely gorgeous, with style like I'd never seen before. His head was shaved, except for two bright purple ponytails shooting straight out from the top of his head. He wore crazy psychedelic clothes— not popular back then, but on him you would've thought they were the newest trend.

Kory and I hit it off right away. He was an amazing and ferocious drummer and a wonderful addition to the band, and his energy was infectious. Our first show was in the afternoon outside of a community art college. This was a defining moment in my life in many ways; it was my first real gig, with a receptive audience that also included my first groupie—none other than Sophia.

I'll never forget that initial rush of being on stage. When we got behind our instruments, I was nervous, I'd never played in front of a real audience. As I gazed out into the crowd, I saw people looking up at me and waiting to see what I'd do, so I clicked my preprogrammed drums and bass, then looked over at Kory and gave him the cue. Instantly, he erupted into a thundering tribal beat that layered right into the synthetic drones that floated from my boards. He pumped out an energy that was primal and the audience exploded, their heads bobbing to the music. I swayed to the beat and played the hooks, rhythms, and melodies that I loved, and Roger twirled on stage as he sang and screamed the lyrics to "Crawler," our first song. When we stopped, the crowd yelled and applauded. It was incredible: They were my peers, and they understood and appreciated what we were doing; there was a connection between the audience and us, and the music we were making was it. The audience moved closer to the stage, smiling and yelling for us, and I fucking loved it; I wanted to play my heart out for them.

I closed my eyes and swayed to the beat of my own melodies, and for that half hour, I escaped to a place that I would love and long for for many years to come: the stage. I felt like anything was possible on stage, that I could step out of my biography and my history and create the person who I wanted to be.

Kurt was there, supportive as always and acting as my personal roadie. After the show, he left to take the equipment back to the house, and Kory, Roger, Sophia, and I went out for drinks at Chi-Chi's, a local Tex-Mex restaurant. We drank margaritas, ate a little, and got hammered, reliving every song that we'd played and how well they'd worked, or not. Then we started plotting a game plan for our next show, until we were too shit-faced to talk anymore. When I finally left, Sophia came with me.

We stumbled to my little yellow Fiat, got in, and slammed the door. Then she grabbed my face and looked into my eyes. "I've been dying to do this," she said, and she pulled me to her and kissed me so deep and hard that I felt my head spin, like Linda

Blair's in *The Exorcist*. When she stopped, I was speechless and felt a warmth flow from my lips all the way down and between my legs.

I quickly looked around to see if anyone in the parking lot had seen us, as Kory and Roger were leaving in their own car. But they hadn't. I sat back, feeling the pounding heat in my body and trying to decide what had just happened and how I felt about it. My first reaction was shock, and then anger. I wanted to push her out of the car because I didn't understand what was going on. But I didn't; instead, instinctively, I moved in close and kissed her again. The ache that I'd always felt in the deep, hollow pit of my stomach was being caressed, and in the following moments, the world made sense. And suddenly I got it: *This was the feeling everyone was talking about!*

We mashed face all afternoon in my car. This was a taste, I thought, of what was possible if I pursued music: I could not only have everything I wanted but also things I hadn't even *known* I wanted. I dropped Sophia at her house that evening and continued home with a feeling of undeniable truth. I had arrived: I was finally alive inside my skin. I'd never experienced this feeling before, and I wanted to hang on and never let go. At home, I got into bed with rock and roll in my heart and Sophia on my lips.

I could hardly sleep that night; I lay in bed reenacting every moment of that glorious day. In the morning, I woke up exhilarated and dying to call her. I couldn't eat anything, and I felt my heart pounding out of my chest, I was so excited. My mom asked how the show went, and I gave her a blow-by-blow breakdown of everything, except what happened with Sophia of course. I called Kory to tell him, but he was still sleeping, so I went out to my piano and played for a while, as that was the only way I felt I could really translate my feelings into reality.

I couldn't wait to talk to Sophia and see what had sparked this and how long she'd thought about it. We hadn't really talked in the car, only made out. Now, I wanted to make plans with her for that night, too.

At ten on the dot, I grabbed the phone and punched in her number. She answered on the first ring. "Rayya!" she said, right away, and then, "Please don't tell anyone what happened yesterday, okay? And it can't happen again."

I was stunned. "But why?" I managed, and I felt my heart sink into my stomach. "Because I'm not like that." She said it so matter-of-factly.

"What is that?" I asked. I had no idea what she was talking about.

"I'm not a *lesbian*," she said.

"Me neither!" I said, quickly. "I have a boyfriend!"

"Great." She sounded relieved. "Then we don't have to talk about it again?"

"Sure. No problem," I said, but a part of me was destroyed. I didn't understand how she could have felt so passionate about me yesterday and now seem to feel absolutely nothing. Was it just at that moment, after a great show, that she'd been attracted to me? Was it the alcohol she'd drunk? How could this be wrong when it felt so right?

And was *I* "like that"? Was *I* a lesbian?

It sounded like a bad word—and I didn't quite understand why, because we hung out with gay people all the time. But they were all men, I realized. So why was it that when guys are gay it was attractive, even charming, but "lesbian" sounded appalling to me?

Obviously, I wasn't ready to come to grips with the word *lesbian* yet. But I also couldn't shake the feelings that I had for Sophia.

SEVEN

SOPHIA PLAYED A good game when she was sober, but when she drank she wanted me, and she let me know it. I couldn't get enough of her, and I didn't care if she only wanted me when she was drunk. I did whatever I had to do to get close to her. At the bars, I'd buy her two-for-one drinks until she loosened up enough to allow herself to be with me. I played this game really well. If you were fucked up and unavailable, then you were the one for me.

Kurt had no idea what was happening, because I maintained my sexual relationship with him. Our relationship had been strained for eight months, and going out (and by going out, I mean making out) with other friends had become normal for me. As long as we saw each other one or two nights a week, he was happy. I had no idea what was happening to me either, and became agitated and depressed. This was good news for me musically: It made me write lyrics that were more meaningful and searching, and helped to elevate the intensity of the music to frenetic climaxes, complex rhythms that helped me soar to places that I couldn't reach in the reality of life. Kory and I dropped Roger; he wasn't singing melodies the way I'd written them. I had finally found my voice and liked it, so I took over the singing. Our new name was Outskirts of Blue and we were a force to be reckoned with. We were a two-person powerhouse of sound and melody, both very androgynous, and together incredibly dynamic. I loved the escape from reality, loved the club scene and getting to live through the songs I wrote, and being popular and adored. I made the clubs my home because I felt seen and understood by the friends that I'd made there. Our common thread seemed to be that we were all misunderstood by conventional society, whether we were gay, straight, punk rock, new wave, or a mix of everything; being at the clubs, together in this scene, seemed to make life make sense.

I started working at Heidi's Salon in Bloomfield Hills, a very affluent suburb of Detroit. Heidi was a Lebanese woman who was an entrepreneur in the business and was opening many high-end salons all over the country. She wanted hairdressers who had a reputation for being forward thinking and edgy, which is why she'd hired me to work for her in the first place. I started assisting for a busy hairdresser named Jasper, who loved the fact that I looked different and was in a band. Four days a week I would shampoo his clients, put on their color, blow-dry their hair, and take care of his every need. I would also tend to his clients while he ran out to screw someone's wife on his lunch break or pick up some cocaine if he needed a little upper. He let me use his chair in the evenings and on the days that he wasn't working to build my own clientele. I sometimes also used one of the two empty chairs in the back that were meant for overflow, or as our unofficial office for small meetings with managers or senior hairdressers. I tried to clock in as much time as possible because I loved being around creative people and learning as much as I could. At first my customers were only club kids and family, but soon I started building a clientele that was a combination of club kids and high-society women. These "normal" ladies loved me because I was different and unusually stylish. It was funny to see a pink Mohawk stepping out of my chair only to be replaced by a woman with a Dorothy Hamill, highlighted wedge. One thing I found quite fascinating very early on, was that it didn't matter who the client was, all women wanted to feel and look beautiful according to their own standards. Also that most people had their own insecurities, no matter how rich or good looking they actually were. My clients came in and explained to me what their idea of glamour was, and showed me photos, either of themselves during a time in their lives when they were happy, and looked great, or of an actress or model they wanted to emulate. I realized then that my job consisted of much more than doing hair. I became their confidant, their therapist and friend. I was the sounding board off which they bounced private thoughts and feelings, and I realized that even though I was having a tough time figuring out my own life, I had the tools to provide them with what they wanted on all levels. All of the experiences behind the chair helped me to create lyrics that were touching and universal.

Our first huge gig was reopening an old famous gay club in Detroit called Tod's Sway Lounge. A promoter, Sterling Silver, asked us to play opening night, when two well-known club kids, Michael and Billy, were getting "married." The wedding would be a spectacle, and it was something Kory and I were very excited to do. I was wearing my dad's 1940s gabardine wedding tuxedo, my makeup was white, and my eyes were painted with tons of eyeliner. My lips were red and smudged, and my hair was teased up: I looked like Robert Smith, the lead singer of The Cure. Kory had on a vintage 1960s tie-dyed dress, his ponytails were let out to feature his mane of hair, dyed back to blond and falling over his face in an undercut bobbed style. He had heavy turquoise eye shadow on, with fake lashes, and looked like a hot sixties model. When we stepped out onto that big stage, the crowd went wild. I took the classic "Here Comes the Bride" wedding song and reworked it into a fist-pumping anthem for us kids who felt like rejects—with hard-hitting drums and powerful synthesizers, it was masterful, droning, robotic, yet melodically inspiring as well as moving and emotional. I loved it so much that I used it as our signature opening song for every set we played from then on.

Sophia had started dating a guy, but she and I had our stolen evenings without the boys, when we'd get drunk and be "intimate" with each other. I always wanted more from her than she was willing to give, but I also liked the fact that I didn't have to identify my feelings, or categorize them as anything more than "having fun." For a while everything moved along seamlessly with my dual careers of music and hair, and most of the time I felt like I was on top of the world.

But after a while, I couldn't shake that underlying need for *more* that it seemed I'd had my whole life. I wanted to be loved by someone who inspired me, I needed sexual expression, and I was looking for a bigger stage. Soon I realized that being in Detroit wasn't gonna do it on any level. I couldn't pry the cage open there and come to terms with a sexuality that I didn't understand myself; I needed space from Kurt, my family, and most of all Sophia, because she couldn't give me what I wanted. I needed to move, preferably to another city far away. But in the culture I came from, an unmarried woman of twenty-three didn't move out of her parents' house, let alone out of the state. It wasn't even a topic up for discussion or consideration.

Still, I was determined to leave. I'd visited New York City with Kurt the year before for a few days. It inspired feelings in me that I didn't know existed. I'd never dreamed that a city could have so much character and energy. It was a living, breathing, microcosm of the world and I wanted to be sucked into it. The streets were vibrant, and the unapologetic nature of the people made me feel comfortable. I was anonymous, yet a part of something huge. I knew what I wanted to do, I'd never let my force of will run so wild, and I couldn't allow my parents to bind me—and soon enough, I found my way.

Every once in a while Heidi would stop by the salon to check in with the staff, and I approached her about a transfer. One day she asked me to come into her office. I was super nervous because I was still a fairly new hairdresser, working in an upscale semiconservative salon. I looked a little like Boy George in the way that I wore loose Japanese-inspired clothing, lots of beads and belts, and makeup that was usually very heavy but flawless. My hair was black and, depending on my mood, either teased up or smooth.

Heidi on the other hand used little makeup, had an accent, and usually wore elegant and expensive suits. Her hair was dark brown and cut into a Vidal Sassoon–like bob.

"What is on your mind, Rayya?" she asked, always pronouncing my name sharply like my own family did.

I took a deep breath, my palms were sweaty and my hands were clenched, but I made myself say it.

"I was wondering if you're opening any places in New York City," I said, "I'd really like to move."

"But this is the best salon around here, and you're doing so well," she said, looking genuinely concerned.

"I want to move out of Michigan." I lowered my gaze to the floor, ashamed of saying it, and expecting to hear a disappointing answer.

"Hmm," she said, "give me a haircut now and let's see how you do."

"Sure!" I said, completely surprised that she would ask me, with all the hairdressers at her disposal, to give her a haircut. I knew it was a test, and as nervous as I was, I was up for it. My dreams were on the line now, and as I've done so many times in life, I was willing to give it my all. I attended to her as though she were the only woman who existed on the planet. The other hairdressers were watching as I shampooed her hair, and meditated while giving her an extensive scalp massage. My inner mantra was, *I am the best, I am the best, I am the best*. Whether I believed it or not, I said it over and over to myself until she was prepped and ready for my chair. When she got in it and I put the cutting cape on her, the salon manager came up to us.

"What's going on here?" she asked, as I'm sure everyone else was wondering.

"Rayya is cutting my hair," Heidi answered directly.

I beamed nervously but didn't say a word and started to comb her hair.

"What are you thinking about for your cut?" I asked.

"I'd rather know what you'd like to do," she answered.

"I'd like to give you an edgier version of your haircut," I said, "to update it a bit so it has sharper lines."

Heidi asked what I meant by sharper lines, so I went on to explain that I'd use a straightedge razor (which no one was using then) to break up the bulk and give her a choppier look. She was a bit skeptical, but very interested in my technique. She asked where I'd learned it, and I explained that I had found my father's straightedge razor from Syria, and decided to use it to cut because my first pair of beauty-school scissors weren't very sharp. She was intrigued and agreed to my suggestions so I went to it. I was nervous at first, but after taking my first couple of snips, entered into my cutting zone, which was always a comforting, safe, and fun place for me to be. I could feel the other hairdressers watching from the corners of their eyes while working on their own clients. Once in a while I'd hear, "oh that's looking great." I didn't pay attention to anything but this haircut. This was my audition to the future and I wasn't going to mess it up. I cut her hair into a perfect A-frame, razor-sharp bob (short in the back, longer and pointed in the front) and blew it out perfectly. I swung the cutting cape off her shoulders and handed her a mirror to inspect the cut.

She looked at it from every angle, scrutinizing the way it fell after swinging it around for a full two minutes. Then, she finally spoke. "I have two salons opening in Connecticut, if you're interested; I'm going to need an art director over there soon."

"Where?" I had no idea where Connecticut was on the map.

"It's forty-five minutes outside of New York City," she said. "Stamford, Connecticut."

"No way, forty-five minutes outside of New York?" I said, "Heidi are you being serious with me?" I was shocked, and scared all of a sudden because it felt like this could actually happen.

"If you want to go, Rayya, then yes, you can have the job." She was so matter-of-fact about it that I was stunned.

The offer from Heidi snapped my dreams into reality. I could start a new life, outside of an exciting city filled with art and music and fashion, but most of all I could be who I was meant to be, without restraints. This could be a dream come true, and I wanted to run with it. But I had no money (I'd been spending it all on instruments), because I was transitioning from assisting to having my own chair (which also meant I didn't have a steady clientele to hold me down and tempt me to stay). I had to talk my parents into this and have them buy into my dream.

To persuade them I used the fact that Heidi was Lebanese, and that she needed me to help with this venture, and that she, of all people, wouldn't send me somewhere that wasn't legitimate. They resisted at first, but then, as usual, my persistence wore them down, and they agreed to let me go. But they were angry and disappointed in the choices I had made so far; after all, my oldest brother was a dentist, my other brother owned his own dental lab company, and my sister had gotten a master's degree and married a Syrian doctor. ("You are my smartest child, Rayoochty!" my father often said to me. "Why do you want to waste your life without an intelligent career?") So they wouldn't give me money or help me financially in any way. I decided I wouldn't let that stop me, either; all I cared about was getting the hell out of there. I'd always said that Detroit was a great place to leave. And in New York—or close enough—I'd be able to express my talent and sexuality without the watchful and judgmental eyes of my family and their community. I was homophobic and judgmental enough about myself; I certainly didn't need a community to reinforce my worst fears. Leaving, I hoped, would help me break free.

Kurt, predictably, was hurt and angry as well, but in his usual generous way he offered to drive me across the country—to Darien, Connecticut, where Heidi would put me up for one month, in the attic of a small flat that they called "corporate housing." I had two hundred dollars in my pocket and a hunger for life that was relentless.

I said my good-byes to Sophia. She seemed genuinely happy for me, or maybe she was just relieved that she wouldn't have to deal with my outward longing for her anymore. Either way, it broke my heart. Yet I knew that on the other side, there was something big and exciting waiting for me: namely, the life I was meant to have. In my heart, I knew I was going to be a star.

EIGHT

LATE 1983 WAS an exciting time in New York City. The vibe was that anything was possible if you were an artist or a musician. Clubs like CBGB and the Pyramid were showcasing local punk-rock bands like the Ramones. You could catch the Cramps, Laurie Anderson, or Sonic Youth at Danceteria. The Roxy was a dance club where really bangin' hair salons like Girl Loves Boy would have roller-skating parties. Area was hot for its decadent themes that changed every month. And the gay bathhouses were booming all over the city. Underground East Village galleries like The Fun Gallery, started by Patti Astor and Bill Stelling (who later became a friend) were trumping the big, slick Soho spaces. They showcased fresh new artists like Keith Haring, Jean-Michel Basquiat, Fab 5 Freddy, and Kenny Sharf.

I couldn't believe that I was both free from my family *and* living forty-five minutes outside New York City. I moved to the small, very proper town of Darien, where it was easier to find an au pair than it was to find a person of color. Heidi had set me up to stay with one of her hairdressers, Kasha, and I slept in her attic for a month until I could figure out how to get my own place.

When I went into the city I usually drove, in my little Fiat, but I also had the option of taking the train right to Grand Central Station. I explored and jumped headfirst into everything new and exciting: the hair scene, the music scene, the art scene, and the club scene (which also happened to be a huge drug scene).

After a month in Darien, I got an apartment in Stamford, Connecticut, with my new friend Jamie, the other art director at the salon. Jamie was adorable and wild, with dirty-blond hair that curled in ringlets, and a chiseled Roman face that made him look like a hip statue of David. He wore skirts with combat boots and had remarkable taste in the same genre of music that I enjoyed: techno new wave. We both loved bands like Depeche Mode, Siouxsie and the Banshees, The Cure, and New Order. We immediately started a band. He was a singer, so again, I took a backseat to singing and just played. We wrote music together and rehearsed during every moment of spare time that we had, and soon I got us our first gig. A deejay that I knew from Detroit, Mark Manino, had moved to New York and was spinning at an underground club called Night Birds, that was tucked into a little alley down in Tribeca. Mark wanted to book live-performance bands to bring more people into the club, and when I reached out to him and told him I'd started a new band called Ancient Beat, he put us first on the list to perform. I asked Kory to fly in and do the show with us because he was such a driving factor in a live performance. He agreed, so I sent him cassette tapes to practice to, and when he arrived, our trio was ready to rock. We had an amazing sound check, playing through the new songs and rehearsing at the club for a couple of hours before the actual gig started. The New York club scene was different: The audience held back and was much cooler and calmer than our Detroit followers. They didn't give up the applause as quickly, but during our third song, with Jamie and me harmonizing on the chorus and Kory beating the drums into a frenzy, the crowd gave it up and burst into applause and movement, which was a sign that we had them. Everyone congratulated us after the show, praising our style and showmanship.

Jamie and I did everything together: hair, music, fashion, and life. We started working with art directors from Vidal Sassoon, who took us to compete against other salons for national hair shows, which we won. I began running ads to find young models who wanted free haircuts or color, then used the photographers I knew, from Heidi's shoots for her salons, to shoot my own ads, in case I needed them down the road. The models loved it because they also got free, beautiful headshots. I also assisted another Sassoon art director, Carlos Munoz, on fashion shoots that he'd booked outside of Heidi's. I was learning from the best and collecting some very creative tear sheets (printed advertisements) that showed my diverse talent for styling, haircutting, and color. It was fascinating being around real models, watching them walk a runway or work a camera. I loved the limelight, and the music was progressing as well.

And yet, as far as my sex life was concerned, I was like a baby just learning to crawl. For one, I was shy about approaching other women unless I was high. I did manage to make an exception one night at the photographer Bruce Weber's birthday party in the city, when I had a quick and staggering one-night stand with a bleached blond, sun freckled, fresh faced, and just-off-the-boat eighteen-year-old Italian model I met there. Since I didn't really get to know this Italian beauty before I disappeared in the morning, it was not an emotional invest-ment for me; I just got to bask in the afterglow of sexual exploration without all the aftermath bullshit. I'd never before been able to just enjoy sex—without feeling love. And now I felt I'd had a fabulous induction into an exploration of the senses, just sex, nothing more, nothing less. Still, it didn't help with my homesickness. Despite Jamie and my other new work friends, and my newfound freedom, which I loved, I'd never lived outside of my parents' home, and I was lonely.

One night after six martinis at a local Stamford bar, I found myself on a pay phone crying to Kurt and drunkenly inviting him to come live with me. He was elated; originally I had told him I needed space and that he couldn't come to New York, and since then he'd continued to tell me how much he missed me, calling me almost daily.

In the morning, I woke up (with a huge hangover) and remem-bered our conversation. I wanted to smack myself and throw up for extending Kurt that invitation, but I also felt I couldn't take it back; it had made him so happy, and I didn't want to hurt him all over again. For the next couple of weeks I dreaded every phone call from him, but I still couldn't bring myself to drop the hammer on his enthusiasm for coming and being with me. I talked to Jamie about it, thinking maybe I could use him as an excuse, but Jamie welcomed another roommate to help with the rent and didn't want to turn him away.

So Kurt moved in with Jamie and me, and things were fine for a minute or two. And then, predictably, I started feeling stifled and malcontent, and soon I was pissy and impatient with him. I didn't want to sleep with him, didn't want to be his girlfriend (I was still keeping my sexuality a secret, and Jamie was the only person I had confided in), and was angry with him most of the time just for being who he was: a nice guy. As painful as it was for me to be with him, I'm sure it was worse for him, because he had no clue why I was being so mean. Still, he moved right in and got a job managing The Stamford Salon

After much consideration, I left and took an illegal sublet in the city by myself. It was a small, dilapidated one bedroom on Mott Street and Houston, painted fire-engine red from floor to ceiling (including the refrigerator). I paid $245 a month—a steal at the time—and was to have it for three to six months, depending on when my artist- and musician-friend Tommy, who had the legal lease, came back from England.

I loved having my own apartment in New York, even if the hallway entering the building smelled like cat piss and the apartment itself came with the meanest cat I'd ever met in my life (which is why it was so cheap). Mr. Milk would hide under the furniture, then come out slinging his claws at anything that moved. Kurt helped me clean the place out, and had gouges on his shins to prove it. Once in a great while Mr. Milk would feel gracious enough to come sit on my lap, which would scare the shit out of me because I never knew whether he was purring or growling. I couldn't tell the difference. Still, I drove my little Fiat to work, commuting to Stamford four days a week, and staying in the city the other three, so I could really sink into my life there. Kurt—who visited me every few days—was like a lifeline to my old self. We still had sex once in a while, which was okay with me because he helped me in many different ways, and I cared for him. He set up a recording studio under my loft bed, and I was happy by myself and extremely creative during that period, writing and recording dozens of songs, without Jamie. I wanted to find *my* musical voice, and get to know the city that I'd grown to love.

I was still in touch with Kory, and after that show with Jamie and me, he immediately decided to move to the city. I couldn't have been happier, since he and I were kindred spirits, soul mates, and each other's muses, and I'd missed him both personally and professionally. When he arrived, I was so pleased, and we jumped right into playing together, rehearsing for future gigs and recording some of our best songs in my little studio. Life was moving me in the direction that I'd always dreamed of, and music became my lover, so much so that I almost forgot about my sexuality for a short time.

And then I met Lana—the woman who would combust my heart and shatter my world.

NINE

I FLEW HOME to Detroit in the summer of 1984 to cut, color, and style some models for a print ad for Heidi that would appear in *Vogue* magazine. It would be a full-page, stark, black-and-white ad, with our salon logo to show that we had our finger on the pulse of what was happening with hair. (Heidi was branching out all over the United States, and I was flattered when, of all her hairdressers who had worked on fashion shows, she picked Jamie and me to do the ad.) It had been less than a year since I'd left, but I already felt different. I was more confident, no doubt because of my success in New York in both the hair and music scenes.

My friend Barry picked up Jamie and me after we finished shooting the ad and told me we were on our way to rescue a friend of his, Lana. He'd often talked to me about this friend he wanted to introduce me to, because he thought we would really hit it off. Lana had been locked in her bedroom that day by her girlfriend, a big old body-building Syrian butch named Mary.

"These two play really weird games," Barry said.

"Cool," I said. We had just eaten some magic mushrooms, and my adrenaline was pumping after the *Vogue* shoot. I was up for anything—and this actually sounded weird enough to be exciting.

We drove through the historic Boston-Edison district, a dangerous part of Detroit that nonetheless had some huge and gorgeous mansions.

At Mary and Lana's home, which was one of the mansions—a three-story English Tudor with overhangs and beautiful front gables—we knocked on the door. No answer. I heard a dog bark from somewhere inside the house. "Whose dog?" I asked.

"Lana's," Barry whispered. "He's a Doberman puppy that barks at shadows."

"Shit, this is getting better and better," I mumbled to Jamie, as he giggled. The mushrooms had completely kicked in now, and the excitement and paranoia from what was happening were sending shivers down my spine.

Barry had obviously done this before. He found the key, hidden in a big stone gargoyle's mouth, and opened the front door.

We tiptoed inside. "Who *lives* here?" I whispered.

"A gay couple that bought and refurbished it," Barry said. "They're letting the girls stay here for a while."

Deep green and purple draperies cloaked every window; rich colors were everywhere—magnificent reds, gold, and browns—with Victorian furniture placed perfectly in every corner of the room. It was dimly lit, but the art was stunning. Huge portraits and impressionist-style paintings with large gold frames hung on the walls. In the corridors were smaller, more modern and abstract drawings and photographs.

We walked down one of the hallways, and the barking got louder.

Barry knocked on a huge wooden door, and the barking exploded, wild and ferocious.

"Are you sure about this?" I asked Barry.

Before he could answer, I heard a soft, sexy voice croon, "Sam, you silly boy. Come here."

Barry turned the big old-fashioned key that had been left in the door from our side, and we all stepped in. The bedroom was the size of my whole apartment—at least six hundred square feet, dim, and painted completely purple. Sam—who didn't look like a Doberman because his ears were intact and floppy— bounded at us, a huge, slobbering, clumsy goof of a puppy clearly hungry for love and attention, and I bent to pat him and let him kiss my face.

Musical instruments were all over: percussion, vibes, steel drums, and synthesizers. They surrounded a huge king-sized bed in the middle of the room. On the bed sat Lana.

My eyes met hers, and I blinked, once and then twice. And then her kohl-lined dark eyes pierced through me and I didn't know where to turn. "I'm Rayya," I managed.

"I know." She smiled. "I'm Lana." She looked me up and down. "Barry's been telling me about you for quite some time."

"Me too," I said, though I could barely get the words out. Her long, curly jet-black hair fell around her shoulders and seemed to be moving like the hair snakes of the Medusa. She was wearing a slip dress, but I don't remember the color, because it wasn't her clothes that drew me in like a magnet.

"This is my good friend Anita," she said, still looking at me, and only then was I aware of another woman who had been in the room the whole time.

"Hi," Anita said, with a quick wave of her hand.

I smiled briefly at Anita, who was a heavyset woman with dark hair and a sweet, curious smile. I looked around to see if I'd missed anyone else, like the butch girlfriend, but she was nowhere to be found. "And this is my friend Jamie," I said, without my eyes straying from Lana's face.

And then Lana tapped her bed, and I sat down and entered Lana land.

Maybe it was the magic mushrooms that intensified the evening, but as I talked to Lana, I felt like someone was finally seeing me for who I really was, rather than making assumptions based on my past or my family, or pigeonholing me by my careers. I had always felt deeper and more complex than just "a hairdresser" or "a musician," but no one had ever taken the time to ask me all about myself: who I was, what I wanted. Nor, I realized, had I ever really stopped to ask *myself* these things. But Lana asked me everything. She urged me to tell her about my exotic Syrian heritage, and I thought, happily, *exotic?* Because that was a first; I'd heard my heritage called a lot of things—freaky, alien—but exotic was certainly not one of them. In fact, before that evening, I'd tried to hide my Syrian background, never bringing it up or speaking about it in the new life that I was creating in New York. But that night, something inside me shifted, and I was able to see my potential through the eyes of Lana. She loved the language, the food, and especially the music of Syria. She wanted to know what part of Syria I was from, as her current girlfriend, Mary—yes, the one who'd locked her up—was Syrian as well.

I was stunned by her interest, almost to the point of thinking it was a trick to get me to open up so she could throw it all back in my face, like the Bracco sisters had done. I just couldn't believe that someone so beautiful and cool—and female—would be so interested in me.

But clearly, she was. We laughed a lot, and played some of the instruments, and watched Sam the ridiculous puppy chase shadows on the walls in the dark. I don't remember where Barry, Anita, or my friend Jamie went while Lana and I stayed on in the purple room; I just remember that we rubbed each other's feet and talked till the early morning hours, with me asking her all about herself, too: where she was from, how old she was, what she did, what she longed for in life. Lana was a second-generation Italian, born and raised in Detroit. She was fourteen years older than I was, had been married and divorced, and had a son who was only a few years younger than me, who lived with her mom. She'd traveled the world, to places that I'd dreamed of visiting: India and Afghanistan and all over Europe. She'd had many lovers, both male and female, and was as eccentric as one could be without being labeled crazy. She'd previously co-owned a really cool clothing store called Phobia in Detroit, and had dreams of designing jewelry and accessories and leaving Detroit at some point. She was a spiritual being, yet conflicted by the need to have another credit card. She floated through life, loving and supporting artists and their dreams, which was her greatest high. By morning, I called her my little fairy girl because she reminded me of a dark, Italian Tinkerbell.

I went back to New York a day or two later, but I couldn't get her out of my mind. We stayed in touch, long distance, through the inevitable breakup with crazy Mary and all the drama that was involved, from the lockdowns to the emotional and physical abuse. I didn't tell Lana that I was in love with her, although it must have become clear to her as I began going back to Detroit once a month or so just to hang out with her, sometimes not even telling my family I was in town. After three or four months we had still not even kissed, but I was completely infatuated.

During one of my visits I was shocked when she introduced me to a guy she'd started seeing. Ty—short for Tyler—a beautiful British photographer who was making a name for himself in the art world. He seemed to me the perfect boyfriend for a bisexual woman, because he was tall yet soft-spoken, with a virtually hairless swimmer's body except for his long, sexy, dyed-blond hair. He also had perfect poise and a great upper-crust English accent that would make anyone, male or female, melt in his presence. He wore makeup (eyeliner, lipstick), which was normal for the eighties art scene, and always had fabulous clothes—duster coats that dragged behind him like the train of a wedding dress, or metal armor with shawls.

I'd never confessed my feelings to Lana, and when I found out she'd started dating Ty, I was crushed. I reminded myself: *How could she really know I loved her, when I also had a "boyfriend" in New York?* I thought that we were working our way toward each other, but I was too slow, too young, and way too afraid of my own feelings for it to happen easily or quickly. But I also wasn't about to give up.

TEN

ON NEW YEARS Eve of 1985, I did Ecstasy for the first time. I thought I'd found heaven in a pill. Ecstasy was legal at the time and made me fall in love with being in love—it transported me to a soft place with no inhibitions. It was intoxicating and sexy, mind-exploding—it took the razor-sharp edge of reality and blurred it, turning the world into a beautiful, loosely rendered watercolor. I wanted to touch everyone, and kiss, hug, and cuddle everything around me, and soon enough Kory and I were hitting the X so hard that my brain felt dislodged from the rest of my skull on most days. There were times when we lost count of how much we took and spent days in my cavernous apartment, crawling in and out of the walls in our minds. It made me feel weightless and mobile. I also felt as though I could talk about anything without fear or malice—let out my innermost feelings without judgment. When I was on Ecstasy, the real world melted away and a realm that was kind and loving took it's place. I loved the drug so much that I wanted to turn everyone on to it, so I started trafficking Ecstasy back to Detroit and supplying my friends while also performing at clubs in the area and swooning over Lana. It was perfect for a while, because it allowed Kory and me to visit home every six weeks or so, and between the shows and the dealing we also were able to make some money.

Our performances became more and more elaborate under the influence of the drugs I was taking as I created them. Unaware of my drug use, my mom and sister came to every one of these shows in Detroit. They sat up front and center, proud, taking in how I'd built huge columns out of papier-mâché that girls would burst out of as we performed, plaster fragments all over their bodies and faces. Amid all the freaks, punk-rock, and goth kids, I'd look out into the audience and see my mother's bright smile following me around the stage, and that gave me power and energy. For the first time in my life, I could see that my family almost believed in me. I also felt that I was on the verge of becoming something special, completely separate from them, but just as successful. I understood, for the first time, that I could do it my way, outside the box, and still win them over. For all that had happened, I still wanted their approval so badly, and now was my chance to show them that their way wasn't the only one.

Lana and Ty were big fans of my music, my drugs, and me, so the three of us bonded. We would drop Ecstasy together and sit around smoking, drinking, kissing, and expressing to one another how in love we were. One of my favorite lines, spoken often by a friend of ours, was "I love you man; you're my best friend. What's your name again?" This was Ecstasy: the love drug. My nickname in Detroit became Madame X.

I was becoming a minicelebrity and couldn't get enough of it. In Detroit, we drew the most interesting audiences to our shows and the top promoter was constantly after us to perform. There were after parties at Barry and Irene's house, and dinners that Kory and I would go to with our entourage of dancers, friends, and hangers-on. Lana was always there, at every show and every party. I was deeply in love with her. She expressed the same to me quite often, and I was sure that we would have an affair at some point.

In New York, we were admitted carte blanche to every club. One time at Area, I stood at the bar between Andy Warhol and John Cage, who were having a conversation that I wasn't listening to because I was too busy snorting lines. We were on most guest lists and frequently invited to VIP rooms. Life seemed to be rolling in a positive direction.

But one night when I was in New York, I got a phone call really late and it was Lana. "We're getting married and we want you to be our maid of honor," she said innocently and happily.

I was speechless. Was this some cruel prank, like the ones from my childhood? But I soon found out it was true. She and Ty were getting married and moving to England.

I flew to Detroit and begged her not to marry Ty. But I was too late. She wanted out of that city as well, and marrying Ty would ensure that she could work in London.

So I agreed to be their maid of honor, and we got married. I say "we" because that's what it felt like to me. The three of us, all on Ecstasy, at Barry's house in front of the fireplace, dressed in robes and pagan regalia with a witchy woman performing the ceremony, and huddled together in every scenario during and after the ceremony. I'm not sure Ty knew exactly what was going on—he seemed like the innocent in all of it—but Lana and I knew. Even though we hadn't had sex yet, the deepness of our relationship and the closeness we felt was stronger than any sex I'd ever had.

I flew back home to New York, heartbroken, and started pining for my soul mate, who was now a married woman.

★

I moved into an apartment in Chelsea, and Kurt moved back in with me. It was the only way I could afford the rent, which was $550 a month. It was a one-bedroom, fourth-floor walk-up railroad flat on Fifteenth Street between Seventh and Eighth Avenues. Kurt built all the furniture in the apartment, including a loft bed, so I could put my studio underneath. It was a great little place, with lots of light, and it was mine. My name was on the lease, and in New York that was a huge accomplishment. I also rented a studio space in the music building on Eighth Avenue in midtown, and started auditioning band members. I wanted the music to become more expansive. I needed to shed the keyboards and become a front person, the singer of my band.

Lana asked if she and Ty could stay with me in New York during their transition to London. Without even consulting Kurt, I said yes. Not that he'd have minded, but I wasn't taking any chances. Though if he had said no, I'd have ignored him anyway.

They had shipped most of their stuff to the UK, but they still arrived with enormous amounts of luggage that cluttered our place. I was ecstatic, but also a bit downtrodden, as it was a double-edged sword: I finally had Lana living under the same roof, but she was sleeping with her husband in the next room.

I was a bitch to Kurt, annoyed with him all the time. I knew he didn't deserve it; he put up with so much. He was still in love with me, even though he now knew I was in love with Lana, as I had told him as much. "I feel like it's another phase, Ray," he had said at the time, but I had shaken him off; he'd sounded like my mother when I started wearing hip-huggers and platform shoes. When I tried to tell him it was definitely not a phase, he mumbled, "She's gonna be gone soon anyway."

That's what I'm afraid of! I wanted to yell.

I used Kurt's love and kindness to my sick advantage. He was a great guy and I should have let him go then, but I still lived in fear of being exposed to my family as a lesbian, and the thought of coming out terrified me and made me hold on to Kurt for as long as possible. My friends urged me to be myself; they saw how much pain I felt because of my sexuality. Everyone assured me that, gay or straight, I was the same person they loved. I didn't believe them. I'd never been accepted completely for who I was, and I'd never met a full-blown lesbian who wasn't called derogatory names. I just couldn't let go and allow myself to be a target, and although I was sure I was deeply in love with Lana, I couldn't admit that I was gay, not even to myself.

Ty got word from England that his father was ill, and he had to leave alone, sooner than expected. Callous as it sounds, I was happy he was going; I cared only about having Lana to myself. I wanted Kurt to leave, too—to go home for a few days—but he wasn't budging; he knew what was going on. The more protective of me he became, the meaner I became. I called our friend Anita and invited her to come for a visit; she would make a great distraction for Kurt, and I was desperate to steal time alone with Lana, without him watching me like a hawk.

Lana and I held hands on walks, kissed on the street in the Village, and behaved like normal lovers. I felt moments of freedom from my past, and tried to shed my fears about the present and future. I was recording in the studio, and, with Lana's support, I started connecting to my heritage. By having the woman whom I loved appreciate my culture, I also started to look at how my character had been shaped by my family and my country's history. How rich and valuable my past was and that in fact it had made me who I was. I started listening to Fairuz again, a Lebanese singer who I'd loved as a child, and my music took another turn, with a Middle Eastern flare that layered chromatic melodies like the ones I'd grown up listening to. It became even more distinct and personal than the music that was generic to the eighties. It felt sexy and I was finally embracing my Syrian background, and soon I started speaking Arabic to Lana, because she thought it sounded really hot. I was finding the little foreign girl who I'd abandoned. I wanted to take her by the hand and prove to her, through Lana's heart and my own, that she could shine. For the first time ever, I had the desire to embrace my culture and my sexuality. Lana and I were inseparable, and Kurt was just himself, quiet, sweet, and understanding. He would brood sometimes and go on cocaine benders, but as long as he left us alone, I didn't care what he did.

Anita arrived while I was in the recording studio, so after my session I met her and Lana for some Mexican food at Mary Anns in Chelsea. I had asked Kurt to spend the night out because we wanted to have girls' night in. We drank some margaritas then dropped some Ecstasy and headed home, stopping at the video store on the way. Lana wanted to get *Lianna,* a film by John Sayles about a married woman who finds her inner self through a lesbian love affair. I was game; in addition to appreciating the topic, I would've done anything to create the mood, because in my heart I knew this was going to be the night that I finally got to have sex with Lana.

When we got back to the apartment, Kurt was still there.

I was furious. "Aren't you going out?" I snapped.

"I don't have anywhere to go, babe!" he said.

"I told you, it's girls' night and I don't want you around," I said. I knew I was being mean, but, sadly, I didn't really care that I was hurting him.

"But I don't have anywhere to go!" he said again.

"Did you call Kory?"

He shook his head no, and looked down at his feet completely embarrassed.

"I told you to call him!" I said. "He's probably out by now."

"Sorry, babe."

I sighed loudly. "You know what? Just fucking forget it. Just stay in the bedroom and we'll stay in the living room. We're gonna watch a movie, so *please* stay out of our way. Okay?" I said, pointing toward the bedroom and waiting sternly until he moved slowly toward the door.

I don't know why he didn't tell me to fuck off and then pitch everyone out, but he didn't. Maybe because he knew he was walking a fine line with me, that it would take nothing for me to break up with him, especially when it came to Lana. He just said, "fine" and went back into the bedroom and crawled up into the loft bed and was quiet. As for me, I felt the tiniest stab of guilt, and then nothing; I was too intent on what I wanted—my night with Lana.

We made some popcorn, and settled in to watch the movie. Anita lay on the little couch against the wall, and Lana and I took the foldout bed. At first Lana and I just giggled and frolicked like no one else existed, and Anita gave us a couple of dirty looks, which made us giggle even harder.

About halfway through the movie, though, we started kissing. They were light and loving baby kisses at first, but soon her breathing got heavier and my heart was beating out of my ears. "I want you," she whispered into my ear; her breath was warm and moist.

I pulled the blanket over our heads and opened her mouth gently with my fingers. I slipped my tongue into her mouth, and when she embraced it, our kiss became so passionate that I lost all inhibitions and moved my hands gently over her body and pulled at her clothes.

Poor Anita sat squirming uncomfortably on the couch in that very small room, high on Ecstasy watching us and/or the movie. She was breathing heavily and muttering with her arms crossed. "You guys are bogue," she said. Something about having Anita in the same room and Kurt right next door made it even more thrilling. The naughtiness of it all was titillating.

We ignored her. Under the blanket, I gently caressed Lana's breast, and then my touch became harder and more desperate. Lana took off her shirt and pulled me close. Under the darkness of the blanket, I could hardly see her body, but I could feel her soft skin and the hardness of her nipples. The blanket slipped off us, and I turned to check on Anita. She was in the same position as before, on the couch, and so pissed off that her eyes looked like daggers launching at me.

I didn't care; this was my chance with Lana. I dove back under the blanket. I had waited so long for this opportunity and wasn't going to let anything stand in my way.

I guess I was higher than I thought, because I passed out during sex and woke up facedown between Lana's legs at four in the morning. I was embarrassed and sheepish, and crawled up to her side to see that she was sleeping as well. Everything was quiet but the hum of the television. I got up to turn it off and saw Anita's slightly open, narrowed eyes.

"That was not cool," she said.

"Sorry honey," I said sweetly, and I meant it. But not enough to keep me from crawling right back into bed with my lover the second Anita fell asleep again.

Lana opened her eyes, moaned with delight at the sight of me, then wrapped me up in her warm, loving arms. This gave me more happiness than I'd ever known. In the morning Ty called and announced that his father had died, and that Lana should stay a bit longer in New York, as he had to tend to his family. I tried to commiserate, really I did try—but I couldn't hide how happy I was that Lana was staying with me for a couple more weeks. She, too, tried to hide her excitement by putting on the sorrow face, but secretly, notwithstanding her sadness for Ty, she was just as giddy as I was that we'd have that much more time together.

I broke the news to Kurt that she was staying, and although he said he was fine with that, I saw his spirit crash. At that moment, I felt great sadness and gratitude for Kurt's kindness, for his gently stepping aside and letting me have this. It was really remarkable, but I was also waiting for the other shoe to drop in some way, knowing I deserved it.

"Thank you, I know this is hard for you," I said, and I reached out and kissed his cheek. He reached out and pulled me close for a hug, then walked away.

With Lana and me both well aware that she would have to leave in a very short time, we took in the city—the streets and shops, little cafés that became home to our intense love affair—as if every day was our last. It was a roller coaster of intensity that was both ecstatic and depressing and served to fuel our passion. I was floating in my own hemisphere, and my creativity was pouring out of me in the studio, on stage, and in bed.

I should've known to run for cover, because of course, anytime you soar that high there's gotta be a huge crash afterward. And so there was. The day came when Lana had to leave for London, and I was beside myself. Driving her to the airport, I felt broken, and it wasn't attractive. I cried and pleaded with her to stay, knowing full well it wasn't going to happen.

Lana tried to be mature and adult about it—she was fourteen years older than me, after all—but she also was devastated. "You'll forget about me soon, and have many other lovers," she said, wiping tears from her cheeks.

"*Never!*" I yelled, and the thought of not being with her made me want to throw up. In retrospect, I realize how overdramatic I was at the time, but this was my first real love affair, and I honestly had thought I'd spend the rest of my life with this woman.

My relationship with Kurt was—and, really, always had been—more of a friendship than a romance. He'd always wanted more than I did; for me, something about it had never felt right, but I'd never known what that was until I'd kissed Sophia back in Detroit. But even then, I still hadn't really believed I was a lesbian. I hadn't known what I wanted, so I'd run away, only to realize that wherever I went, there I was: same person, same desires, same pain. But now, with Lana, that truth stared me right in the face: I was in love with Lana, not Kurt. I was in love with a woman, not with my boyfriend, or with any other boy, ever. I was a lesbian, and in my heart, I knew this was my truth.

Back home from the airport I lay in a fetal position on the floor of my closet under my hanging clothes, inconsolable. After an hour or so, Kurt came into our room. "This will help with the pain, trust me," he said, and he held out a pipe and a tiny dish with rocks rolling around on it that looked like natural pearls. He had graduated to smoking cocaine, though I had been so wrapped up in my own drama that I hadn't even noticed.

I took the pipe, lit it with the lighter he handed me, and took a hit. My head instantly got sucked out of the darkness, and everything went bright. I stood up to allow the mindless feeling to flow through my body and felt an electric charge take over. And it did help for a minute or two, temporarily dulling the pain and making me forget, until the darkness came back black as vengeance, making me paranoid and uncomfortable, with the depression still cutting into me. Afterward, I took a Valium, which always took the edge off after a coke high.

My phone bills to London were double my rent. (Alas, this was before the advent of e-mail or Skype.) I wrote an endless number of depressing love songs and sent Lana a cassette of them every week. Ironically at this low point in love, the music couldn't have gone better. My band was coming together with Kory still at the helm on drums; Gerald Collins, an accomplished guitar player also came onboard. Pete Sutos, a kick-ass bass player who I'd known from Detroit signed on, too. I was looking for the perfect keyboard player to take on my parts and we'd be all set. One of my hair clients hooked us up with a producer to record an EP as soon as we were ready, and the name of the band was Rayya.

★

Lana told me that she was in love with me and wanted me with her. She also told me that she'd told Ty everything.

He finally sent me a letter stating his love for Lana and professing that he loved me only a bit less than he loved her, which I found quite strange. Then he asked me what my intentions were toward her and our situation.

I was honest. I thanked him for the opportunity to be forthright and told him that I was in love with Lana and would do anything I could to be with her. I also told him that I had tried to get her to stay with me in New York, but that she'd been committed to him. My hope, I told him, was that he would allow me to find a place for the three of us to live together, so we could all be happy.

He wrote back saying that Lana was miserable without me, and asked me to come and stay with them for a while. I jumped at the chance to go to London, be with Lana, and explore our relationship.

Being an art director at the salon had its perks, one of them being that I was able to take a leave of absence, telling Heidi that I wanted to go to London for inspiration and to bring back new techniques and styles. The next step was to get Kory to move into my apartment with Kurt and help with the rent. (Kurt was so numb from freebasing he didn't really seem to have an opinion anymore, though he may have been happy to see me go because it would give him more opportunity to party.) I was twenty-five years old and again throwing caution to the wind, leaving every-thing in my life behind for love and passion.

I moved into a huge loft with Lana and Ty in Notting Hill Gate, which was like Alphabet City at the time: a neighborhood that was still dangerous, but cool because a lot of young artists and musicians were living there, as it was not yet gentrified and still very cheap. We traveled first, taking some side trips through the countryside dropping a lot of Ecstasy as we went. The three of us slept together in the same bed every night. Lana slept in the middle, of course, while I slept on her left and Ty on her right.

Lana had rules to ensure that no one got hurt. I was only allowed to have sex with her when Ty wasn't around. I'm sure she told him the same, although he and I never talked about it. We did everything as a threesome, but each of us got one day a week to spend with her alone. And she and Ty were the primary relation-ship, but Ty and I honored and respected each other.

★

Despite all this, I still don't think Ty really knew what was going on between Lana and me. He seemed oblivious to the fact that Lana and I were together sexually, probably because our sexual relationship was still mostly hidden from him. We held hands and kissed in front of him, but I was never allowed to talk around him about having sex with her. The whole thing was doomed from the beginning, because Lana basically controlled the whole dynamic. I was happy to do whatever she wanted, and so was Ty.

I was content with this arrangement for a while. And then, predictably, I wanted more.

I started feeling horrible jealousy when I saw them kiss and hold each other. It burrowed so deep that I was miserable even when I was alone with her. Also, it seemed to me that she protected his feelings more than she did mine.

"He's very sensitive and vulnerable," she would say. "You're a strong woman, Rayya. Look at how mighty you are."

She knew how to pacify me, and I loved that she thought I was strong, but inside, I was dying. I was weak for her, and I didn't want to be the strong one anymore. I wanted her to protect my feelings and tend to my needs.

I stayed for as long as I could, which was less than a couple of months, since I couldn't work in England. By then it was apparent that Lana wasn't going to leave Ty for me, and I was depleting my bank account. So off I went, back to my lonely existence in New York, with an inconsolable heartache and an appetite for destruction.

ELEVEN

KURT WAS A full-blown crackhead by the time I got back to New York. When he picked me up from Kennedy Airport, I almost didn't recognize him, broken out as he was with sores and blisters all over his face and body. He looked like a homeless person.

He tried to deny the drugs and even tried to have sex with me when we got back to the apartment. I was repulsed; I could hardly look at him, much less deal with his drug-induced shame and paranoia, especially when I had my own wrist-slitting heartache to tend to. I pushed him away and retreated to our room in disgust.

But soon my disgust turned to rage. Kurt had been fired from the billing firm he worked for on Wall Street—the drugs, no doubt—and hadn't bothered to tell me that he had no money to pay his share of the rent, or that he'd now be in the apartment 24/7. (Kory was gone; he'd vacated the week before because he couldn't take Kurt's drug habit anymore.) But the straw that broke my back was when I found out he had drained my bank account of the little money I'd had in it: He'd found the ATM card I'd left at home and knew my access code because we'd always been casual about that. So I was broke, brokenhearted, and living with a guy I couldn't stand to look at, with payment of both shares of the rent approaching fast. Though I still loved my job and was happy at work, the minute I returned to my apartment I felt trapped in this horrible existence with Kurt.

And yet, one night after work, to give myself some energy—because I was already exhausted and still had to go to the music studio in midtown to work on our EP (which I'd borrowed money from my family to record)—after continuously asking me to free-base cocaine with him, which I had done once, I finally gave in again and smoked crack with Kurt. He said it was different from coke—cheaper, and much more potent. It was my first time with crack, and I was shocked at how all my feelings of despair were instantly erased by the rush of the poison; how, when I was high, that numbness was all that mattered. After that, Kurt and I became crack buddies for a little while, but I was still going to work, while he stayed home, smoked, then methodically sold everything he could to get more money for drugs. (One night, I arrived home to find two Irish thugs I knew from Detroit carting my expensive professional gig speakers out the door and into a truck because Kurt owed them $550.) He also borrowed money from my family and my friends, all without telling me. We fought constantly about his addicted state, and finally one night, during a huge confrontation, I became so angry I pushed him hard out the door of the apartment, and he was so fucked up that he fell down a flight of stairs in our building. Not a proud moment for me. Then I called his father in Michigan and asked him to please come and collect his son.

Two days later, a cousin or aunt of his arrived to pack up what little stuff he had left and take him back to Michigan. And that part of my life, the Kurt part, was finally over, except for the one thing he'd left behind: his drug habit, which had become *our* drug habit. Which was now my own to deal with.

★

The drugs fed my broken heart, and my broken heart fed the need for drugs. Meanwhile, Kory moved back in, and in many ways he was my saving grace. We did everything together: clubs, girls, music, drugs, and life. Meanwhile, despite the pain and jealousy I'd endured in London, I begged and pleaded with Lana to come back to New York, insisting that she and Ty could live with me as I had lived with them in London, and promising her we'd be happy. After a few months, they agreed to come; she was miserable without me they both said, and their marriage felt the strain. I was ecstatic. I didn't care that Ty was coming, too—or at least I told myself I could deal with it, since it was my only choice. After all, in addition to Lana, Ty and I both loved music, art, books, New York, and drugs. And Lana *was* my drug, like that first amazing hit you keep chasing again and again, knowing deep down that eventually pain will ensue, but not letting that stop you.

Kory, for his part, hated what I was doing with Lana and Ty and kept trying to talk me out of it. I told him he didn't understand how much I loved her and what I was willing to do to have her in my life on a tangible level.

"That's what I'm worried about," he responded. "I scraped you off the pavement last time around, buddy. You're finally starting to feel a little better, and here she comes again, like a roller coaster plowing right in."

"She loves me," I said.

"Yeah, well she loves him, too, remember?" he replied, not willing to make eye contact.

"She makes me happy," I retorted.

"Yeah," he said. "Until you're not."

He was right, of course. But the lifestyle I was living with him was also killing me. He worked at Danceteria, where I would hang out, drinking and doing drugs, almost every night. I also commuted to cut hair four days a week, and also worked on fashion shoots for Heidi. On top of that, I had band rehearsals three nights a week and would go out and party afterward, doing crack and sometimes heroin if we couldn't find Valium. At the end of every night, we went home and nursed ourselves with porn, watching it together.

We sometimes brought girls home and had sex with them together; some fell for him and some for me, but in the end I always dumped the ones who liked me. My life was like a garbage disposal unit: Everyone who came in got sucked into the whirl-pool that ended in obliteration. I was going insane waiting for Lana to come back to me; losing my mind, but passing the time while I waited by having fun.

And it wasn't just strangers who got pulled into my vortex. One night, for example, I showed my old friend Anita a time she's still less than thrilled to remember. She and I had become close friends.

She'd visited me in New York before, but this was the first instance when I was a full-blown drug addict.

Kory and I had little gatherings on Saturday nights for the usual motley crew of friends: Jamie, of course, and also a couple of punk-rock kids who Kory worked with, a fashion designer and musician friend of his, and an artist I'd made friends with in the East Village. We hung out and listened to music, drank, smoked and did drugs—cocaine, heroin, crack—and then we all went out to after-hours clubs together. When Anita arrived, Kory and I were in the bathroom smoking crack while the little party was happening; I'd completely forgotten she was coming. "Holy shit, hurry up and hit this," Kory said, ignoring the buzzer. "It just melted the hair off my balls, it's so smokin'!"

I quickly took a hit and felt that chemical rush penetrate my lungs and then my mind. For a moment, everything was bright and intense, celebratory and happy and perfect. And then, as quickly as it came, the high left, and I was fucked up and irritable, nervous and tense and neurotic. I plopped down on the side of the bathtub, sighed, and stared at the pipe again, craving another hit.

"I need some downers," I sputtered. Crack was unforgiving — the pull to do it was out of one's control—and the only thing that softened the edges was Valium. But lately Valium had been hard to score, so we'd resorted to snorting a tiny bit of heroin, as it was easier to buy on the street and also worked much more quickly.

"I know man," Kory said. "This shit is strong."

The buzzer rang again as I took another hit of crack, and then a third. "It's Anita!" I heard her whine through the intercom. "Rayyaaa . . . let me in!"

Back then—1985—Chelsea was a cesspool of squats and drug dealers running a neighborhood that wasn't yet gentrified. I pictured Anita hovering at our door as she glanced around nervously. "Oh no!" I said to Kory, half laughing and half panicked. "I totally forgot she was coming!"

He began to laugh, too, and then harder and harder—I must have looked terrified—until he was practically choking. "What is she, your mother?" he said, gasping for air. "Don't be so paranoid, Ray! Anita *likes* to party!"

I shook my head. "She doesn't know about the crack, Kor'."

"So what?" Just give her some to try. She'll dig it. It *rocks!*" And he resumed with another hit as he sat on the back of the toilet with his feet on the closed toilet seat.

I shook my head again. I knew I *was* paranoid—that was the crack—but also, though Anita did love to party, there was something about her that was almost grandmotherly. (We actually called her bubba, because she was so much like a *bubbe,* or Jewish grandmother.) I had a feeling she'd disapprove of this scene, and I didn't want to disappoint her. Neurotic as she could be, Anita was also loyal and loving and a hoot to have around, a good, longtime friend.

But then I had a thought that cheered me up: "Hey!" I said. "I bet she has Valium!" Anita always had Valium. She couldn't sleep without it.

"Cool," Kory said, and then, as he listened—the outside door was right next to the bathroom, so you could hear people coming up the stairs—"She's still tryin' to get up the four flights of stairs, poor thing."

We both broke out in laughter at the thought of Anita pulling her bag up to the fourth floor of our walk-up. She was lovely but a bit uncoordinated, kind of like a Weeble that could never make a graceful entrance. She made an easy task look really hard.

"I wonder if she ran into the retard yet?" Kory said, and we started guffawing all over again. Tony was a thirty-something, mentally challenged guy who lived on our floor and who, every time he heard our buzzer, went into the hallway to greet whoever it was, drooling and trying to grab them until his ancient mom came out, yelling in Spanish and pulling him back into the apartment. He was harmless, but if you didn't know him, he could be quite freaky and intimidating—especially for someone like Anita.

I heard the *click-bang, click-bang,* of first her feet on the steps and then the bag being dragged up after her. Then I heard Tony charging out into the hallway, and then a suitcase tumbling loudly down lots of stairs—and then Jamie opening the door and stepping out to go retrieve Anita's bag as she made a break for the door and rushed in. Still in the bathroom, Kory and I were completely hysterical.

"*Hello?*" Anita yelled, sounding panicked. "Rayya? Where *are* you?!" She stomped into the living room, and then I heard her coming back toward the bathroom and bedroom as I took another hit of crack.

"Rayya? Rayya!" She was at the bathroom door now, pounding on it. "What are you *doing* in there?!"

"Hi Sweetie!" I called. "I'll be right there, I'm just talking to Kory for a minute. Honey, do you have any Valium?"

"What?" she said, and then, "Oh—yeah, hold on, let me get my purse." She sounded annoyed as all hell.

I heard her grab her bag hard off the kitchen chair—everything overamplified in my state—and I opened the door and saw my friend standing there, her brown curly hair bobbed with baby bangs, brown glasses framing her face. Her lips were bright red with lipstick. I stepped out and leaned in to give her a kiss on the cheek, then grabbed her purse, ran back into the bathroom, and shut and locked the door. "I'll be right out, hon," I told her.

"Hey! That's not nice!" she said.

Who said that being on crack made you nice? I thought, as I raided my friend's purse for her Valium. "A-*ha*!" I yelled to Kory, pulling out a little plastic bottle with blue pills inside. "Here they are."

There were eight pills left. I gave Kory four and popped the other four myself, slugging them down with the warm beer that had been sitting in the bathroom since we'd locked ourselves in forty-five minutes earlier. "Ahh," I said, as the pills went down, because I knew I'd feel better soon.

Anita had begun pounding on the door, and after we'd taken the pills, I opened it and let her in. I was tense—I knew she was mad—but Kory jumped off the toilet to give her a big bear hug, and immediately she softened. Kory had that effect on most people; everyone loved him. "How was your trip, bud?" he asked.

"Exhausting!" Anita said, with her Michigan Jewish accent. "And," she dragged her words out, "that creepy guy scared me!"

"Oh, sweetie," he said and gently brushed her face, "I got your back Niters." As he spoke, he loaded a big rock of crack into the pipe and moved it toward her mouth. "Here babe, hit this," he said, as I lit the torch.

Anita did as she was told. The second she inhaled, her eyes bugged out and her face turned bright red. She sat down, hard, on the toilet. "What *is* that?" she asked.

"It's crack," I said. "Isn't it great?" I leaned over to finish her hit.

"Crack?" She looked stunned. "Don't they say that *crack is whack?* I saw that big billboard on the highway." She was talking about the huge installation by Keith Haring on the FDR Drive. My heart melted for her when she said it; she was so sweet and naive and childlike. But she also looked terrified. "Honey, it's fine, don't worry," I said. "We do this once in a while. It's fun!" Kory nodded, then took yet another hit.

Anita shook her head. "I don't like this," she said. "It feels weird. Like a bad coke high. I don't like it, Rayya."

She was right, of course. If I'd stopped long enough to think about what the high was really like instead of constantly trying to chase the first three seconds of the first hit, I would've completely agreed with her.

"Where's my Valium?" Anita said. She stood up and grabbed her purse, which was now sitting in the sink. As she lifted it, the prescription bottle, severed from its lid, rolled around empty in the basin.

Anita looked at me in disbelief. "You took *all* of them?!"

"Kory and I split them," I said, hoping that throwing him into the mix would soften the blow. "You have more, right?" I added.

"*No,* you fucker! That's all I had!" She stood up and punched me in the arm, snorting and stomping her feet. "I hate this feeling!" she yelled. "It's *horrible!* I need my Valium!"

Kory and I exchanged a look of guilt, but I wasn't too worried; I knew I could rectify this situation, no problem.

"Here, take another hit," Kory said. "It'll get better, I promise."

She obeyed him. But by the look on her face, I could see that it wasn't getting better.

"Look," I said, taking over. "I'll go out and score us some downers. Okay? I was thinking about doing that before you got here anyway. Just hang out with Kory for a little, and I'll be back as soon as I can. Don't worry, babe. We'll fix you up in no time."

The Valium had started to take effect, making me calm and collected and wiping out all the neurosis from the crack. I left my apartment, jumped into a cab, and headed for Eleventh Street between avenues B and C: Alphabet City. This was where I copped all my good drugs. When I arrived, I handed the cabbie a twenty and crossed my fingers as I asked him to wait. Cab drivers hesitated to hang around in that neighborhood because it was dangerous—few people other than junkies or hookers went east of First Avenue in those days—but a twenty sometimes did the trick. He agreed to wait, albeit reluctantly.

I scoped out the scene and soon saw a Latina chick who looked like one of the dealers who usually hung out there. She was thin and dirtier than most of the dealers I'd dealt with. I slowly and cautiously approached her looking around to make sure there were no cops. "Do you have Valium?" I asked.

She shook her greasy, rag-covered head. "Only coke and dope," she said.

I handed her forty dollars. "Give me four bags of dope, then."

She handed them to me quickly. The little wax baggies were ink stamped with a brand I was familiar with: the Statue of Liberty, celebrating her one-hundredth birthday with a facelift that cost 250 million dollars. Even the drug dealers were cashing in on Lady Liberty that year. I jumped back in the cab, happy and relieved. It had been a quick, easy score—and the heroin, which would actually work faster than Valium, would take care of my girl Anita.

Back on Fifteenth Street, I ran up the stairs with sheer excitement at having copped "the Liberty," not just because of the name but because I knew it would be good. Anita was so desperate as she sat on the floor rocking back and forth twirling her hair, that by the time I walked into the bedroom of my apartment she didn't care what I had, as long as it brought her down from that bogue high. I ripped open a bag, put it up to my nose to smell it . . . and panicked. "It's *beat!*" I yelled, tasting it. "It's fucking *beat!*"

"What does that mean?" Anita whined. "And what's in the bag?"

"It's supposed to be heroin," I said, throwing the bags on my dresser, "but it's fake. I got ripped off. Anita, I'm so sorry." On top of everything else, I was starting to lose steam, feeling the Valium penetrating my every fiber.

"Heroin?" Anita yelled. "I don't want *that!* I'll get hooked! I just want my Valium. I need it, Rayya! Can't you just get me that? Doesn't anyone here have a stupid Valium?"

The sheer look of madness in her eyes was enough to reignite my commitment to her cause. "C'mon, let's go get some!" I said. I grabbed her arm and pulled her up. "C'mon, Kory."

"Uh-oh, here we go," he said, but he gamely grabbed her other arm. "It's gonna be a fun night out, I can feel it," he added, nervously laughing.

"Fun for *you*," Anita moaned. "You're high on *my* Valium. I can't go out like this. No way."

Ignoring her comment, we pulled her out the front door and flagged another cab back to Eleventh Street and B. "Kory, you stay and hold the cab," I instructed when we arrived. "Anita, you come with me."

She opened her mouth to protest, but nothing came out except a huge sigh. Taking that as a yes, I jumped out, pulling her along. Within seconds, I'd spotted the Latina chick who'd ripped me off; she was down the block pacing in front of an abandoned building smoking a cigarette and drinking a tallboy.

With the remnants of crack, the adrenaline of anger, and the calming powers of Valium coursing through me, I felt pretty invincible. I ran up the street, Anita waddling in a speed walk behind me, and came up on the girl, dying to get what I was owed and also to show my friend that I was in control, that nobody fucked with me. The girl was really tall, in her late twenties, wearing crusty, extra-tight clothes and beat-up sneakers. She was tough looking, like someone who'd just gotten out of jail. When she saw me come up, she looked more shocked than scared. I doubt this chick was afraid of anything, given where she hung out. I grabbed her by the neck and threw her up against the dilapidated redbrick tenement building, clutching her throat with my hand and pushing all my body weight into her. I am not a small person, and she looked stunned and very alarmed. "Okay, okay!" she spluttered with her Puerto Rican street accent. "Whatchou' want chicka?"

I shoved her once more. "I want my money back, you fucking bitch!" I yelled. "That dope was beat!"

"I ain't got it, putta!" she said shoving back, but not enough to make me lose my grip.

"You fucking liar," I said, and I shoved her again, banging her head against the building. There was nothing I wouldn't do to this girl if she didn't give me either my money or some real dope.

I heard Anita's voice, almost a cry. "It's okay, Ray," she said. "We can go somewhere else."

"We're not going anywhere," I yelled, spitting in the girl's face. "We're getting our shit right here, right now. Right, Mommy?" I tightened my grip on her throat, feeling my heart pounding in my head. In the background, I heard Kory yell from the cab at the top of his lungs, "Get 'er, Ray! You get 'er!"

People had started to gather at the sight of two white girls in Alphabet City, one pinning a Latina chick up against a building, the other looking terrified. Suddenly four guys—one very handsome Latino, buff, clean, and in charge of the other three, who were black, gangsta'-looking roughnecks, and obviously his cronies—stepped out of the crowd and approached us, two grabbing me and the other two her. I knew what was up: The main dope dealer and his boys didn't like anything attracting attention on their block, because that was usually followed by the NYPD.

The guys pulled me off the Latina while also keeping her from attacking me. I looked at Anita, and for a second I felt as desperate as the look on her face. But I couldn't give up yet. I turned to the main guy, who happened to be holding me. "She ripped me off," I said, and to prove it, I pulled the four bags of heroin from my pocket and threw them down, the opened one spilling the fake white powder at our feet.

"What are you crazy, Blanca?" he said, gripping my arms even tighter. "Throwing bags of dope at me on the street?"

But I could tell he was listening now, and that gave me courage. "Well you ain't getting busted, 'cause that shit ain't real," I said. "It's stamped Liberty. That's your stamp, right?"

Had I just dug my own grave? Accusing him of running a dope spot? But one of his boys picked up the bag and inspected it, first smelling and then tasting the powder. He gave the main guy a nod.

The guy loosened his grip, then turned his attention to Latina. "I'll take care of you later," he snarled at her. "Meanwhile, give her back the forty dollars."

"I don't want the forty back," I yelled. "I want four bags of Liberty!"

He looked at me for a long moment, as if trying to decide whether to punt my ass across the East River or just give me the stupid dope. Finally he sighed and nodded at one of his boys, and the guy handed me four more bags. "You got some *cojones,* Blanca," he said, almost admiringly. "Now get the fuck outta' here with your freaky friends."

I tucked the four bags of dope into my bra, knowing it was legit, and hooked my arm into Anita's. "Let's get the fuck out of here, babe!" I said. Lady Liberty had never looked so good, stamped on that little folded waxed bag.

We speed walked back toward the taxi, where Kory was standing with the door open, his fists air-boxing with triumphant blows. "If you do come back, make sure you see my boy," the main drug dude yelled after me. "He'll take care of you next time."

I raised my arm in acknowledgment. I was triumphant, but also, now that it was over, shaken to the core, though trying not to show it.

Anita looked like she was in cardiac arrest as I pushed her into the backseat of the cab. The driver was waving his arms and cursing and yelling that he'd been sitting for too long; his body odor permeated the cab. I climbed in after Anita. "Back to Chelsea, Swami, Fifteenth Street between Seventh and Eighth Avenues!" I said, and I shut the bulletproof divider on his fury and his odor. Then I reached into my bra and pulled out a beautiful and well-deserved bag of dope. God, I loved America. "Beautiful," I said.

Kory pulled out his wallet and rolled up a bill while I carefully opened one of the bags and poured some out on the back of my hand. He handed the rolled bill to Anita. "Here bud," he said. "This should take the edge off."

She didn't argue or resist in any way, just took the rolled-up bill, leaned into my hand, and snorted the pile I put out for her. She gagged, swallowed, and then leaned back into the seat, looking flush.

I smiled. "Just breathe baby, 'cause this definitely gets better," I said. "And honey? Welcome to your weekend in New York!" I reached around and gave her a huge hug.

She almost smiled back as she allowed me to hug her. Then she pulled away, looked me straight in the eye, and said, "Can we eat soon? I'm hungry."

Kory and I collapsed against her, snuggling and laughing at a job, of some sort, well done.

TWELVE

BY MAY OF 1986, my drug schedule looked mostly like this: I'd try and stay straight from Wednesday through Saturday, which were the days I worked (though sometimes I couldn't wait until "my weekend" and had to do a little crack, and Valium, on Thursday to get myself through). By July though, I began copping drugs almost daily, spending fifty or sixty bucks a night doing crack, Ecstasy, and Valium, and snorting coke in between. I did whatever I could get my hands on and soon I was snorting and smoking so much that Valium and other downers didn't work anymore, so I switched to snorting heroin, which was quicker at numbing the pain. For some reason I thought I could outsmart it, keep it under control and not become addicted. It worked for a little while, but by September of 1986, I was a mess.

My parents came to visit me in New York—something that took me weeks of cutting back on my drug use to prepare for—and broke some devastating news: My mother, then fifty-five years old, had been diagnosed with leukemia, and would start chemo when they returned. I was destroyed, and blamed myself: Stress, as far as I knew, played a huge role in causing cancer, and as my mother's one child who didn't exactly have her life together as my siblings did, yet managed to be the most self-centered of them all, I thought that I was probably her biggest source of stress. I used her illness as another excuse to completely jump off the deep end, and started using drugs with even more of a vengeance than before I'd cut back.

★

Kory brought a girl home from Danceteria one night later that fall. I was brooding in the living room while they were having sex in the loft bed, so he invited me up. I joined in, but more as an observer. It was fun, and the girl, a superhot Persian chick named Marney, ended up liking me instead of Kory. I was still pining for Lana but started dating Marney anyway, being completely honest with her about my love for and devotion to Lana and the fact that, once Lana and Ty moved back, it would be over between us. She was willing to be with me anyway, but occasionally protested: "She has him, why can't you have me?"

I thought about that and it made sense. I wondered how Lana would feel about it, but was afraid to say anything for fear she would cancel her move to New York. (They were coming, but hadn't figured out exactly when yet.) In the meantime, I spent quite a bit of time with Marney, and we became very close. She was smart, fun, really sexy, and obviously uninhibited, and I loved how easy and light our relationship was: no heartache, no drama, the life I thought I'd wanted. . . . That is, until Lana arrived back in New York.

I was secretly very nervous, and spent days getting the apartment ready. I wasn't sure how we would all get on, especially since they'd been living alone for some time. I took a week off work so I would be available for all of her needs. I was ecstatic when they arrived, and planned all my time with her/them. When I returned to my job, I couldn't wait to get home, and on my days off, I'd walk twenty-two blocks to the Garment District, where she worked in a showroom helping Eric Beamon, a well-known jewelry designer from Detroit, make his beaded suede pieces, and pick her up just so we could walk home together. Our apartment was small, but the same rules we'd followed in London applied to our relationship now, and things were fine for a while. I was so grateful Lana was with me that I didn't allow myself to want more. Ty got a job as a doorman at Nell's and was gone early evenings, so I'd have her to myself until the wee hours of the morning. But after a while, his presence in his absence got me feeling moody and depressed again.

It was Valentine's Day and Marney caught me at home. I'd spent the holidays with Lana and had been avoiding Marney's phone calls for weeks and putting her off, not wanting anything to spoil my honeymoon period with Lana. Now, I told her that Lana and Ty and I had plans to go to a friend's party.

"Don't you want your own date?" she asked, in a way that pierced me. I thanked her and said I'd take a rain check. "Okay, but if you change your mind, I'm available," she said.

Later, I mentioned to Lana that Marney had called to ask me out. "I couldn't believe she thought I'd be free," I said, practically sneering.

Lana paused thoughtfully. "Maybe you *should* go out with her," she said, finally. "Ty is taking me out for a special dinner tonight. We can meet at the party after."

I was stunned, and couldn't hide my anger. "And you didn't think to tell me?" I said. "Or ask me?"

This hadn't come up yet, as last year they'd still been in London on Valentine's Day. Now, I wondered: Would I always play second fiddle on birthdays and holidays? Would I always be the one meeting them at the party? "I thought for sure we'd spend it together, since it's our first," I said weakly.

"Ty took the night off from work to spend it with me, so . . ." She seemed guilty but resigned.

"I don't get it," I said, my voice getting louder. "You *want* me to go out with her?" I couldn't believe she wasn't jealous enough to ask me not to go out with another girl.

Tears welled up in her eyes. "I can't really ask you not to, can I?"

"Yes!" I yelled. "You *can* ask me, and I'd do it! Just say 'Rayya, please don't go out with anyone else.' And I won't!"

The look on her face gave me the answer I didn't want.

So I called Marney and accepted her invitation. Then, because we were all insane, as soon as Lana found out, she got jealous and took it out on Ty, being snippy with him while they were getting dressed and ready to go, acting like he was her obligation. Meanwhile, I primped for my own date, pretending I was excited and that my heart wasn't crushed.

We went to dinner at Café Orlin, a little bohemian restaurant on St. Marks Place in the East Village, and Marney looked beautiful. Her dark almond eyes sparkled, and her smile was infectious. I would've been perfectly content with her if I hadn't been consumed with Lana and Ty, wondering what they were doing or whether they'd gotten to the party yet. When Marney and I finally arrived, they were already there, and the drugs were flowing freely. Marney wanted to leave right away, but I wanted to stay for a while, so we stayed. It was cruel what I put Marney through, what we all put one another through. I would go into the bathroom with Lana, where she would confess her undying love for me, and we would snort lines of cocaine and make out, and I would confess my undying love for her, and then we would go back out into the party and to our dates for the evening.

Marney knew what was up, and she wasn't particularly fond of drugs or the people who did them, so she kept tugging at me to leave. But Lana wanted me to stay, so I stayed. Eventually Marney walked out, and I didn't try to stop her.

Things got worse quickly as I fought to keep my triangle going, knowing the only way to hold on to Lana was to keep her jealousy fueled. One night, I flew Marney with me to Detroit for a huge music/performance-art piece: Over prerecorded tracks, Kory played drums and tribal percussion and I sang. The fashion designer James Coviello painted the set, and made every piece of clothing for Kory and me—from an elaborate headdress and the bustle and train of a long priestess gown, all the way down to my four-inch platform boots, Jimmy created a modern, punk-rock onstage version of a medieval landscape and I pulled off the look perfectly.

The piece was called the "Spiral Dance," inspired by a pagan book by Starhawk that Lana and I loved, and I needed dancers on stage whose bodies I could paint. Marney volunteered, and she was amazing, with a veil over her face and her hot naked body painted with black-and-white spirals, making her look like an optical illusion. Jimmy also danced nude, and the show was hailed as the performance of the ages and so were the designs; the press was amazing. We were rock stars in Detroit, and Marney, Jimmy, Kory and I loved every moment of it.

But then Lana flew to Detroit with Ty to surprise me, which of course made me so happy, even if Marney was, justifiably, less than thrilled about it. And predictably, Lana eventually had a meltdown, saying she didn't want me with Marney, that I was hers and she wanted Marney to leave. I was mortified that she was behaving this way toward Marney, but at the same time, sadly, didn't argue, because it felt so good to finally have Lana fight for me. Marney flew home alone the next day, and that was the end; she never spoke to me again, and I could hardly blame her.

Still, I wasn't able to pull away from Lana and that toxic love triangle, or the insanity I equated with love at that time. When I was with her I felt whole, elated, and full of life, and when I wasn't, I was a complete mess. I didn't want to go to work, and I rehearsed with my band only when I couldn't be with her. When I did go to rehearsal, I moped around doing more drugs than music. When Lana and Ty were in London, I had been able to funnel my sadness into lyrics, and music had become my lover. Now, my music suffered because all my energy was spent obsessing about Lana, where she was, what she was doing, and how I could manipulate more time with her. I was insecure and crazy—and of course, the drug use only got worse. Finally, Lana and Ty moved out of my place, inviting me to live in a bigger apartment with them. Thankfully, I knew enough not to leave my home, especially to move into a place that would really be theirs. Eventually we drifted apart, and I continued to drown myself in pity, sorrow, and drugs.

★

Kory came over one night and dragged me out to a party at an art gallery called Provenance on Eighth Avenue between Seventeenth and Eighteenth Streets in Chelsea. It was hosted by a wealthy eccentric named Michael Mugerian, an art dealer who loved to spend money on emerging artists of all kinds. I'd been intrigued with him for a long time because he represented my friend Alan Sanchez, a budding painter and excellent musician from Detroit.

It was Michael's fortieth birthday party and Alan's first major solo show in New York. As a birthday gift, I grabbed a cassette of three songs I'd just recorded with my band. (There were five of us now, though Kory alternated between mine and another band he was starting that was more hard-core rock and roll, less new wave.) At the party, someone popped in the cassette, and Michael danced over to me raving about one of the songs, "Infatuation." He was so taken by it that he asked to manage me, and of course I said yes.

Immediately, everything started moving very fast; Michael was extremely proactive about making my career. He had me picked up in limousines and driven to different designers' showrooms to choose clothes for shows, and he made sure I was on his arm at every party, fashion show, and important art opening—a whole new level of red-carpet entry that hadn't been available to me before. The type of decadence that we shared at that time was not unusual—it was the eighties after all, when music, art, and fashion collided and created a scene that everyone openly indulged in. Michael was no exception, he loved to party as well, and we spent an afternoon freebasing in Fabrice's showroom, who was a very well-known Hatian clothing designer, while picking out a beaded, mirrored, spider-webbed jacket for a showcase I was performing in. Michael paid fourteen hundred dollars for it—more money than I'd ever seen spent on an article of clothing.

My excitement grew along with Michael's attention to and confidence in me, and soon I'd completely bought into the glamorous rock-star image and was spinning out to thoughts of getting a record deal. I did everything but practice the music that had actually gotten me to this point. Meanwhile, Kory, who was heading in his own direction with his new band, couldn't bear to watch me getting caught up in the glitz and hype of a career that wasn't a reality yet. He kept telling me to work harder—that it would take everything I had to make it—but I didn't listen to him, just as I hadn't listened when he'd warned me about Lana. He was my voice of reason, but I was having too much fun for reason, and I stupidly shut him out.

I had a huge solo show coming up that Michael had promoted for the New Music Seminar, and I would be playing without Kory, at a new club called Private Eyes, in front of all the major record labels. I was nervous and depressed about not having my buddy, my muse, and my best friend with me. To make it worse, Kory didn't come to my performance, as we had been a bit competitive lately seeing who was going to "make it" first. I was devastated by this, but tried to convince myself that I didn't need Kory, or anyone else for that matter. This was going to be the night that would launch my career as a solo artist, and nothing could ruin it.

I was wearing that gorgeous, sparkly, and mirrored Fabrice jacket as I stepped out of the limo into a swarm of media covering the show, cameras flashing. In the dressing room, I had a couple of shots of Southern Comfort, which always relaxed my vocal chords, and snorted a bunch of cocaine to prime me for such an intense social setting.

When I stepped out onto the stage, on the most important night of my career, I was alone: no familiar faces in the audience, and no band, drummer, or dancers to provide depth or energy or a security blanket for whatever might happen when I started singing. I knew I looked great in the flashy outfit and glamorous makeup and hair, and the club was packed, which was a dream. But it was a suit-and-tie zombie crowd—record executives who looked like they belonged on Wall Street, waiting for the next Sade or Celine Dion to appear—and the prerecorded tracks that had always been the backbone of the performance felt like not nearly enough. I was an East Village goth-wave performer pretending to be a pop star, and suddenly I wasn't sure I could do it.

I took the microphone and tried to find a face to connect with so I could at least make my performance real. But the only person I could see was Michael, who was flitting around talking to the suits and ties. "Hello," I said tentatively into the mic, and the crowd rose to their feet and cheered, moving closer to me. That helped some—this was it, they were ready—so I gave the signal to cue the music and launched into crooning "Hymn 11:11," which was a dark ballad Kory and I normally did together.

I knew right away I wasn't pulling it off, so after I finished "Hymn 11:11," I launched into my anthem rock song called "Nothing Matters," which always made my audience happy. Without Kory's drumming, or my band behind me, and the right audience to feed off of—I felt small on that big, empty stage under the halos of blue and red light—my voice seemed flat, and my performance felt empty, lacking the soul, heart, and grit that usually drove my shows home. I knew the music well enough though, and during "Nothing Matters," I was able to put up a good front— dancing and grooving—letting go of my insecurities enough to create a buzz that this audience liked. But deep down, I knew I was off my game. If my usual crowd had been there, there was no way I'd have gotten away with that performance.

Typically my shows moved so fast that even by the last song it would still feel like we'd just started to play, but tonight, by the second song—with four more still to go—I felt it was never-ending. "Infatuation," destined I'd hoped to be the single on the future record, and a hit, couldn't come fast enough.

After the show, although everyone praised me, I was embarrassed. I felt I'd lost some of myself. The hard work and practice that usually gave me an edge and pushed me to a stellar performance had not been done this time around, and it showed. My preparation had gone into a pipe full of freebase, a snifter of Grand Marnier, a Fabrice jacket, and a stretch limo that lied to me.

★

I was a full-blown garbage head by then—doing everything but addicted to nothing except to checking out in every way. I would do as much as I could for as long as anyone around me had drugs, it didn't matter what kind they were. What had started out—way back in seventh grade—as a way to fit in and feel better, to not feel so uncomfortable in my own skin, had taken over and was now ruining my life and everything I'd worked so hard to achieve, from making music to finding love and friendship. What's more, for the first time in my life, I was truly alone. Michael was busy with other projects and had no time to micromanage my life and career; I'm sure, when he signed me, he hadn't expected me to fall apart before his very eyes. Kory—my dearest friend and bromance, the heartbeat of my music, and the spark that had inspired me in the past—wasn't speaking to me, because he couldn't bear to watch me wasting away; he had done his share of drugs, too, but his true addiction was music, and he'd never let himself fall to a level anywhere near where I was now.

I was blowing a lifetime opportunity, the development deal that Michael had given me. But I didn't know how to stand up, brush myself off, and proceed. And I was so numb from all the drugs that I didn't even really care.

THIRTEEN

WHEN I MET Kim, the new manager at the salon, I hated her.

Although she was kind of cute (under the heavy makeup and trashy bleached blond hair), she was wearing a matching pink sweater and skirt suit that I thought was revolting, and she was uptight and bitchy. You could tell she enjoyed her position of authority, so I copped an attitude toward her right away. She tried to act cool, but she was a tacky little Jersey girl managing our happening salon, and after a while I just ignored her.

One morning, nursing a hangover after the New Music Seminar weekend, I went into the massage room to take a little nap while the assistants were setting things up for me to start teaching. (As an art director, part of my job was teaching the other hairdressers new cutting and color techniques, both at our salon and at others Heidi owned on the East Coast.) I didn't have any more coke to keep me going, so I was fading fast, and the room was dark and smelled sweet with aromatherapy oils . . . perfect for taking a little snooze on the massage table. I was just getting comfortable when I heard the door open, and then dim lights illuminated the room. I looked up to see Kim looking over at me with a big smile on her face.

"Long night?" she asked.

"Uh—just tired," I groaned.

"Do you need a bump?"

I couldn't believe what I'd heard. My first thought was that it had to be a trap; she wanted to get rid of me because she knew I didn't like her.

Still, my eyes were wide open now, wondering where this was going.

Kim pulled out a vial. "You don't mind if *I* do, do you?" she said, and snorted a bump right in front of me.

She had just incriminated herself, so I figured I might as well take advantage, and I joined in and did a couple of lines. That got me up and running, of course; I soared through the four-hour class, and then Kim and I and a few of our co-workers went out for drinks.

A blizzard had been brewing all day, but I was enjoying myself and had no intention of leaving quickly to try to beat the snow and get home. The blizzard hit while we were having drinks; by the time we stepped out of the bar, the snow was so deep there was no way I could dig my little Fiat out and drive back to New York. "You can stay in the company condo with me," Kim offered, almost eagerly. All night, she'd been feeding me from her ample supply of cocaine as well as subtly flirting with me. I was pleased, but still not at all interested in her in that way.

When we got to the condo we did more lines, then poured some vodka and tonics and sat down on the couch where I would be crashing. I was drunk and drugged out, yet still had a little steam left as long as the coke was flowing. We talked for a bit, and then she asked if I wanted to come up to her room while she showered, saying she had some downers to help me crash. I had a bit of heroin stashed, because I knew I couldn't get by without it, but a few more downers were always welcome.

So I went up to her room, thinking I'd just get the downers and maybe a T-shirt to sleep in. While she was in the shower, I looked around. Somehow, the room felt familiar, even though I'd never been there: the way things were placed on the shelves, and the smell of the T-shirt she gave me . . . and then it hit me. It was Lana's smell, the scent of Opium perfume.

Not that Opium was all that original, but still, I couldn't believe it. "Are you an Aquarian?" I shouted through the bathroom door, just for the fun of asking.

"How'd you know?" she responded.

I blinked. "Just a guess," I said. "What day?"

"Guess again."

I didn't respond, just sat down on her bed, slightly excited now. If I couldn't have Lana, at least I could have someone who had her sign and smelled like her. The water went off, and a few minutes later Kim came out of the shower in her white robe with her wet hair slicked back. She looked extremely sexy. "Guess what day," she said, smiling.

I shrugged. "February ninth?" It was Lana's birthday, of course. Her mouth fell open. "How'd you know?"

"I didn't." I stood up and walked into the bathroom with the T-shirt she'd lent me for the night, my adrenaline pumping. The shirt had I LOVE THE JERSEY SHORE printed on it. I shook my head, pulled it on, washed my face, and went back out.

She had put on a sexy, short, lilac-colored slip and gotten into bed. "Here's a couple of Valium." She smiled holding out her hand. "You can sleep here if you want," she said, patting the space in the bed next to her.

High, lonely, and hurting from a relationship that had taken everything from me, I laid my Armani suit on the chair and got into her bed. I took the two little blue pills, knowing they wouldn't make a dent in the pain, but still grateful for them.

Immediately she rolled on top of me and kissed me, long and hard. It was a total turn-on. I returned the kiss and we began making out.

She told me she'd never been with a woman before, but I didn't believe her; I thought she was just trying to get me fired up. Still, the sex was hot. She was assertive whereas Lana had been passive, and I felt wanted and needed, and as satisfied as I could feel these days from anything other than drugs.

In the morning, still sound asleep, I woke up to Kim's frantic voice. "You have to get up!" she whispered. "My fiancé is outside! It's his birthday, and we're supposed to spend the day together." He had been knocking at the door for almost an hour, she said. She then proceeded to tell me her fiancé was a thug in the mob who would kill me if he found me here.

I sat up, not sure if she was fucking with me. But then I heard angry voices yelling her name from outside the front door, and I shot out of bed and started throwing on my clothes while she went down to let them in and make coffee to keep them at bay. My heart was beating out of my fucking chest, and I was frantic and furious. Why hadn't she told me she was engaged? That was the last thing I needed right now, after the situation with Lana and Ty.

Finally, I came downstairs to find her mom, Patty; her mom's friend Kelly; and Vincent the mob thug fiancé sitting in the living room staring at me, while Kim nervously made excuses about why I slept in her room instead of downstairs on the couch. Her mom and Kelly clearly didn't buy it, and Vincent was giving me the old stank eye.

Groggy, needing drugs, and desperate to get out of there, I asked Kim to take me to the train station because digging my car out of the snow was unthinkable. Vincent ominously offered to come with us, but her mom—maybe feeling a little sorry for me by now—asked him to stay and help with getting brunch together, and Kim and I finally escaped to her car.

All the way to the train, she looked like the cat who ate the canary. I was angry and unforgiving, but she was extremely apologetic, telling me over and over how attracted she was to me, and eventually I simmered down enough to peck her good-bye before I got on the train.

Everything about Kim was wrong for me, not least the fact that she was straight and engaged. Still, when I went back to pick up my car, I ended up sleeping with her again. She was seductive and soothing, and I was too much of a mess to resist. I ended up having a relationship with her for the next few years, during which she finally got rid of the fiancé, though not before he threatened everything and everyone I knew—including Lana and Ty and my family back in Detroit. Vincent finally left us alone after her old-school Italian family told him to back off.

Kim's mom, in contrast, was awesome. She and her partner, Kelly, had been together for eight years—living as "roommates" for six of them—yet they'd never properly "come out," even to Kim, who was an only child (and had lived with them before taking the job in Connecticut). It couldn't have been easy living in Perth Amboy, New Jersey, and being from an old Italian family; I understood that. But when Kim and I came out to them at our first Christmas—as if they didn't know—they, in turn, came out to us, in an evening that was warm and wonderful. That's probably one of the few positive memories Patty and Kelly had of the years their daughter spent in hell with me.

FOURTEEN

KIM AND I were a train wreck. Her needs and my baggage were perfectly codependent, and the drugs fed everything. A first-time lesbian, Kim wasn't about to have anyone rain on her parade, so she became obsessive with me. She wanted to show me that she could hold her own in my environment, and put up with the still-lingering Lana and Ty scenario. This worked for me because I'd been so tattered by having to share Lana that I enjoyed her possessiveness.

She moved into the Chelsea apartment shortly after our first night together, and we hit the ground running. The sex was astounding and the drugs were debilitating. She had money, and so did I, now that I'd stopped taking care of two other people. I acted like a high roller and used my tips, which were a good hundred dollars a day, to keep us going. Kim was a partier, obviously, but had never been exposed to this kind of rock-and-roll lifestyle, and she loved it. We had a two-seat Mercedes Benz convertible hardtop, and lived high on the hog as long as we stayed high on drugs, too.

And then the inevitable happened. Inevitable and horrifying.

I was in Connecticut teaching a hair color class one day when I felt like I was coming down with a cold or the flu. I'd been up with Kim as usual the night before, smoking cocaine and then snorting a bit of heroin to come down, and we'd driven to work that morning, also as usual, hungover and tired. A few hours into the day, my nose started running and my stomach started to hurt. I had no drugs left—I had figured I'd cop as soon as we got home from work—but now I knew I really needed something to make myself feel better. Within another hour, I began throwing up and had bad diarrhea. *Definitely the flu*, I thought, and I took two Tylenol and began the drive home, leaving Kim to take the train later. It was a long drive, and I was fading in and out of consciousness on the highway in between stopping to throw up on the side of the road. By the time I pulled onto Fifteenth Street, I thought I was going to explode from every cavity.

I left the car double-parked, door open, and ran up to the apartment, where I called Pappy Johnny—the local heroin dealer on the next block—to please come over or send something for me. I wasn't sure why I called him, because I did think it was the flu, but I guess I figured the heroin would make me feel better anyway.

When Pappy came and saw the state I was in, he quickly broke out a ten-dollar waxed bag, ripped the top off, and laid out a line of dope for me. "I locked your car for you," he said.

I nodded my thanks. "I must have a really bad bug," I said weakly.

"This should help." He wagged his chin at the torn-open bag, then sat back and watched.

Half wondering why he said this (and half knowing he was right), I rolled a bill and vacuumed the line of heroin. I gagged hard, then inhaled; immediately, everything calmed down and eased up. It was like I'd hit the reset button, and everything went back to normal in my body.

"Thanks," I said, and I sighed.

"I knew it was gonna do the trick." He smiled.

But I wasn't smiling. In fact, the realization at that moment was terrifying: All the months and years I'd managed to evade the ball-and-chain nightmare of addiction had come to an end. I was an addict.

Still: "Does this mean I have a habit?" I asked stupidly, hopefully, desperately, praying he'd laugh and say "Of course not, sweetheart."

Pappy looked at me, his gray eyes cloudy and sad, then said, "I'll go move your car, be right back." He collected the rolled-up ten, turned away from me, moved out the door, and shut it behind him, leaving me alone to sit in the hell of my thoughts.

So this is what it will be like now, I thought, with nothing short of panic. I never wanted to be that sick again, and for that to happen, I would need to have heroin. All the time.

Kim was still fine, at least—she'd only done heroin a couple of times, both with me—and I didn't want her to follow in my footsteps and get hooked, too. So for a while, I tried to lay low with the dope, and sometimes hid it from her while we partied, giving her only Valium and other downers when she wanted to come down. But she caught on fast, getting angry and resentful that I wasn't giving her what I was taking. When I tried to explain the woes and danger of what I was doing, it didn't work; nothing stopped her longing and bitching about wanting to be on the same page with me. If I was a junkie, she said, she'd be one, too. And that's how we both ended up addicted to heroin, though I never got over the guilt of being partly responsible for her descent.

I stopped teaching at the salon, and only made it to Connecticut once or twice a week to work on clients (who were getting tired of my cancellations), where I'd get through the days by doing drugs constantly. I cared only about getting and staying high. I wasn't making enough money now to pay for my drugs, or my rent, so I resorted to selling cocaine out of my apartment and at clubs. I would go out to the Pyramid, or to Save the Robots—places where everyone knew me as an up-and-coming musician—and hang out and sell cocaine to whoever was interested.

By the late eighties—Chelsea was infiltrated by South Americans who were bringing huge amounts of coke into New York. They all knew me from living on the block, and they were willing to front me large amounts of the drug.

I hadn't paid my rent for a while, and every month I'd go down to the courthouse and the judge would give me an extension, providing I went back the next month to report my nonworking status. Hairdressers are in the self-employed category, so there was no unemployment to collect, but Kim was still able to get to work as long as she had enough coke and dope to get her through the day. I would send her off each morning with a half a bag of dope to hold her, plus whatever coke I could spare while still leaving enough for me, then go back to sleep until late in the afternoon. Then I'd get up, do a hit to get my day going, and start wheeling and dealing the drugs.

★

When I think about it now, the downward spiral seems so obvious, but let's just say that my foresight then was a bit more blurry than my hindsight is now. First, I became unable to sell as many drugs as we were consuming. Then I missed a court date for the apartment, which meant no more monthly extensions and certainly an eviction. Worst of all, though, I owed a man from Cuba, named Cuba, $2,800. And Cuba was a short, pumped-up local dealer with a shaved head and beady little eyes who was not to be fucked with.

He showed up one night at my apartment to collect the money, which I owed him for a big eight, three and a half ounces of cocaine. When I answered the buzzer, my stomach fell as I heard his voice. "Cuba," he said with force, in his accent. "Let me in."

I buzzed him in, then ran around trying to hide all our drug paraphernalia. None of the big coke dealers used; it was a business to them, and they frowned on others who were selling and using. Kim went into the bathroom to clean herself up, as we were both looking pretty strung out. When I opened the door for Cuba, he walked in as if he owned the place —picking up mail then tossing it back on the kitchen table.

"You got my money?" he asked, with his back toward me as he continued to look around.

Kim came out of the bathroom, hair slicked back and sporting a little lipstick. She flashed a big smile at Cuba. "Sit down," she said. "Would you like something to drink?"

He looked around as if he wouldn't be caught dead sitting on our furniture. "Nah, I'm good, just waitin' for my dough," he spat, and then, "You're two days late."

"I know, Cuba," I said, shooting Kim a look of panic. We didn't have the money—or enough coke left, if he asked for the product instead.

"Doesn't Michael have the money?" Kim said.

"Who's Michael?" Cuba turned around and glared at me.

"Michael is my music manager," I responded. "He took some on credit, but he's good for it."

"Call him." Cuba said.

I shook my head. "I'll get it from him tomorrow." I was desperate not to get Michael involved. "He's definitely good for it," I added. "He's loaded."

"Now!" Cuba sputtered, leaving no room for discussion, then pulled a gun to prove it. Immediately, I called Michael and told him my situation. "I'm coming over," I said in a panic.

Cuba squeezed into the Benz with his gun. I sat on his lap, and Kim drove. I'd never seen a gun that close, and I was terrified, shaking and sweating. At Michael's Park Avenue apartment, Cuba and Kim waited in the car while I ran up and got a thousand dollars to hold him off for a few days. Michael was furious, but he gave it to me.

The next day, I woke up to an eviction notice taped to my door: We had ninety days to leave the premises. After staring at it vacantly for a while, I snorted a couple of lines for a wakeup, and tried to think. I needed a way to make money fast, so I could keep doing what I was doing.

For the past month, I'd been storing large amounts of drugs, in lockboxes for the dealers, because Fifteenth Street was such a hot spot. They needed the drugs close, so when they sold a large amount, they'd come up to my place and re-up. They would throw me small amounts of coke to keep the safe in my apartment. Now I reasoned: The drug dealers would surely want my lease if I offered it, so they could use the apartment themselves as a holding space. I rummaged through my old papers and found the original lease to the apartment, then used Wite-Out to make it a blank template and made copies of it.

I asked Cuba to come over first, telling him I had a proposition.

He was interested, but automatically thought he would get the lease for the remaining $1,800 I owed him. But the lease was worth more than that, plus I hated him for the scare he'd given us the night before. So I sent him packing.

When Cesar, the Colombian drug lord, heard I'd met with Cuba, he sent over one of his boys and asked Kim and me to dinner. When we accepted, they picked us up in a limo and took us to a private club and restaurant in the meatpacking district. The place looked like a dive bar when we walked in, but upstairs, the vibe was completely different. A large round table had been set up in the middle of the room, with six place settings on a white table-cloth—for Kim, me, Cesar, and three of his Colombian goons—and beautiful flowers in the center.

I was nervous, but Kim was smooth as silk; she was used to this wise-guy crowd, and she had enough knowledge to know how to work the room, even charming the owner of the place (a forty-something Spanish woman who looked like she came off a flamenco dance floor, waltzing back and forth, to and from our table, and bantering with Cesar in Spanish). Kim flirted with the guys just enough to rock their cocks, but held them at bay because she was there with me, and only to do business. At the end of the appetizer course, I pulled out a legit-looking lease for the apartment that was dated for one year. Cesar could hardly contain himself and ordered a bottle of champagne. I could see his ego inflate at the fact that he was being chosen over Cuba and would have a stronghold on the block. I had him right where I wanted him.

We negotiated over the entrée and ended up striking a deal over dessert. He would give us $7,000 in cash and a half ounce of cocaine for the lease, but it would stay under my name because they were illegal immigrants. They would continue to pay the rent of $550 a month to me, and I would pay the landlord. I filled the lease in with one of their names as a co-occupant, then signed it, finished the bottle of champagne and dessert, and went home for the night with the seven grand. The cocaine, he had told us, would be delivered the next day.

The next afternoon, I went to pay Cuba the rest of what I owed him. He lived in Queens, but no one had that address; when I needed him, I was to go to an apartment in the Chelsea projects, which he shared with his city squeeze Hilda—whom he some-times referred to as his puta—a battered-looking junkie who lived there. "Cuba got busted last night," she said, when she opened the door. She looked stressed and tired, like it had been a long night.

"You can leave the money with me."

I laughed. "Ah, I don't think so," I said, and I started to walk away.

Hilda stepped into the hall. She wore only boxer shorts and a wife beater, and her arms had so many bruises and tracks running down them that she could have passed for a crossing station at Grand Central.

"Leave it with me!" she said, trying to sound threatening even as she almost keeled over from her smoker's cough. "That's what he'd want!"

I gave her a look. "If that's what he wants, he can send me a message," I said. "He knows my address." I walked away, leaving her ranting that he would kill me if I didn't leave it. I wasn't too worried. As a huge drug dealer and an illegal immigrant, I figured he'd be away for quite some time.

Kim and I packed up the apartment and moved to Jersey City, New Jersey, leaving no forwarding address. Jersey City was far enough from the dealers, yet close enough to get into the city when I needed to score. Then we put the Mercedes up for sale, because we needed the money for more drugs.

Two weeks later, the Benz was stolen out of a Shop Rite parking lot while Kim's mom was showing it for sale.

The insurance—which, amazingly, we hadn't let lapse—paid off the loan, but we lost our down payment. Kim's mom felt so badly that she gave us her car, a little Honda Civic hatchback that we would use and abuse like everything else.

The first month came and there was no eviction at Fifteenth Street, so I collected my rent from the Colombians and spent it on drugs. I thought we were set for at least another month—I was so clueless I didn't realize an eviction could happen any time, not just on the first of the month—so I kept going to Fifteenth Street to cop my drugs. One afternoon, I was stopped at a red light at Fifteenth and Eighth Avenue when a huge Hispanic thug with baggy clothes and a gold front tooth ran up to the car. He whipped out a gun and held it to my window, aiming at my head.

Kim saw him first. Her eyes grew wide, but when she tried to tell me, her lips moved but nothing came out. Finally, I turned and saw the barrel, just inches from my face. But instead of cowering, my adrenaline and instinct took over. I rolled down the window and faced the gun head-on, literally.

"Pull over, you fucking bitch," Cesar's guy yelled. "They raided the place this morning."

The marshal had obviously come to enforce our eviction, found the drugs, and taken everyone in.

I started to cry, fear and anger and desperation at the state I was in, finally catching up with me. "If you're gonna shoot me," I yelled, "then just fucking shoot me right now." I grabbed the barrel of the gun and put it to my forehead. "Pull the trigger. I don't care. Just fucking *do* it!" I was screaming at the top of my lungs as tears streamed down my face.

A car behind me blew its horn. The thug turned quickly toward the car, then pulled his gun away from me and shoved it into his jacket.

Kim was silent, her eyes closed. Maybe she was praying, or maybe she couldn't watch me get my brains blown out.

"Drive, bitch," the guy finally yelled. "Get the fuck out of here, puta." He waved me along, trying to look inconspicuous to traffic.

I pulled away, engulfed in a spasm of terror and relief. I didn't look back or reenter that block for a good decade after that.

FIFTEEN

AT SOME DESPERATE point, Kim and I agreed it was time to get into a methadone program.

A few words about methadone: It was designed and developed by Germany during the Second World War to keep their troops pain-free; after the war, the United States took control of the German factory that produced it and renamed it Dolophine (a combination of the Latin *dolor,* meaning "pain," and the French *fin,* meaning "end"). In 1947 the United States began clinical trials, thinking Dolophine/methadone would be revolutionary as a pain-killer, but dropped the ball until the late sixties, when heroin use was rising fast, and nothing that doctors used seemed to counteract the withdrawal symptoms. They started experimenting with meth-adone and realized that it was the best replacement to help people stop using heroin. The research found that tolerance was slow to develop, so the all-encompassing methadone maintenance treat-ment program was born. The problem for me with this program is that people get on methadone maintenance and then often are unable to get off because the effects last much longer in the system, which makes the detox excruciating. What's more, everyone I knew back then on methadone maintenance used it to double dose, meaning they took the methadone as a cushion while still shooting heroin and cocaine; the methadone merely kept them from constantly getting dope sick.

Kim and I were no exceptions to this, at least when it came to cocaine. With free drugs on a daily basis from the State of New York to keep our habit at bay, we did more cocaine than we'd ever done before. We did as much as we could possibly afford. As for heroin, I couldn't fully kick it with the initial doses of methadone—they start you on a low dosage (usually around 10 milligrams) and build you up until you're taking enough to not be sick anymore from heroin withdrawal, and it took me a while to get up to that amount, even though they increased my dose fast. (I was up to 70 milligrams within a couple of weeks—the highest they'd give back then was 100—and that was rare.) So for the first month, I subsidized by snorting some heroin, though not as much as I had been. Then I had a month or so where I didn't need any heroin, but after that the cocaine starts to eat up the lingering effects of the methadone in your system, so that by the next morning, it was as though you'd never had it at all, and you have to run back to the clinic and get dosed again. What's more, I started to find—again, likely because of all the coke I was doing—that the methadone couldn't hold back my heroin addiction anymore, and I gradually began adding heroin, first in small, then in larger amounts. I'd heard that if I shot the heroin, it would last longer, but I was still afraid to try that, even though I was intrigued by the concept.

Meanwhile, since we'd had to get on Medicaid to ensure we got in the methadone program (Medicaid being free government health care for low-income families), we now also got welfare, which gave us each $210 plus $140 in food stamps every two weeks. The food stamps came in handy, because when the cash ran out I'd take them to a bodega and cash them in, seven dollars for ten, then have money to buy more drugs. And trust me, I needed the drugs; there were times I was so sick that I couldn't get out of bed to hustle. Again, the amount of cocaine we were using ate up all the methadone in our systems, and left us dry, like we'd never had it. Knowing I had money waiting at check cashing always made it easier to ride out the pain.

I wasn't just physically sick at this point; I'd become neurotic, and I had constant paranoid delusions that someone was after me. (Though in retrospect, I can't help wondering if maybe they weren't so delusional after all!) We had acquired a dog, a black lab/mutt mix named Hanzi, who I was afraid to take out and walk (so he shit in the kitchen), and two cats whose litter box was never changed. In short, our place was a (literal) dump. On top of that, we were smoking so much cocaine that one night Kim's lungs crystallized and collapsed. She went into convulsions and was rushed to the hospital, where she stayed for a week; when she came out, she had to stop working. (She also needed an asthmatic inhaler, which she'd have to use for the rest of her life.) That didn't help our financial situation, and soon enough we stopped paying rent and started getting eviction notices. We were in deep shit, and I didn't know how to fix it. So I decided we'd run.

We gave the cats to a friend, packed up the dog and all our stuff, and hit the road for Detroit and my parents—the only people who would take me in at this point. Since we were "in the system," we could now drink our methadone at the local Detroit clinic, while also collecting money from welfare to do whatever else we wanted while we were there.

A few more words about methadone: When used correctly—as detoxification from heroin—methadone is in effect the best thing since sliced bread. A small dosage, taken on the first day of detox, eases the withdrawal symptoms simultaneously, then if you slowly reduce your intake of the methadone, in seven to ten days your dependence on the heroin should be gone as well. Methadone is used on a regular basis in detox facilities and actually helps heroin addicts kick dope. Unfortunately, this isn't how the methadone maintenance program in this country works. *Maintenance* being the operative word. For one thing, you have to be on methadone maintenance for one year before they consider detoxing you—and you have to comply with the regulations of the program, which means taking it every day, otherwise you get dropped. The government has studies showing that higher doses of methadone given over long periods of time can keep patients in treatment, and reduce criminal activity. Of course that's true because it fucking keeps you numb and builds up in your system. Most everyone I knew started the methadone treatment program because in addition to being addicted to heroin, they were also addicted to shooting coke or smoking crack, and since methadone was free, it provided a blanket of opiate cush in one's system, making it possible to enjoy those other drugs even more. You show up at a government-run clinic where registered nurses dispense methadone tablets dissolved in juice that you drink in front of them over a counter. (In recent years, they've replaced the orange tablets with a cherry-flavored liquid.)

I'd worked myself up to 90 milligrams per day, which was a very potent dosage of methadone, and that got me higher and was much more consistent than street heroin, because it was synthetic, pure, and cumulative in the system; it also had a numbing quality, which is why it helped with the pain of heroin withdrawal. But unlike heroin, which moves through your system very fast, methadone leaves opium deposits deep in your tissue and bones for long periods of time, which then take longer to clean out. It also happens to be a nightmare to detox from because it takes so long to get out of your system. Most of the people I knew were never able to get off it.

Not that Kim and I had any particular interest in doing that anyway.

On arrival in Detroit, we moved into the basement of my parents' house. My mother was doing intense chemo at the time, and they were so busy with her medicines, hospitalizations, and blood transfusions that they didn't notice what a mess we were. She was in the hospital once or twice a week, and weak and sick when she was back home. Still, I never thought that she would actually die. I never thought anything, really. I just continued getting high and didn't pay much attention to what was happening around me.

But when my sister, who never overreacted to the sick and dying (because her husband was a doctor and they minimized illness to a fault), called one day and asked me to meet her at the hospital, I knew it had to be bad. When I arrived, the Syrian Orthodox priest from our parish was there in the waiting area saying prayers, and a couple of very close family friends were there, too. My brothers and their wives were on their way.

Mom had been moved to a special part of the ICU because she couldn't hold the blood they were giving her. It was one of those rooms with a big wall of glass that you could look through but couldn't go into unless you were prepped. My father was in there, looking broken sitting next to her bed in a sterile robe, cap, mask, and rubber gloves. When he glanced up and saw me, he got up and came to the door. A nurse had given me all the gear to put on, and now she patted me on the back while ushering me in.

I couldn't believe this was happening. My mom—an elegant woman with velvety Mediterranean skin and perfect Chanel-red lips at all times, a woman who, if you happened to catch her at home when she wasn't yet dressed or primped, would still have on a lovely nightgown with a matching robe—was now a tiny gray figure lying in bed, tubes going in and out all over her. It seemed as though she had been fighting so hard, yet here we were at her deathbed.

I expected her to be completely out of it as I sat down next to her. But as soon as she heard my voice, her eyes opened, and there it still was: that sparkle I loved so much, the sparkle my dad had fallen in love with so long ago. "You came," she said, putting her hand out to me.

With my rubber-covered hand, I reached out and held hers. "Of course!" I said. "Where else would I be?" I started to cry.

"It's going to be okay," she said.

"I don't think so," I said.

She might have been dying, but I saw now that she was still beautiful. I, in contrast, felt disheveled and ratty, ugly and high, and borderline sick since I hadn't been able to get to the methadone clinic yet that day.

"How are you doing?" she asked.

"Shouldn't I be asking *you* that, Mom?"

"We can see how I am," she said, trying to smile.

I sniffed. "I'm fine," I said quietly, still teary-eyed.

"Well, you don't look so well," she said, and I couldn't believe that even sick as she was, my mother was still trying to ease my weary little existence. "Talk to me, *habibity*," she said then. "Tell me things."

I shifted, suddenly feeling a different kind of nervous. "Like what, Mom?"

"Oh, I don't know. Anything."

We sat in silence for a moment. I was trying to find something interesting and positive to tell her, but I couldn't think of one thing.

She probably knew that my life was full of pain and chaos— really, how could she not?—but I knew this wasn't the time to launch into a discussion about my welfare dependence or my cocaine and methadone addictions, or how I'd been evicted from my last apartment. My mind was racing, and yet I was speechless.

"I need to ask you something," she said, finally.

"Anything," I replied, almost relieved.

"You, *habibity*, are a lesbian. Right?"

I swallowed hard. A long time ago, going through my old things after I'd moved to New York, my mom had found a letter declaring my love for Sophia. She'd been disgusted and irate and had called me in New York to confront me; I'd been so traumatized by her accusations and anger that I'd put Kurt on the phone to talk to her.

"Mrs. Elias, don't you think I would know if Rayya was a lesbian?" he'd said to her. "She's my girlfriend! I can assure you she's not." (Poor guy, he didn't have a clue at that time.)

My mom and I had never broached the "lesbian" subject again. But by now, it was understood by everyone in my family that Kim and I were a couple, even though nobody ever talked about it. Kim traveled with me, lived with me, and got wasted with me; we were almost never apart. When we'd moved into my parents' house, my father had given me a look but didn't say anything, and that was that.

I snapped back to reality. "What do you mean, Mom?" I asked, trying to stall.

"A lesbian, *habibity*. Isn't Kim your lover?"

I cleared my throat under the mask and tried to look anywhere but at my mom's piercing eyes. Heat was rising through me, and I wasn't sure if it was my own heart I heard beating or the actual heart machine my mom was connected to. I looked at the machine and realized that the little peaks and valleys were perfectly sequenced with the noise in my brain.

"Please tell me the truth," my mother said. "I have so many

questions." She squeezed my rubber-covered hand, the gloves showing islands of sweat through the powder that lined them.

"Yes," I said finally, in a whisper. "I am." I stared at the ugly painted concrete blocks and the tiled gray floors, trying to find comfort in the institutional monotony.

My mother smiled, victorious, and then continued, clearly using her circumstance to get me to burst open and tell her everything she'd always wanted to know but was afraid to ask. "What do you do?" she asked.

I swallowed. "What do you mean?"

I had a feeling I knew what she meant, but I couldn't wrap my head around it. Could my proper and graceful Syrian mother, with her flawless etiquette and perfect French accent—my mother, who'd never spoken to me about sex in my life, even back when I wanted her to—could she really want me to tell her what sort of lesbian sex I engaged in?

"I mean how do you *do* sex?" she said. "How do you—"

"Mom!" I pleaded. "C'mon! I don't do that!"

"What do you mean, you don't do this?" she said. "You don't kiss?"

"Well—yeah," I confessed. "I mean, we kiss, but . . ." I stopped. I was drenched in sweat.

The door opened, and I'd never been so happy to see my dad. He stood in the doorway, wanting to come back in, but Mom said, "Zachary, please leave us alone for a little while."

My dad looked at me suspiciously. But he must have seen the fear in my eyes (and taken it for concern about my mother's health), because he softened, then said, "Don't look so frightened, Binti. Everything will be okay."

Obviously, he had no clue as to what was going on. "Dad!" I said, grabbing at my lifeline. "You can stay! Really!"

"No," my mother countered.

So my dad left again, the door closing and locking behind him, and I was a hostage to this uncomfortable conversation once again: heartbeat monitors, tubes, none of the drugs I so needed by this point, and my mother's sexual curiosity, a dying wish that I couldn't deny. "So tell me," she said, picking up where she'd left off. "You kiss, yes? On the lips?"

I sighed. "Yes," I said.

"Do you touch her breasts and kiss them, too?"

"What? No!" I lied.

"Then what do you do? How do you, you know . . . make love?" She almost smiled. "Don't look so shocked," she added. "Your eyes are going to land on my bed."

My eyes already felt like they were all the way across the room. I was sweating ferociously now, and I thought for sure I would choke on my words. But it was my duty to grant her this dying wish, no matter how inappropriate, and she didn't let me forget it. "I am dying, *habibity*," she said. "And I want to know these important things about you."

So I took a deep breath and spilled the goods—or at least a select few of them. I told her that yes, we did kiss, and yes, we made love and gave each other orgasms and slept naked together, too. She asked questions, and though I was as discreet as I could be, I tried to answer them as best I could, and she pulled more out of me than I would've ever thought I would tell.

Thankfully, the mask acted as a bit of a shield from the

humiliation of giving my mother explicit details about my sexual relationship with my girlfriend. It wasn't fun. But it was interesting in that what intrigued her the most was the emotional and sexual role-playing. She wanted to know who was topping whom, and why. Amazingly, I had never really thought about the intricacies or the psychology of this business myself, and I realized after this conversation that there were many things about myself that I didn't even know. As with everything else, with sex, too, I usually acted on instinct, certainly never reason, and that was it.

One of the sayings my father always repeated to me was, "know who you are, Binti, because this is where the foundation of your character is." This was another lesson that would take me a lifetime to learn. Many years later, when my father was in the hospital, on his dying bed, I apologized to him for all of the pain and trouble that I'd caused him. "Are you happy now?" he asked.

"Yes I am daddy," I said, crying with my head on his chest.

"And you are well?"

I nodded my head yes.

"Then I have done my job well," he said, patting my head gently. This was my father, clear-cut, with only a few words, that meant everything.

Somehow, I got through the rest of the conversation with my mom without dropping dead of either drug withdrawal or humiliation. And I don't know if it was the chemo or the salacity of the information she got out of me, but something ignited my mother's adrenaline, and—miraculously—she recovered and eventually left the hospital and lived for three years after that. The narcissist in me still likes to think that the sexual detail sparked an excitement in her that made her fight to go on. At any rate, our relationship shifted after that and became more of a friendship. We never talked about it again, but forever regarded each other with reverence for having had a conversation never to be forgotten.

Years later, when my mother did pass away, I was clearing out some of her stuff and found a copy of *The Joy of Sex*. I flipped through the many sketches of sexual positions with a smiling heart, glad I'd been the one to find it; I felt it was meant to be that way. "*Habibity*, I was just interested in sex, period," I could almost hear her say, and as much as I wanted to share this information with my sister, for a long time, I didn't. For once, I had something with my mother that my sister didn't have, and for years I kept that special bond all to myself.

SIXTEEN

AFTER MY MOTHER recovered, my parents asked Kim and me to leave and get our own place. I couldn't blame them. For one, I was twenty-seven years old—not a kid anymore. But also, between the borrowing money and never paying it back, our dog who still wasn't trained, and the running in and out in the middle of the night to score, Kim and I did nothing but add stress to their lives. So we left and moved briefly into the base-ment of my old friend Bobby, who, conveniently, was also our drug dealer. I'd driven the twelve hours to New York once and copped ounces of cocaine for him (because it was so much cheaper than in Detroit), but this time, when he asked me to do it again, I took the money—twenty-five hundred bucks—and left with Kim, staying in New York and not coming back with his drugs. Whatever guilt I felt, which was a lot, was countered by the fact that taking Bobby's money meant we could start over again. Plus, I'd left all my music equipment in his basement and knew he could sell it to recoup at least some of his loss.

★

Back in New York, I rented us a room in a huge apartment on 138th Street until I could figure out what we should do next. This cockroach-infested place turned out to be a crash pad for Jamaican mules bringing ganja into New York. I couldn't stand being so far uptown, especially under those conditions. So I searched for an apartment that was the right fit downtown, in Alphabet City.

For a while, being on methadone gave me the opportunity to look for a job without constantly needing money to chase a heroin high. I found one at a salon on Seventh Street, and I stayed away from the cocaine just long enough to wow the owner into giving me a bunch of his color clients. I found Kim and me a great apartment on Second Street between Avenue A and Avenue B, conveniently located across the street from Lucky 7—the biggest dope house on the east side. Besides that perk and the fact that I could walk to work from my new apartment, we were far enough away from the old Chelsea drug dealers to be safe; this was organized, east side heroin turf, too tough for even Cesar and his gang to tread upon.

My first paycheck was nine hundred bucks plus tips. Things seemed to be looking up . . . except that immediately I started blowing the money on cocaine again. What's more, because I was now on such a high dose of methadone, the street heroin I was snorting didn't work as well, and soon enough I started to need more and more of it—or something more potent—to not get dope sick. There was a way to stretch the dollar, and I don't know how I'd avoided it until now: shooting up. I'd thought about it for some time, but never quite had the nerve—even more desperate times made the decision for me. So I decided to pay a visit to my friend Tommy, who I knew could teach me how to do it. I brought the drugs, ready to share, which I knew would most likely persuade him.

"C'mon, Tommy, I just want to try it," I said to him, after we'd said hello and sat down to do a couple of hits. He'd started fixing to shoot his up and I wanted a lesson.

But Tommy shook his head. "I can't, Ray," he said. "It's not right."

I had expected this; I'd actually asked him about it a few times before. I was becoming more and more intrigued. He'd always said no, trying to deter me from the needle the way I'd tried to scare Kim about heroin. I was curious and afraid in the past, so I would let it go, content on getting high by snorting. Now, I wanted and needed it, and I was determined, ready to fight him for the chance. "I'm snorting it anyway," I said. "Just do it for *me, Tommy!* What's the big deal?"

Once more, he shook his head.

"Fuck it, then," I said. "I'll do it myself."

I snatched a syringe off the table. I had no idea what to do, but I was determined. I poured some heroin into a burnt-out spoon that had a wet piece of cotton sitting in it, yellowed by its previous use.

Tommy grabbed it out of my hand. "You're gonna fucking hurt yourself," he said.

"Then do it for me."

Once again, my persistence paid off, and in that moment, it wasn't just about stretching the dollar, but an urge to share this ritual of self-absorption and destruction.

He bent his head and sighed, realizing he was defeated. "Fine," he said.

I was nervous as hell, but also wild with excitement. I'd been getting high for as long as I could remember, but shooting up was a whole new level: the ultimate plunge into the dark and beautiful world of drugs. Everyone I'd looked up to and admired growing up was a junkie: Keith Richards, Janis Joplin, William Burroughs. . . . All the artists, poets, and musicians who had had the most influence on me had either OD'd or were alive and using junk. It was part of the rock-and-roll fantasy I'd read about and romanticized. Little did I know how little glamour there actually was in it.

I watched Tommy closely, trying to remember every step of this incredible ritual. First he removed the soiled cotton. Then he poured a little heroin in the spoon, and opened up a bag of cocaine and dumped in some of that, too.

"Put more in," I bossed automatically.

"No!" he said. "You don't need more than this, Rayya. Trust me."

I did trust him, but I also couldn't believe it would take so little to get off.

He picked up a brand-new, double-sealed set of works (needles) from the table and ripped off the plastic exterior that was vacuum packed around the syringe. "Don't ever use one that isn't double sealed," he warned me.

He popped the orange cap off the needle with his teeth, drew a little water into the syringe (about 20 cc's) from a glass that was sitting on the table, and squirted the water into the spoon. He took a lighter, lit it, and placed the flame under the spoon for a second until the water heated and both white powders melted. Then, holding the syringe with his teeth, he un-plunged it and used the plunger to stir the liquid inside the spoon with a piece of cotton he'd previously bitten off of the filter of a Marlboro.

"Why do you have cotton in there?" I asked.

"To filter it," he said around the syringe.

"Oh. Right." I smiled nervously.

He put the plunger back into the syringe, pointed the needle into the spoon, placed it gently on the cotton, and drew in all the liquid until the cotton turned white and dry. Then he flipped the syringe over, tapped it, and squeezed out the bubble until a small drop of liquid clung to the point. He looked at me with sad eyes. "Are you sure about this?" he asked.

I nodded with anticipation, though not quite as certain as I had been just a few minutes earlier. The reality of the needle piercing my skin was scary, but not enough to change my mind.

"I'm gonna give it to you slow," he said. "Let me know when you've had enough. You don't have to take all of it."

His place was dirty and crowded, with a path leading through the clutter to a mattress on the floor. This wasn't as glamorous as I'd hoped shooting up would be, but I idolized Tommy, who was once a famous guitar player in Polyrock, a band that I loved, and I was happy that my first time was with him. I sat on the mattress, rolled up my sleeve, and smiled nervously. "I'm ready," I said.

"Always make sure there are no air bubbles," he instructed. "Just one can kill you."

I nodded. "Okay."

He took off his belt and tied it around my arm, just above my elbow. My veins popped and he felt around for the biggest one. "You have to register first to make sure you're in," he said.

I had no idea what he was talking about but I didn't really care. I watched nervously as he stuck the needle gently into the big vein and drew in a bit. Blood rushed into the syringe and mixed with the yellowish white fluid that was already in there.

"Okay, here we go," he said.

He pushed a bit in and watched me. The first thing I remember was the taste rising into my mouth as the essence of the chemicals flowed into my bloodstream. Then came the rush, cocaine first, cold and bright and picture perfect with edges so sharp that my vision seemed neon.

"Are you okay?" he asked. "Is this enough?

"More," I ordered, not as automatically this time but at least partly in deference to my lifelong creed: never enough.

He plunged the syringe a little farther. An instant rush washed over me, warm, ambient, and comforting. Tommy stopped and pulled out the needle.

The high was more pure and authentic than anything I'd ever experienced. I felt myself float into an amazing abyss. It was like what I imagined being risen from the dead would feel like: passionate and sensual and free of terrestrial angst. I felt as though I could touch everyone and everything with my mind and my heart. Maybe this is what Jesus felt like when he said: "I am the way and the truth and the life." Anyway, I wanted to live in this place. My mind swirled with fragmented stories and pictures of beautiful images and people I loved while I lay in that dirty bed on the floor.

"How long will this last?" I asked. My voice was loud, as if it came from someone else and invaded the room, so I fell quiet.

"Quite a while," he said.

I wanted it again instantly, that first rush—it was dynamic and unparalleled, and after about ten minutes had dissipated into merely the awesome heroin zone that I normally felt.

Naturally, I became a quick study—exactly what Tommy had been afraid of. I also got the mechanics down so well that I'd do it to Kim, because she couldn't hit herself up. The ritual was exhilarating, and made me feel like I was in that special club of underground urchins who most people were afraid of. This was before needle exchanges were legal in New York City, so I quickly became a notable fixture in the neighborhood as I learned the ins and outs of acquiring works that were safe to use.

At first, I only had to spend a fraction of the amount of money to get the same feeling as I did prior to shooting up. But things deteriorated quickly after Tommy's, and once I started shooting speedballs on a *regular* basis I couldn't stop chasing the high, and soon everything started moving so fast that days blended into nights and vice versa. I wouldn't stop until I ran out of money, and then I'd think about going to work, but only to make more money so I could start the process all over again. Soon I lost my job at the salon and started finding ways to make ends meet on the street.

In other words, I started hustling like never before. Since I was well versed in buying and selling drugs, I took it a step further. I would hang out on a street corner, waiting for some poor victim from Jersey or Long Island to drive by looking for drugs. Then I'd offer to cop for them, skimming a little off the top for myself, and they would pay me. All the other hustlers were getting busted right and left, but the cops seemed to stay away from me. Though I was strung out, I was a white chick, who looked like any other artist living in Alphabet City, not at all like the scraggly homeless dudes who were usually out there hustling. But that came to an end on New Year's Day, 1988.

We'd been up all night getting blitzed, and had run out of drugs around seven in the morning. I told Kim that I'd go out and see if anyone was around, as, it being New Year's Day, there would probably still be stragglers lingering trying to cop. Otherwise, there was only one "official" cop spot open that time of morning, and only to buy coke: a bodega on Third Street.

I went out into the bright, crisp first day of the new year. I loved mornings like this, where the city looked like a war zone: everything—bottles, clothes, take-out containers—discarded as if in the aftermath of a great battle. I walked over to my corner to see if anyone was out, but no one was. After waiting about ten minutes, I decided to go over and see what was happening at the bodega.

As I walked, I scanned the pavement for the lost wallets, money, or drugs that were often dropped by drunk and wasted people during a big night of partying. Passing piles of trashed furniture and garbage bags of old dirty clothes, among other things, I stopped at a heap of discarded toys and saw a black plastic gun that looked like a miniature Uzi. I smiled, then picked it up and put it in the pocket of the red and black plaid wool hunting jacket I wore.

When I got to the bodega, I saw that it was dark, but there were people milling around inside. Someone had broken into the store, it turned out, and people from the neighborhood were looting food and everything else they could get their hands on. I thought I could take some stuff, go down to St. Marks Place and sell it, and then buy drugs. We also had nothing to eat in the apartment, so I'd get food so we could have a nice New Year's Day brunch.

I found a shopping cart down the street that a homeless person had been using, dumped the stuff inside it onto the sidewalk, and rolled it down to the bodega. There was a punched-out hole in the glass, so I parked my grocery cart and crawled through the hole, making sure I didn't cut myself or tear my coat.

I must have looked crazed from being up and wasted for at least twenty-four hours, because people were giving me looks of fear and then quickly leaving the bodega. Ignoring them, I walked through the aisles and grabbed sponges and rubber gloves, Ajax and Palmolive, roach motels, Crest toothpaste, and lots of bottles of Nyquil. I loaded up my cart and went back for cans of pork and beans, Dinty Moore beef stew, Chef Boyardee Beefaroni, Kellogg's Frosted Flakes, milk, cheese, Skippy peanut butter, and bread. Finally, I began filling a brown paper bag with nickel candy. I took handfuls of orange slices, Now and Later, Swedish Fish, jawbreakers, and individually wrapped gum balls.

When I was almost done, a youngish kid who I'd seen before working behind the register walked in through the actual door. When he saw me, he froze. Recovering, he looked me up and down, and then I saw his eyes rest on the right pocket of my coat. I looked down and realized that half of the toy gun was sticking out. When I moved to push it back in, the poor kid raised his hands in surrender.

I thought fast. As I said, this was normally a morning drug spot, and the kid had no doubt come to open the store and start selling. "I want the coke," I said, keeping my hand on the plastic gun.

He reached down slowly and grabbed a brown paper bag from the inside pocket of his heavy winter coat, then held it out to me. Amazed at my luck, I reached for the bag and grabbed it. He slid to the side, away from the door, taking mini steps to get out of my way, and I walked out of the store backward, hand still firmly planted on the toy gun protruding from my pocket. I wanted to take my cart filled with all of my goodies, but in the end I decided to take only the bag of candy I'd laid on top of the cart. Then I hustled my ass out of there and down the block. I could feel the little packets of coke in the brown paper bag, and I couldn't wait to get home and show Kim. I'd sell a bunch of them, buy some dope, and hang out for a banging New Year's Day.

About a block and a half from home, I started getting sweaty; I needed a hit. I walked faster. Then, from out of nowhere—I was half a block from home at this point—two police cars pulled up from opposite directions. Cops jumped out of the cars—at least four or five of them—and one of them yelled, "Get down and put your hands up!"

I was scared shitless, as this had never happened to me before. "Why?" I yelled, trying to play innocent.

"On your knees!" the officer yelled back.

I sunk to the ground, petrified. One officer held me, another cuffed me behind my back, and a third grabbed the paper bags—one full of candy, the other full of cocaine. One of the officers patted me down and asked me if I had any knives, guns, or needles on me.

"No!" I said, starting to cry. I was terrified and in shock. The officer reached into my right pocket and pulled out the plastic gun. The other cops stepped back for a second until the officer who was holding it started laughing. "It's a fucking toy," he said. He tossed it to one of the other officers standing there, and, the tension broken, they all started to laugh.

"Of course it's a toy, officer," I said. "It belongs to my nephew Sami, who's visiting. I went to the store to buy candy for him. See?"

"This is some kind of candy?" This from one of the officers, who'd pulled out a handful of yellow bags with cocaine lumps in them.

I pretended to act shocked. "I have no idea what that is," I said.

"Here's the candy," said another officer, as he dumped out the other bag.

I widened my eyes. "Sir," I said, "I picked out a bunch of candy, and the guy in the store gave me both of those bags. I was just going back home now."

"Well, you ain't going home till we get this sorted out," the main cop said. "Happy New Year. You're under arrest."

They threw me into the squad car and took me to the precinct, where I spent the afternoon and evening answering questions and getting fingerprinted. Since I had no prior arrests and no record, they eventually decided to "believe" my story. They'd wanted to bust that bodega for a while, and now, with what they'd found in the bag, they had good cause to raid them. So they let me go.

I walked home, exhausted and shaken and very relieved. But the relief was short-lived, as that wouldn't be the last time I was busted. In fact, from that morning on, I was pretty much a regular in the system.

SEVENTEEN

KIM WAS AWAY at her mom's for a weekend, and I was dope sick and waiting in the alley of a dilapidated building on Ludlow Street to cop. The dope dealers on my block were closed down for a couple of days after someone tried to jump off the building they used to sell drugs from. It was around one thirty a.m. when I saw a tall blond chick make her way down the dim hallway of the ratty building next door, notorious for use by hookers, and out into the warm summer air. The August stench of Chinatown was welcoming compared to the smell of the trick she'd just finished off; I could tell by the sigh of relief and the deep breath she took.

I followed her through the alley. I'd seen this chick before, both in my neighborhood and out at the clubs. She was mysterious, cool, and attractive, and I'd always wondered what her story was. I'd had no idea she was a hooker; I had thought she was an upscale club kid with cool clothes and good hair—a hairdresser, maybe, or a makeup artist.

Usually she gave me an I-know-you nod of recognition, and I'd nod back. But that night, perhaps embarrassed by what I'd discovered, she didn't acknowledge me. I followed her out onto Hester Street, curious. "Hey," I said, stepping up behind her.

"Hey yourself." She said this with a thick Norwegian accent that knocked me back; I hadn't expected that.

I looked her up and down. She was a classy-looking, hot number, expensively dressed, with manicured nails and an upscale bleach job—something I might have done. This chick didn't need money, you could tell.

She pulled a pack of baby wipes from her purse, removed one, and wiped her hands and neck. Then she muttered, "Once in a while you get a real stinky one, and ya never really know till you get right up in there."

"What?" I asked.

She looked at me like I was a space vampire.

"I was trying to cop," I whispered, suddenly intimidated.

Her expression softened, and in that moment, I realized she was out here for more than drugs or a trick: I saw, in her pretty, tired face, an ache for something, maybe the same need I had: to be loved and loved and loved.

"I'm Ray," I said, gently.

"I know. I'm Sasha."

This girl knew me? "How?" I said, and I started to walk with her.

She tripped off the curb, then scowled at the left heel of her shoe. I quickly reached out to steady her, but she shook me off stoically. "I'll go to Fiorucci in the morning and get new ones, if I stay up long enough." She spoke to herself, as if I weren't even there.

"I love Fiorucci," I responded.

"I see you in the neighborhood a lot," she said, finally responding to my earlier question.

We were both quiet as we turned onto Canal Street. Then she said, "If we can get to Crusty Mike's before two a.m., we can cop and get straight; otherwise, we'll have to go to Avenue B and find him in that godforsaken hole Save the Robots. You in?"

I had no idea she was a junkie, but I couldn't have been more thrilled: a score and some time with this girl, all at once. "Sure," I said.

Save the Robots was an after-hours club that people usually funneled into from other clubs around three or four a.m. It was right near my apartment, and housed the finest underbelly of the Lower East Side drug addicts and an occasional up-towner who liked to call his problem "freebasing" as opposed to "crack smoking," even though they were basically one and the same. Crack being totally ghetto and less pure, with many more chemicals; like minute steak compared to a filet mignon.

Sasha raised her arm in a perfect *Heil* Hitler. Two yellow cabs came within inches of a car crash trying to pick us up. After sizing them both up, she went with the older driver.

The clock was blazing; we had to get to Crusty Mike's before he split. "Avenue A and Thirteenth Street, handsome," she purred, and then she fell back into the seat next to me.

The driver was an Irish Bronx guy in his midfifties. He had a cross hanging on his dashboard, which seemed to amuse Sasha. She whipped out a fresh roll of bills from the evening's activities and began waving it around like a dirty dishrag. "Patrick, were you named after the cathedral?" she flirted, after looking at the driver's medallion.

The man looked uncomfortable. "No, St. Patty's Day," he said. "My parents were big drinkers."

"Oh—so are you a recovering Catholic?" she asked.

"A what?"

"Never mind, hon. It's not important."

I could tell she was educated and street smart, cultured and well traveled. Most Europeans are when they end up in New York in their twenties. I was infatuated.

We pulled up to Crusty Mike's building, and she handed the cabby a twenty and asked him to wait for us for a minute. Then she checked to make sure no one was prowling around, as everyone knew about this cop spot, and two white chicks getting out of a cab was a sure sign of a good vic (victim).

I didn't think she was as concerned about losing her money as she was about getting beat up. Turning tricks got rough on girls sometimes, and I remembered seeing her a while back with a bruise on her face. She'd had huge Jackie O sunglasses on to try to cover it up (to no avail), and I recalled thinking then that she probably just fell at a club, or something. Now, I thought otherwise.

No one was lurking, so we got out of the cab and she rang the buzzer.

"Who?" a male voice blared on the crackling intercom.

"It's Sasha," she said.

The buzzer rang; Sasha took off her left shoe, jammed it in the door, and ran back to the cab to give Patrick a huge tip. "Anything else I can do for you?" she flirted, as I watched her with sheer delight.

"Ah, no," he answered, with a nervous smile.

"Whatever you say," she said, but she reached inside the cab and gave his cock a firm stroke, then cupped his balls and whispered, "Anytime you want, Patrick, you can find me on Allen Street."

Patrick adjusted his hard cock quickly, then took off, looking over his shoulder as if he might just do that sometime. Sasha took her shoe out of the door, pushed the door open, grabbed my arm, and quickly pulled me inside, then she slipped the shoe on her foot and started climbing the stairs to Crusty Mike's. I followed.

Crusty Mike's door was slightly ajar. Sasha pushed it open slowly, looking unsure of what to expect when she entered his place. As she did, a Yuppie dude in a suit pushed past us and out into the hallway. He rushed down the stairs, yelling, "I've been here before! You just sold to me two nights ago! Come on, man, I ain't no fucking pig."

Crusty Mike walked calmly out onto the landing and stood watching as the Yuppie stomped down the stairs, continuing to yell all the way. You could tell that Crusty Mike wasn't the type of guy who needed to threaten you, because everyone already knew he was crazy enough to do some sick-ass shit to you if you crossed him (thus, the Yuppie's fast descent as he yelled). You could also tell where he got the name Crusty Mike. He had what looked like crusted saliva in each corner of his mouth, the kind where you wanted to tell him to wipe it off, except it was literally unwipeable: two scabs, one on each side of his mouth. Though you could see that he had once been fairly attractive, his face was now deeply lined and weather-beaten, like freeze-dried beef jerky. Dirty, shaggy blond hair framed his face, and his faded blue T-shirt was dirty and torn. His jeans were filthy yet tight, revealing his stringy body all the way down to the studded, beat-up cowboy boots he always wore. He had a faded tattoo on his bicep, a heart that, naturally, had Mom written inside of it. His teeth were yellow and brown with nicotine stains, and his eyes were so bloodshot they looked like the red lines on the map of the Northwest hub coming out of Detroit Metro Airport. I couldn't tell how old he was—maybe thirty, maybe forty—but I knew he was an angry man with a chip on his shoulder.

Sasha and Crusty Mike looked at each other as the door to the building slammed shut a few flights down. "This is my friend Ray," Sasha said.

I nodded at Crusty Mike, and his empty, cold stare said it all: *You'd better fucking be cool, or you're dead.* That's what I heard, anyway.

We walked into the apartment, me following Sasha, who seemed all too comfortable in this shit hole with this lunatic. The place was your typical if slightly more disgusting shooting gallery and cop spot. It smelled like an old folks' home—like old people's pee—a smell that gave me dry heaves. Soon enough, I saw the source of the stench: A piss bucket sat on the side of the sofa, presumably so Mike didn't have to get up to go into the bathroom when he was getting high. On the couch sat two young boys who looked familiar to me—maybe from Danceteria, I thought. They were nodding out, and probably had no intention of making it out of there that night.

Sasha walked past them, and I followed her and Crusty into the kitchen. The ugly smell grew even thicker as I got closer to the bathtub, which—typical of many East Village apartments—was in the kitchen, wedged between the stove and the fridge. As we approached, I saw that the tub contained soaking dirty laundry, soiled dishes, and pieces of food. God only knows how long that filthy puddle had been sitting there rotting.

Crusty sat down at the table. He reached into his shirt pocket, took out a fresh pack of Luckys, tapped the bottom, and launched into a coughing spell that shook the table. Then he undid the plastic, tapped out a smoke and lit it, still coughing. "Third fucking time the cops have tried to get me this week," he wheezed, with the drawl and gurgle of an old junkie combined with the quintessential New York accent.

I didn't care if the Yuppie was really a cop or not; as a matter of fact, I would've bet that he wasn't. But I'd heard that Crusty was always paranoid and delusional and usually thought someone was watching or following him—which is one of the reasons I'd avoided this cop spot for as long as I had. (I had enough delusions of my own without getting involved in other people's.) "Ever since I was put on that FBI list," Crusty added, "the pig traffic has been out of control in here." He pulled another drag off the Lucky and flicked it into the bathtub.

"Who the fuck is this?" said a voice, and I looked over to see a woman standing at the kitchen counter with a pile of money and some plastic baggies.

"Take it easy, Peggy," Crusty snapped, and then, to us, "That's my old lady." A twinkle came to his eye as he lit another cigarette. I could tell he thought Peggy was the cat's meow. She actually did have a rocking body, in her wife-beater and jeans, but her face was weathered, and she had a missing front tooth and a really bad bleach job, the drugstore kind that leaves you patchy and orange in spots. I could tell this chick was a hawk, that she was the one who took inventory of everything and made sure no one got off with anything they weren't supposed to.

"I'm Ray," I said, and I nodded at Peggy, trying to seem both friendly and not too friendly at once.

She ignored me. "What can I getcha' Sash?" she asked.

Sasha later told me that Peggy blamed Crusty for the tooth every time they got into an argument. They also always tried to get Sasha to side with one of them during an argument. She'd resist, as it was a lose-lose situation, but it often took her forever to get her drugs and get out of there.

"A bundle and two twenties," Sasha said. She turned to me. "And you, Ray?"

"Three bags and a twenty," I replied, talking to both Peggy and Sasha.

"Coming right up," Peggy said. She walked out of the kitchen and into what was likely the bedroom, where the larger amounts of drugs were obviously kept. As we waited, Crusty talked to himself in a low voice, mumbling about the two boys nodding off on the couch. "I should charge those fuckers room and board," he said, taking another long drag off his cigarette.

Sasha kept quiet.

Crusty looked at her, and then he took another long, hard look, as if he were just seeing her for the first time. "Damn, you sure are one hell of a good-looking bitch," he said.

"Thank you," she replied.

"You know, me and Peggy, well, we've been talkin' about havin' a little fun, you know, with someone else. What do you think about that?"

"I think that sounds like a good time for the both of you," she said, with so little hesitation that I think even he was surprised.

Oh my god, I thought. *Is he actually asking her to have a three-way with him and his toothless wife?* I couldn't wait to talk to her about it later—if we ever got out of there. The smell was really getting to me. Every time Crusty moved, a waft of BO and piss smell slapped me in the face and made me practically throw up into my own mouth. Plus, I was really sick at this point and badly needed a hit.

Peggy came back in with the goods. Sasha counted her money and gave it to Peggy, and I did the same. Then Sasha asked if we could do one hit before we left. I'd been praying she'd ask; I wasn't sure if I'd make it home in this shape.

"Sure," Peggy said. "Just leave a five on the table when you're done."

We went into the living room and each pulled out our gear: I used a small leather pouch that I normally tucked into my sock for portable use. It housed my works—which were clean and still good as new with a sharp point—a bottle cap, which was much more portable than a spoon to melt down in, a filter from a Marlboro that I'd used bits of previously, and a very small travel-size three-ounce bottle of water. I bit two small pieces of filter off the butt and handed one to Sasha to use.

Sasha picked up the one boy's head that was leaning into his lap, and I could tell that she, too, recognized him. The other boy had a cigarette butt burned down between his fingers. There were two charred blisters, one on each side of the butt.

"Ooh! That hurts," Sasha said, looking at it.

We both looked over at the table and judging from the empty wax bags, saw that the boys had done quite a bit of heroin. We squished in on the couch between them. She felt really good up against me.

First she did her hit, and then I did mine the same way, tying up with the belts we took off our jeans. We sat and enjoyed the rush for a moment, then left a five spot on the table, grabbed our gear, and split.

Outside, the summer air felt balmy. It was late, and as we walked down Avenue A, we contemplated whether to call it a night, go home, and chill . . . or to go to Robots. The dope was good—too good to be walking around, I thought, and especially too good for a hellhole like Robots. We stopped on the corner of Fifth Street and Avenue A.

The homeless man with his pack of dogs had been sleeping here for as long as I could remember. At night, they all lay in a pile on top of one another. It was sometimes hard to tell who was who, because they all blended in together. "Hey," Sasha said to him.

The guy opened his eyes and gently nodded at her.

Sasha bent down to pet one of the dogs and immediately drifted into a gooey nod. This was no strange site to anyone on Avenue

A. The dogs surrounded her and sniffed her hair as it fell in her face, and she smiled, looking peaceful, like she was in heaven— dog heaven, dope heaven. For a few moments, everything was quiet.

I stood by and watched her, for what felt like a calm eternity— so maybe I nodded as well. I couldn't remember what I'd been doing before the moment I met Sasha that night, nor did it seem relevant or important. "C'mon," I said, finally. "Let's go to my place. I want to sink into a nice hot bath. You game?"

Her face turned up in surprise, as if she'd just woken up. She tucked a ten-dollar bill in the guy's gloved hand, then stood up. "Lead the way, my friend," she said, and she hooked her arm into mine, giving me a look that inspired many things inside of me that I couldn't quite identify.

Back home at last, I held her in the bubble bath. I didn't have sex with her, though I certainly wanted to. Instead, we talked softly through the night and into most of the morning, which was something I'd missed. I couldn't remember the last time Kim and I had such a tender and intimate evening. I'd been right about the fact that she came from a family with money and had a huge inheritance. She lived in an awesome apartment on Ridge Street, in lower Manhattan, that was paid for by her trust. She'd been study-ing costume design but had lost interest, and now found that studying "human behavior," through her own experience and interaction, was much more fulfilling. (She said this half kidding and half serious.)

Sasha and I became good friends after that evening—or as good friends as you can be in that world, anyway. She loved hanging out at our place, but, predictably, she didn't like Kim at all; most people didn't, as she was demanding and manipulative.

Kim, in turn, couldn't stand Sasha and the fact that I had a friendship with her. But my life had shifted to the streets in a way Kim's hadn't, since I was the one hustling all the time, and Sasha's life was there, too. And, being foreign, Sasha understood cultural differences in the same ways I did, which led to a common mind-set and intriguing conversation between us. None of the drug dealers and hustlers I was now hanging out with knew that I'd been a hairstylist or rock musician, that I'd made a record (that was never released) and played for huge music-industry crowds, or that I had traveled to Europe and the Middle East and spoke different languages. They just saw me as another junkie, living on the Lower East Side and hustling to stay high and alive. But Sasha at least understood that I was someone, that I'd had a colorful past. And at that point in my life, that was a lot. Almost more than I could ask for.

EIGHTEEN

MOMMY WAS A tough old lady who lived in the neighborhood. She would smack you upside the head and tell you to wake up if she saw you nodding on the street when she walked by. Her son had died of AIDS a few years earlier from using dirty needles, so her mission was to make sure that junkies had a safe place to shoot up with clean works to use.

As I said, I was a hustler at this point, meaning that I acted as a middleman for people—often of the suit-and-tie, Wall Street variety— who came down to my neighborhood to score drugs but couldn't, either because no one would serve them, or they didn't want to take the risk of getting caught. So I was out on the street before and after office hours, when they drove through the neighborhood looking for someone to cop drugs for them, and I'd offer my services. The choice of hustlers on the streets was slim: Either me, the cute white girl . . . or a bunch of scary-looking, multicultural men, most of them jonesing for a fix themselves. I won out most of the time.

One night a client of mine was hanging out at our apartment with Kim while I was out copping for him. He liked to snort cocaine, and he had no idea that we shot our drugs; in fact, he had quite an attitude about junkies and was very vocal about it—but he paid so well that we put up with his bullshit. Kim did her part and sat with him at the apartment, letting him brag about all his great accomplishments. Our tag team worked well, because these guys didn't have to wait in their cars; they had a place to hang out and do a bump if they needed to, in the safety of our apartment.

It was unusually easy to cop that day, and things went smoothly. I was able to get all the drugs the client asked for as well as my own, with plenty of time left to stop at the neighborhood shooting gallery to do a quick hit and still get back home before he got restless. Sometimes a quick stop, during a long, hard night of hustling and running, was a needed oasis for me.

Mommy ran the neighborhood shooting gallery, you see, and as a result I was someone she knew pretty well. She was a small black woman whose age was a mystery. (Depending on the day, her stress level, and the style of wig she wore, she could look anywhere from fifty to seventy-five.) On the off chance that you caught Mommy with her dentures out, she'd bitch you out as if it was your fault that she had no teeth. She usually wore a floral housedress and slippers, and shuffled around policing and cleaning up after people, making sure no one was tweaking too hard, or overdosing in her living room. She was direct and to the point, almost crotchety, unless you were a regular at her establishment and then she could be somewhat pleasant. There were always lit candles and flowers on a little altar in her living room, along with a framed photograph of her son. She knew everyone in the neighborhood, past and present, where they'd moved to and what their kids were doing. The cops left her alone because they felt sorry for her, allowing her to make a buck in this unorthodox way. It cost five dollars to use her place, and since she was a diabetic, she always had clean needles that you could buy for an additional two dollars— unless you didn't have enough money, in which case she'd give you the works on credit. Sometimes the cops would watch the building to see who came in and out and bust people outside.

That night Mommy introduced me to Kevin, a tiny redheaded guy, no bigger than a dwarf, with a smiling face, polka-dotted with freckles. After we'd said hello, we sat at the table next to each other and peeped over to see what the other was doing.

When he disappeared into the bathroom for a few minutes, he asked Mommy to watch his stash, which is when she took the opportunity to tell me that Kevin was harmless—basically just a sweet guy. He was a cat burglar by trade, and had been incarcerated for many years. He had no intention of living a straight-and-narrow life, she said, because he had no idea how to live in the real world. He had done so many stints in penitentiaries since he was a teen that he was completely comfortable in the system and even enjoyed being able to count on "three hots and a cot," especially because, since he was so small and knew his place in the food chain, no one in prison really fucked with him. (None of the inmates would bully a dwarf because it made them appear weak.)

Kevin came back to his enormous pile of heroin and cocaine, and quickly, we both realized we liked to get high the same way: a little bit of each and straight up the arm. After we both did a shot and settled into heroin bliss, Kevin told me that he was out on parole from Sing Sing and needed a place to crash. I already liked him—he seemed well mannered and good spirited. Now, I took one look at the wad of money he was fondling and the drugs he'd already bought and told him that he could move in with Kim and me and crash on the couch. I rented the couch out to different people all the time, mostly drug addicts who lived on the street and needed a place to shower, get off, and sleep for the night. Knowing that Kevin had been in prison for so long almost made him more credible, more trustworthy. He accepted graciously, and was so grateful that he loaded my syringe with a big fat hit before we left.

When Kim met Kevin she liked him right away, too, so he was in. And we all lived together harmoniously for a few days, everyone happy because the drugs were flowing freely. (Kim and I were still on the methadone maintenance program, so we always had a small buffer—unless we skipped a couple of days of the methadone, and then the pain was excruciating, ten times worse than any heroin withdrawal I'd ever known.) But one morning, as I shut the apartment door behind me on my way to the clinic, the elevator door opened and four cops stepped out. They grabbed me and said that they had a warrant for my arrest because I had missed a court date for a past drug charge. I had no idea, but it was true, so they cuffed me, called me an ugly dirty junkie, and hauled me down to the local precinct, where they fingerprinted and booked me. Twelve hours later, they hauled me downtown to the bullpens.

The bullpens—or tombs, as some people aptly call them—are the hellhole that consists of endless holding cells in the bowels of

100 Centre Street in lower Manhattan. Every criminal in New York City gets processed through the bullpens, whether he's in for murder or jaywalking. So drug addicts, OWS protesters, embezzlers, and hard criminals alike are subject to the same conditions: bologna-and-cheese sandwiches, bad coffee, cockroaches, mice, rats, and filthy toilets and urinals (which you use with no privacy in front of the population of prisoners) are standard. The women try to give you space while you're using the bathroom, though less because they care about privacy than because the closer you are to the toilet, the more it smells like shit. The courts, of course, convene upstairs, where everything is proper and the justice system is hard at work sealing everyone's fate.

I'd been processed through the bullpens a few times by then and knew that during the 1980s there was nothing you could do on the street to constitute a *real* sentence, unless you were a hardened criminal (which I wasn't at that point; I was simply a drug addict who'd found herself in the wrong place at the wrong time, way too often). So I knew what to expect: three to seven days in the bullpens, depending on how overcrowded the system was, ending with a quick slap on the wrist, a "time served" verdict, and freedom to go.

The biggest pain in the ass about getting busted was that I would have to go through a few days of withdrawal: kicking and screaming and sweating on a cement floor in jail next to a bunch of hookers and crackheads, until it was my turn to see a judge. Still, false confidence came easy to me at that point because as fucked up as I was, I still looked better than most of the people who were in the same game, so I felt like a thoroughbred amid a bunch of donkeys. The drugs made me feel invincible, and I believed I was smarter than everyone else because I could turn on the charm and use proper vocabulary and etiquette to blend in with the highest of the high and the lowest of the low, in order to get what I wanted. I knew what I was doing was wrong, but I needed to be able to get away with drug scams, major drug deals, and even robbery, and as long as no one got hurt, it was okay. I'd do a few days in the bullpens and come out unscathed.

Kevin took care of Kim while I was in the slammer that time, which was no small feat: She required huge amounts of intravenous drugs to maintain her head, and if she didn't have them, would go into a crying frenzy, smashing things in the apartment and threatening to go out and find drugs herself, and since she didn't know how to hustle or cop, it was always my responsibility to take care of both of us. I was kicking hard those three days in jail, and the night I came home Kevin had my drugs waiting for me, cause he knew how physically sick and fucked up I would be. This was proof that Kevin was a guy I could really count on and trust, and after that he was welcome to stay as long as his generosity lasted.

Marty was our next-door neighbor, a quiet, tech-head type of guy, sweet but a total geek. He was the poster boy for Yuppies and gentrification, with a lot of money and the dream of living on the edge within a cool artist community.

While Marty was on vacation, we came up with a plan that could only work with an expert cat burglar such as Kevin. In the middle of the night, he would scale the side of the building to the third floor, open the window into Marty's apartment, and climb in. Kevin would then unlock the door so we had access to Marty's place during the day, while the other two neighbors on our floor were at work. Not that they'd care, or probably even notice; Patrick, next door to Marty and to the right of us, was a fashion photographer who was also a junkie, and Jonathan, to our left was a record producer from Australia who always had music blaring and chicks streaming in and out. In fact, Kim, Kevin, and I looked completely harmless compared to what you saw in the Alphabets at that time. Still, just in case, we stuck to daytime hours to make our plan happen.

The rest of the plan was this: We would sell off Marty's stuff, piece by piece, day by day, depending on how much money we needed. Which we did—and alas, with our insatiable appetite for drugs, poor Marty was left with nothing by the time he got back. I even let go of his record collection: four huge milk crates of great vinyl classics were taken to Sounds, a record store on St. Marks, and sold off crate by crate. I don't get a warm, fuzzy feeling when I imagine the look on Marty's face when he got home and discovered his apartment had been cleaned out.

When the police came to take the report, I tried to be as helpful as possible so they could find whoever did this to Marty. I told them everything I knew—which was nothing, of course. No one heard or saw anything unusual. I told Marty I would keep my ear to the ground on the street and see if anyone knew anything about the robbery. This is the difference between an alcoholic and a junkie. They'll both definitely steal your money, except the junkie will help you look for it afterward. Thank god Marty had renter's insurance. (Who but a nice Yuppie from the Upper East Side would've thought about insurance at that time?)

About a week later, Kevin stole a car and was using it as an airport taxi to make money. He'd been getting a little sloppy and strung out lately, not to mention less generous: He'd come back to the apartment with just enough stuff for himself and maybe a little taste for Kim and me. Having him around was becoming more of a liability than an asset, and I was planning to ask him to leave soon; I just wasn't sure how. In the meantime, we still had two pieces of Marty's left to fence: a cool stainless-steel sculpted side table, and a lamp. I had found a modern art furniture store in the West Village that I thought would be interested in both; they were one-of-a-kind pieces and would definitely attract attention, plus across town people had more money to buy this sort of stuff—and there'd be less chance of Marty walking by the store and seeing his table and lamp displayed for sale.

The pieces were fairly small, so I put them in pillowcases and set off on foot to the West Village. As I stepped out of our building, Kevin pulled up in the stolen car, a gray, four-door sedan. He rolled up behind me and stopped. "Get in!" he called. "I'll give ya a ride."

A ride would've been great—the stuff I was carrying was heavy—but I knew better than to get into a stolen car, especially with my track record. "No thanks," I said, and kept walking.

"Come on, Ray," Kevin said, continuing to drive along beside me. He was being nice, I'm sure, but I knew he also didn't want to miss out on the payoff for these two pieces and the drugs that we could buy.

Again, I shook my head and kept walking down Second Street.

But Kevin wasn't having it. He continued to trail me, until finally I walked over to the car to talk to him.

He smiled in his good-natured way. "Just get in the back, like a gypsy cab," he said. "What's the big deal?"

"It's a stolen car Kev," I said. "I can't get busted again."

He looked around. "Don't worry," he said. "If anything happens, I'll play driver."

I gave up and got in the backseat.

We drove a couple of blocks up Avenue A, then took a left, heading toward the West Village. And then it happened: First I heard a siren, and then two cop cars with flashing lights headed us off, which made Kevin slam on the brakes and come to a halt. One of the cops got out; the other, through his bullhorn speaker, yelled, "Please step out of the car."

I instantly freaked out. "Oh my god," I said. "Oh my god. I fucking knew it! What are we gonna do?"

"Don't worry," Kevin said, totally calm. "I got this."

I *was* worried. This was a felony, and I wanted nothing to do with car theft. I looked out the window and saw the officers with their guns drawn. "Oh my god," I said again. Heart racing, I stepped gingerly out of the car. Immediately, the officers threw me on top of the trunk and handcuffed me behind my back, then pulled me up and walked me over to the side of the car. I looked over and saw Kevin on the ground, facedown, arms being cuffed behind his back.

"What is going on here?" I cried.

"Do you know this man, miss?" the officer asked.

"No, sir!" I said. "I was just taking this cab! I was on my way to a furniture store on the west side and I couldn't get a yellow cab, so I flagged him down."

They picked Kevin up and laid him down on the hood of the car, bent over, with his head sideways pressed so hard into the metal that his face looked contorted.

"Is this true?" the other cop asked.

Kevin hesitated.

"Officer please!" I said, desperate now. "I have no idea who this guy is!"

Just then, Kevin yelled out. "She's tellin' the truth," he said. "She got in the car thinking it was a gypsy cab. She doesn't know me from Adam."

The cop hesitated a second, then turned me around and uncuffed me. "Go," he muttered. "You can leave. But next time, make sure it's a yellow cab."

I wanted to cry with relief. "Thank you so much, Officer," I said. "Can I get my stuff from the backseat?" At that moment, my entire future was in the hands of an ex-con who I'd known for only two weeks—if he wanted to, he could sell me up the river and I'd be over. Like every other choice in my life, I'd put myself in this position, without thinking at all, and once again I was bound in a tangled web of circumstances, supposedly "beyond my control," but actually completely of my own making. It takes situations like this for me to realize that my persistence has real consequences. Life-altering consequences.

Without answering, the officer reached into the backseat of the car and pulled out the pillowcases. He opened them and glanced in. I held my breath. "Cool stuff," he said, finally. He handed the pillowcases to me and motioned for me to walk away.

I turned quickly on my heel and walked as fast as I could down the street without breaking into a sprint. When I was a safe distance away, I turned around to take one last look at the redheaded leprechaun named Kevin, a character who could easily have walked out of a Peter Jackson trilogy. He turned and saw me look, and I swear that when our eyes met, he smiled and winked as if to say, "It's okay, Rayya, I got this." That was the last time I ever saw or heard from Kevin.

NINETEEN

BACK IN DETROIT my sister, Maya, who I hadn't seen or talked to in almost a year, woke up in the middle of the night in a cold sweat. She'd had a dream—a nightmare—that I was sitting on a dirty blanket in front of a store begging for change, my bare feet black with dirt, sores and bruises all over them. Maya sat up and looked around her lavish bedroom with a sigh of relief. It was just a bad dream; nothing more. Still, lately she'd been having these dreams about me every night. *Why?* She wondered.

She knew that the last time she'd seen me, I'd been in bad shape. She thought about how lucky she was to have her comfortable life, all her children safe and taken care of, and she wondered why her little sister seemed to have gone so far astray. She felt that the dream was a sign that I'd fallen into even worse straits and needed her help.

So she explained to her husband that she had to go and find me, and then she hopped on a flight to New York. On arrival, she took a cab down to East Second Street, the last place Kim and I had lived before we'd been kicked out and Gary had taken us in briefly. Maya had been there before, a few times, to try and visit, but I would pretend no one was home because the place was not exactly up to her standards: There were always filthy clothes lying in piles all over the floor, and sometimes in order for the dirty dishes not to smell, I'd put them in the fridge because there was never any food in there anyway. Used drug paraphernalia lay around in so many different places that it was impossible to clean up quickly if someone was at the door. So Maya would wait outside, hoping I'd come out. Eventually she'd get tired of being harassed on the street, and she'd leave a note stuck to the front door of the building asking me to meet her for dinner. Sometimes I'd show up and other times not, depending on what my needs were. When I did show, it was only to ask her for money, of course, which she would give to me unwillingly and make me swear not to use it on drugs. I would promise anything if I had to, on my life if necessary, whatever it took to get the money. Then off I'd go, not to be seen or heard from for long periods of time.

None of this mattered to her now. She was worried about me, and she wanted to find me and tell me I was loved and that help was available if I wanted it.

The taxi stopped to let her out. But she just sat there—over-dressed, out of her element, and slightly panicked. *This is a terrible place*, she thought. *There are scary homeless people everywhere and heroin addicts on every corner.*

She asked the cabbie to please wait for her, and then she ran to the door and buzzed. As usual, no one answered, so she got back in the cab and went up to the St. Moritz and checked in. She changed into jeans and a T-shirt, sat down on the bed, and thought a moment. Then she pulled out her address book, flipped through it, and called Kim's mom, whose number she'd had from before when I'd spent Christmas with them.

After Maya identified herself, Patty told her that I was not doing well. We had been evicted, and that something had happened to me. She wasn't sure what, but that I wouldn't talk about it. She also told Maya that she tried to get me to stay with them, but after sleeping there for a couple of days and eating a bit, I'd disappeared. Kim thought that I'd probably gone back to the old neighborhood.

Maya was crying and trembling on the phone, she later told me. "Can you help me?" she pleaded. "You and Kim, to find her. Please?"

Kim knew exactly where to find me after the Frank incident. I told her I'd be staying with Tommy, who I knew lived at the park, he pitched a tent in the homeless artist community section.

The riots were starting at Tompkins Square Park again; for New Yorkers, it had become synonymous with the city's increased social problems. For me, it was home. The park was a high-crime area, with camps of squatters and homeless people. It was also the center for drug dealing and heroin use. The police were trying to shut it down; the city was trying to take it back from us, and news crews were there 24/7 to document the struggle. People I knew were constantly being brutalized by the police, arrested, and then put back on the street, with nowhere else to go but right back to the park. When the police surrounded the park and were ready to storm in, Tommy and I would find somewhere else to sleep for a night or so, then come back to our home, our park.

★

I had seen what happened at the last riot, two weeks earlier, when I stood on the outskirts of a political mess afraid only that my dealers could be busted. Some people I knew had been beaten up pretty badly. I wish I could say that I'd cared about the politics of the situation, but my interests didn't lie in the injustice of gentrification, or the real estate mongers. All I wanted was somewhere to crash at night and blend into the chaos during the day, somewhere I could shoot my drugs and wash up if I wanted to without the scrutiny of "normal" society.

Now, Kim took both her mother and Maya to Avenue B and Seventh Street, then left them on the corner and entered Tompkins Square Park by herself. She wanted to spare them having to walk through Tent City, seeing all the homeless junkies and freaks—and me, one of them.

I wasn't surprised to see Kim—I had figured she'd make her way down there sooner or later, as she couldn't stay away from either me or the drugs for very long—but when she told me her mom and my sister were waiting just outside the park, I was shocked and enraged and told her to get the hell out and never come back. I wasn't exactly in meet-the-folks condition. I'd looked bad enough before we'd been evicted—skinny and pale, with constant cold sores on my face and track marks on my arms— but since the Frank incident four weeks earlier, I'd really let myself go and even I knew it. I hadn't showered or changed my clothes in weeks, and I couldn't remember the last time I'd eaten. I was so thin that my size four jeans hung off me. My hair was matted and I had sores on my face from picking my skin (something that happened when I shot too much coke, which was always). My hands were bruised and bloodied from trying to hit the veins on them after the ones in my arms had quit on me. I tried wiping my hands on my filthy jeans, but the blood was dried and only flaked off.

Kim, on the other hand (I couldn't help noticing), looked pretty good since I'd left her mother's place. She was clean and her hair was freshly highlighted. She'd put on some weight, which took the hollow look out of her face, and she was sporting an outfit I'd never seen before. I was a bit jealous and skeptical—she'd cleaned up before and always sunk back into addiction over time—but when she sat down next to me and kissed me tenderly on the lips, I forgot my envy and just felt happy to see her. She smelled so good, too: like Oil of Olay and Opium perfume. "Are you okay?" she asked.

"I'm fine," I said, letting her put her arms around me.

"I think you should talk to your sister, Rayya," she said, after a moment. "She wants to help. And what if she wants to give you some money?"

I didn't answer, though I was thinking about it. Finally, after sitting quiet for a few minutes, Kim said. "I'm really worried about you, baby."

After a lifetime of ignoring red flags and smashing the alarm bells, after my many years of absolute headstrong conviction that my will was the only power that could drive me, somehow those six words stung my heart. I stood up slowly and walked out of the park with Kim to find my sister. As I exited the park, walking through trash and people as though I were in the aftermath of an apocalypse, I saw Maya standing at the far edge, just outside the fence, her figure shaking, taking small steps to get closer and then finding her composure and standing still. I wanted to run into her arms and melt, but I also wanted to be strong to prove that I didn't need her or anyone. As I got closer, I realized that she was crying, holding her hand over her mouth. She looked terrified, and I could tell she didn't know whether to hug me or shriek and run away from me. She held out her arms to me. I held my ground, like I was under attack.

"Why are you here?" I asked Maya, looking only at her. I couldn't look at Patty, as I wasn't sure if she'd known about the gold necklace I'd taken from her jewelry case to pawn when I left, and I didn't want to deal with that.

"Because I'm worried about you, *habibity*," Maya said. "Will you come and stay with me in my hotel?"

"Uh, I don't think so." I looked at myself up and down, then tried to jam my bloodied, dirty hands into my pockets, but winced at the pain.

Maya continued to beg me to come to her hotel, even for one night, and let her take care of me. Finally I agreed, but I told her I needed money to score so I could stay straight and not be in pain through the night. As long as I stayed in the park, I could still get my drugs by copping for other people, generally people who drove through and waited in their cars for me to deliver. I also ran errands for some of the dealers on Second Street and made money that way. Tommy let me stay in his tent, while he slept on a bench. I used it purely to get high in, because it was rare that I slept at all. Every third day or so, I'd get so exhausted I'd start hallucinating and then pass out for a few hours, then would wake back up and start the ride all over again. It had been a few hours since I'd used anything, and I told Maya the truth.

She gave me the money, knowing it was the only way to get me alone with her, and on my word, I went in, copped the drugs that I needed and a clean set of works, and came right back. Kim and Patty waited long enough for me to turn the corner, then drove away—fine with me, as I didn't want to share any of my stuff with Kim anyway (and I'm sure Patty was thinking the same thing). I didn't give a shit about anything or anyone at that point; all I cared about was the dope and coke that kept me high and numb so I wouldn't have to face the reality of my life. As we walked away from the park trying to hail a cab, my fellow street urchins/junkies eyeballed my sister. She looked like a walking ATM, and I was both proud and embarrassed to be with her. (I was also worried; she could easily have been jumped at any moment.)

★

We took a taxi to the St. Moritz hotel. Had I not entered the lobby with Maya, they surely would have thrown me out, but she took me by the hand and walked me to the elevator. I was pain-fully conscious of what I looked and smelled like: I was filthy, reeking of intolerable odors, and there were track marks up and down my arms and big gaping sores all over my face. It took me back to when I was nine years old again, the freak at school, and I almost broke out of there in a frantic run. But Maya squeezed my hand and steadied me till the door opened, and then, despite having always been a germ-a-phobe, she put her arm around me and walked me into the elevator and then into her room. Immediately, she went into the bathroom and started running a hot bath. When she came out she said, "It's all yours."

I walked into the bathroom and locked the door.

"Please leave the door unlocked," she called. "Don't worry, I won't disturb you." She sounded so somber and earnest that I unlocked the door, though I kept it closed, because I didn't want her to have to see me like this.

I fixed myself a shot, not to get high but to get well—and trust me, there is a difference. Something inside me stirred with humility, and I wanted to give my sister back the respect that she'd given me. But I also didn't want to spend another moment being dope sick.

The moment the heroin took hold and I felt warm and cozy, nothing looked as good as the brewing bubble bath.

"Are you okay?" Maya's worried voice came through the door.

"Yup," I said.

"Can I help you with anything?"

"Nope. Not now."

The bathroom was lined with mirrors, which I didn't notice until after my get-well shot. Though I'd known I looked bad, I still was horrified seeing myself. My frame was gaunt, my skin gray; as I removed my shirt, the pain from the scabs being pulled at by my sleeves made my whole body twitch. The track marks and face sores were even worse than I'd thought. I wondered how my sister could look at me in this state and see through to the person who she loved and remembered.

I sat on the toilet seat and removed my combat boots, then peeled off the socks that had been stuck to my feet for a good two weeks. They stunk horribly, and my toes were so blue and mushy they looked as if they'd fall off at any given moment.

Everything hurt and felt good at the same time: in the bathtub and in my life. I lay quietly, submerged, for some time, almost hoping the water was magic and would erase all the pain.

Then there was a gentle knock at the door.

"Come in," I said, but I closed my eyes. I couldn't look. Maya walked in quietly. I heard the toilet seat close, and then the door close again.

I opened my eyes. She had laid out clean clothes for me—her clothes, clothes so beautiful I couldn't imagine wearing them.

I began to cry, equal parts gratitude and shame.

"Are you hungry?" Maya said through the door, and then, "Let's order room service."

She knew how much I loved that, because as kids, our parents never let us order room service.

"Okay," I said.

"Oysters on the half shell?"

"Yum," I said, though I wasn't really hungry.

I heard her call down and order two-dozen raw oysters and a filet mignon with all the trimmings. And in spite of it all, I couldn't help thinking how much money she was wasting on room service and oysters, money that would be better spent on my habit.

After the bath, I did another quick shot, just to maintain my head. Then I got dressed in her clothes, which draped on me like I was a hanger without a frame. I came out of the bathroom with slicked back hair and pushed out a smile.

"Can you believe how big your clothes are on me?" I asked. "Did you ever think this would happen?" I was nervous; now that I was clean, there was nothing to hide my appearance.

"No *habibity*, but it's too much!" Maya said. "You're *too* skinny."

"No way!" The former fat girl in me couldn't help but be a tiny bit pleased.

We ate in the room and spent some time trying to talk, but it wasn't easy. We'd always been from two separate worlds, and this absurd setting and circumstance further complicated things. I could see her fear every time I went into the bathroom, which made me feel even more guilty and ashamed than I already felt. When I came out high, she would look away, afraid to engage in a confrontation that might scare me away.

Eventually, she asked if I would consider coming home for help and support, and I promised to think about it.

I slept in a warm, clean bed that night, and then, in the morning, I slipped out and away, though with more money and some information she'd left me on the desk. There was a nonrefundable airline ticket in my name, and the name of a car service for me to use to get to the airport. I didn't want to say good-bye, nor did I want to deal with any last-ditch attempts to persuade me to go home. Maya had planted the seed, and I knew that I could turn to her if I chose to. I knew my mom and dad would be there for me as well. When they'd asked Kim and me to move out when we'd stayed with them, there was no drama, or fight, just an under-standing on both our parts that it was time to go. My mother had tried to contact me, but again, I didn't want any contact, I was too ashamed, so I'd stayed away.

Now, though, city workers were starting to build a fence around the park—police escorts in tow—and I knew our time had come. Tommy was gone; he'd started crashing with some chick on Seventh Street. I looked around, but there was no one else I could turn to, not even Sasha, who had allowed me to crash on her couch a couple of times.

After using, abusing, and exploiting every person I knew in Alphabet City, I was defeated and still homeless. So I went home to Detroit and my family.

TWENTY

GOING BACK HOME got me a lot of uncomfortable glances. People looked and then looked away. At five foot five, I weighed one hundred pounds. My eyes looked huge in my gaunt face. The sores were still there as I hadn't stopped picking my skin, and my arms and hands were intersected with dark, bruised, scabby track marks. Everyone tried to look beyond the mess I was and say something kind so they wouldn't offend me. I wasn't offended. I knew what I looked like.

My parents let me stay in the studio apartment that was connected to their house, and gave me a car to drive, and food to eat. Their only condition was that I go see a counselor at St. Joseph Hospital rehabilitation center and ask for help. I did, but since I was on methadone, they couldn't take me; I had to be completely off all drugs to enter their forty-five-day rehab program.

It took me weeks of rest while detoxing painfully, my only consolation and outings were driving to the methadone clinic to drink my (ever-smaller and diminishing) daily dose. At home, I ate peanut M&Ms continuously; my mom bought two-pound bags, which I went through daily, sitting in bed popping them morning, noon, and night while watching TV. I couldn't have a conversation that resembled anything normal, and it was hard to relate to my friends, as they were afraid of the way I looked and were guarded at best around me.

Maybe worst of all, my new life bored me. As insane as it sounds, I missed the freedom, excitement, and chaos I'd left behind. I didn't really want to stop using drugs; basically, I was home only because I had nowhere else to go. I wanted to feel better and look better, of course. But not at the expense of having to stop shooting up.

Also, though I knew that my life was a mess—how could I not?—I really didn't know how to change it, and I wanted it to be unpredictable again. When I went to the methadone clinic in the mornings, in a shitty neighborhood just outside Detroit, I felt a comfort seeing the gaunt faces that I knew were like mine: those of the junkies, who just barely dragged their asses out to get their daily dose and scope out the situation for opportunities to score illegal drugs and get high. There were the others, too—the people there for serious detox, who were always dressed in crisp, clean clothes, usually with bling on. (They loved to show it off because it meant they weren't hocking all their gold for drugs.)

I'd started to put on some weight, which made me neurotic about my appearance. My clothes were getting tight, and I hated that feeling, but I also couldn't stop eating sugar, which made me feel better. Sugar increases the dopamine levels in your system and that's part of what you need when you're detoxing. I was coming down slowly and painfully from methadone, 5 milligrams less every two to three weeks, which made me sick to the core, walking around in a constant state of muscle pain—back aches—and unable to stay warm no matter what the weather. I couldn't sleep because of the constant dull aching pain that ran up my legs and into my groin. Every junkie I knew whined about this while detoxing. That's probably why I'd never known anyone who had successfully gotten off methadone. It would take me a good six months to completely detox, and then I could start my recovery process at St. Joseph's center.

At the methadone clinic, I hooked up with one of the haggardlooking junkie dudes, who helped me cop some dope in the Cass Corridor (a really bad part of Detroit). I started using heroin to minimize the pain from the methadone detox, and was off to the races again—but this time, living with my family, supposedly trying to get to a place where I'd check myself into a rehab program.

I started stealing money again, from everyone I knew. I OD'd in a shooting gallery in downtown Detroit and woke up with ice in my bra and a sore jaw from being slapped awake—at which point the guy I was with told me that the only reason I was still alive was because he didn't let the thug at the shooting gallery dump me out in the alley. (I blinked, then nodded. I didn't remember anything, just wanted more drugs.) Then I disappeared with my Dad's car for two weeks, attempting to sell it at the end of that run. (I couldn't because I didn't have the title.)

I ended up at my old friend Anita's house, completely obliterated after just having ripped off a coke dealer and missing many days at the clinic. I was hallucinating wild and unimaginable things even as I sat on her toilet shooting drugs—all while she paced the place trying to get ready to go to our friend's daughter's fifth birthday party. I kept screaming that someone was coming in through the shower curtain to kill us. Completely freaked out, Anita called Barry, the person who'd introduced us.

Barry came, drove me to a hospital in downtown Detroit where the homeless were sleeping just outside the doors, and left me in the waiting room, hoping they would take care of me. When they said they wouldn't give me methadone, I had a fit, throwing pens and clipboards across the room. Then I left, cussing them on my way out.

It was pouring rain, and I took a taxi back to Barry's house, telling the driver my friend would pay him when we got there. When the driver realized I had no money, he took me back to the hospital, where I sat in a wheelchair outside in the rain while they called Barry to come back and pick me up.

Barry took me to his and Irene's house, where I had married Lana and Ty years before, then he called my parents and sister.

There was no methadone left in my system—I hadn't had it in days—and I'd run out of heroin, so a really violent detox was happening. I was weak and sick, my hallucinations vivid and wild.

My parents came. They took one look at me—writhing, convulsing, wrapped in blankets in a freezing cold sweat—and rushed me to their hospital, where, this time, kicking and screaming, I had to let them admit me. I never promised I'd go easy.

They gave me the methadone at last, but they fast-tracked my detox, which was excruciating. I lived through it, as I tend to do, and soon I was discharged from the hospital and admitted to the forty-five-day rehabilitation program at St. Joseph's in Pontiac, Michigan.

It was 1990, the start of a new decade, and my first time ever in rehab. I spent a good six months of that year horribly, physically sick, as my body went through wave after wave of vomiting, diarrhea, convulsions, and hysteria, crying constantly and shedding the years' and years' accumulation of toxins that were inside me. I was numb for so long that my emotional state was extremely fragile as well. I had no idea why I'd ended up this way. At the peak of my addiction, I had been shooting heroin and cocaine into my veins every twenty minutes, sometimes around the clock. At thirty years old, I hadn't been off drugs and alcohol for forty-five straight days since I was eleven.

When I got out of rehab, I agreed to go to a six-month halfway house in East Lansing. I didn't care where I went at this point (and it's not as though I had a ton of options); clean or not, I was still in intense physical and emotional pain, and I couldn't even recognize myself because I didn't know who I was, much less deal with any social situation. I could hardly utter a sentence without stuttering or crying. I spent my days listening to an advanced copy of Kory's forthcoming record, and one song in particular, called "The Losers." It went like this:

> Here's to the losers
> The substance abusers,
> To the rejects,
> All the imperfects,

'Cause I think we're beautiful,
'Cause I think we're beautiful,
'Cause I think we're beautiful,
No matter what anyone says

I cried and cried, clinging to the music like a life jacket.

Being in a halfway house in Lansing was no party either, though I was lucky to be there. If I hadn't been on the Medicaid program, none of it would have been possible. I saw so many people being released early from the forty-five-day rehab because their insurance wouldn't cover them any longer. Medicaid covered everything.

The center was a regular little house in the suburbs of Lansing (the grayest city in Michigan). An all-women, backwoods kind of recovery house, and I hated it because it was out in the middle of nowhere. Most of the women were mandated by the courts: some for DUIs, others for crack. Two of the girls constantly fought for dominance in the pecking order, then picked on the weaker women, which reminded me too much of my childhood with the Bracco sisters. But now, as rough as I looked, even the bullies left me alone.

The first thirty days were spent getting acclimated to chores and doing group and one-on-one counseling. There were three bedrooms with three women per room. Our schedule was pretty much as follows: Wake up, make beds, eat breakfast, exercise in the basement, group therapy, talk about feelings, eat lunch, group therapy, more feelings, one-on-one counseling, eat dinner, more group therapy, feelings, feelings, feelings, then bed. On Friday nights, a van would pick us up and take us to AA or NA meetings in smoke-filled church basements, or school cafeterias, where they served cake and coffee and everyone talked about their problems and feelings even more. We were allowed no interaction with family or friends for the first forty-five days, so the meetings eventually became an outlet that I looked forward to, even though I thought them strange. It was good to know there were other people like me in the world, and I didn't have to do anything but show up and listen.

On my third day, one of the daytime counselors told me that I needed to open up more, that I was too shut down, so she made me carry around a big bucket filled with rocks. I had to take this bucket everywhere, even to the bathroom and outside of the house to meetings. Every time I exposed something about myself, I could take a rock out. This felt like abuse to me because as much as I got the symbolism, I didn't want or need to tell these people my stuff. I was better than this, and didn't need to reveal myself.

I connected with two women right away. One was a nighttime counselor named Terry: an ex-junkie who everyone was afraid of because of her tough exterior (which I loved). The other was my roommate Mary-Ann, an alcoholic and single mom, whose ex-husband was from New York City. Mary-Ann was so kind, straightforward, nonjudgmental, and unpatronizing that I liked her right away. Without these two women I wouldn't have lasted a week in that place.

One of the girls, Lisa, got an instant crush on me, and though I wasn't attracted to her, I feigned interest just to get an emotional stroke, which was some relief, however momentary, from the therapeutic hell I was facing. A week later, they caught us kissing and tossed her out of the program. (Since she'd been there longer than I had, they thought she should have known better.) I hung in by the skin of my teeth.

After forty-five days, I was allowed to start making seven-minute phone calls. They told me not to contact Kim. Of course I did anyway. We spoke a few times, but she wasn't really interested in my recovery as she was still on methadone and using heroin. She was angry with me for leaving her, and was moving on with her life. It hurt, but I knew there was nothing I could do about it.

All my issues were glaring at me. And now I had nothing but food to try to stuff back or drown out my feelings. The painful questions that I had to ask myself on a daily basis were, who was I, and why did I hate that person so much? What did I want out of life? And perhaps the most bewildering: Why would I hurt *myself* worse than anyone else had ever hurt me? I was interrogated by psychologists, social workers, and peer groups, rummaging into my behavior like it was an old attic, trying to find answers that I didn't have. But in the darkness of the sleepless nights that followed, I often wondered, *What the fuck happened to me?* A question I'm not sure that even now I have the answer to. By the time I finished my six months, I had blown up to a size sixteen and was horribly uncomfortable in my own skin.

I moved in with Mary-Ann, and lived with her and her eighteen-year-old daughter for about a month, and then realized that there was nothing in East Lansing for me. So I left, moved back to Detroit and into my parents' house again. I got a job as a stylist at a very popular salon called Mario-Max in West Bloomfield, and found AA and NA meetings to go to. But I felt out of place and alienated at the meetings, and it didn't take long for me to stop trusting the process.

I'd been sober for nine months, but still, every day—every *hour*—I yearned for a drop of substance that would help me escape the stark reality of my life: living in my parents' basement, working at a suburban salon with Anita, inhabiting a body I couldn't stand, and white-knuckling every party and event I went to in order not to pick up a drink or a drug. It was not what I wanted my life to look like, nor was I happy.

I was at a meeting one night when a tall, blond boy named Darren, only three days clean, started talking to me. We talked about New York (where he'd lived for a couple of years), and dope, and shooting up, and how sick he still was. To be honest, I saw him coming a mile away, but I didn't care: I wanted to get high with him. He needed a ride home, and I volunteered. We talked all the way, and then I popped the question. "I'll buy if you fly?" (Read: I'll pay if you can get it.)

I had the money, because I'd been working. And I knew he'd know where to get good dope, since he'd only been off for three days.

To the races we went. And can I tell you how good it felt? To be high again, and feel that floating, carefree, painless existence after nine months of torture . . . it was absolute bliss. I spent the night at his house, where, along with nirvana and a refuge from anyone I knew who might find out I'd used, he gave me an excellent facial.

Darren and I hung out briefly, but my friends didn't like him. They knew something was off, but I lied to them and assured them

I was okay. And somehow, I was able to pace myself and not get a chippy (the beginning of a habit), just doing drugs every few days or so. Darren inspired me to start making music again, and I recorded and mixed a few songs in my parents' basement with a good old-fashioned four-track cassette deck that I'd bought used. It was an old machine and perfect for what I wanted to do, but much different from the equipment in the studios in New York that I'd become accustomed to. I took the songs to a club promoter in Detroit, who booked me for a huge show at Industry, a club in Pontiac. It was an Absolut vodka–sponsored fashion show, and they wanted a live performance piece, Rayya style. I had a local Detroit artist help build stage props, and started creating a show that would put me on the map again.

It was hard, but I managed to maintain using a couple of times a week for a few months. Since going through detox and rehab, I'd learned a lot about addiction and relapse. Before then, I didn't know I was an addict, no one had told me or explained the disease of addiction to me. I just thought I was a fucked-up human being who was incapable of living a pedestrian life. I knew I was physically addicted to heroin and cocaine, but had no idea that once I stopped using, I'd have to stay stopped completely, in order to get better. I'd also learned that as an addict, once I started getting high again, it wouldn't take long for me to hit the skids. So the guilt that I felt for using even periodically during this time was insurmountable. And yet, like the full-blown addict I was, I kept doing it.

TWENTY-ONE

I FIRST SAW Jan at a Christmas party at a crowded loft in Detroit. She was tall, gorgeous, sexy, and exotic, with a smile that could make you forget who you were. Which, of course, was exactly what I needed. I honestly don't think I'd ever seen a woman this beautiful. She looked like a young Sofia Loren, or Anouk Aimée in *La Dolce Vita*. She was dressed in a black leather skirt and perfectly sequenced black bustier, which showcased her beautiful bosoms, small waist, and perfect legs. Everything about her was dreamy including her almond-shaped brown eyes, an authentic Italian nose, and her mouth: I'd never seen a mouth so large and perfect on a face before.

Our eyes had locked at the party, but I hadn't been able to speak to her, I was so taken aback. Yet, watching her as she moved gracefully around the room gently smiling and talking to people, I knew I had to get to know this woman. I asked a friend who she was, and if she was gay, straight, or bi. My friend replied, "Oh, that's Jan, she has a sordid past, and you guys look like you could be sisters."

Meanwhile, I had booked a trip to New York because I wanted a few days alone with my drugs without fear of my parents or friends catching me. My parents couldn't really say no; I was thirty-one years old, after all. In New York, I spent four days in a friend's empty apartment shooting drugs and having sex. I ran into Marney on the street one day while I was copping drugs, then met her at her place later on and slept with her. I called Kim, and she came into the city from Jersey, got high with me, and we had sex. (Though I was angry during my sexual exchange with her, because I knew she'd been dating someone else and my pride was bruised.) I missed my plane home, ran out of money, and had to call Kory to loan me forty dollars so I could get to the airport and catch another flight. He threw the cash from a third-story window above the Great Jones Cafe and wished me good luck.

I had a huge abscess in my hand from shooting so much cocaine; my poor, dilapidated veins couldn't handle it. My hand swelled so much it looked like a clubfoot. Back in Detroit, I told everyone I'd smashed it in the door of a yellow cab. But I couldn't cut hair for a week, so there I was again, sitting in my parents' house. I took a breather and stopped using, which felt good because whenever I stopped I felt powerful and in control—as if I could stop anytime I wanted to.

I'd only been back from New York a few days when I was invited to a show with some friends. As I made my way through the row of seats, holding my swollen club hand close to me so I wouldn't knock anyone out with it, I realized that my seat was right next to *her*. Jan. I stopped breathing (even as my abscess pulsated with pain). We exchanged smiles, and I sat down, heartbeat banging out of my ears for the rest of the show. Afterward we all went out for drinks—I couldn't take my eyes off her all night— and later, my friends told me she had commented that I had nice eyes and a beautiful smile. That was all the ammunition I needed to beg my dear Anita, whose roommate was a good friend of Jan's, to have a dinner party and invite her.

She brought a date to the party, a guy, but at some point we found ourselves talking alone, and she told me that she'd been with women, too, though would never consider having a real relationship with a woman. I told her I felt the same way—that I just loved to have fun in bed with chicks. I'd lied about my sexuality for so long that it didn't seem too far-fetched to tell a lie in order to be able to sleep with Jan, if that's what it took. We flirted all night, and at the end of the night I whispered to her that I wanted to cook for her. She said yes.

I was still living with my parents, and she lived with her father, so we set up another dinner at—where else?—Anita's place. I brought my mom's famous grape leaves, and Jan brought some Italian food. We stayed at Anita's together that night. (Poor Anita, always getting dragged into my girl drama!) In the morning I drove her home, and when we stopped in front of her house, she gave me a long hard kiss. That was the beginning of Jan and me.

My mom was weak and constantly ill at that time, and my spirit was broken with grief about her condition. Jan was amazing, helping both my mother and me cope with her illness. Sometimes Mom would be up at night pacing, in pain, or unable to sleep because of the chemo. Jan and I would sit and talk to her, or Jan would give her a manicure to take her mind off the pain. Her sensitivity toward my mom was profound and generous.

As much as I loved being with Jan, I hated being in Michigan: I felt like the place was sucking the life out of me. So I asked Jan to move with me to New York—and she said yes. It wasn't an easy decision, as I felt guilty about leaving when my mother was so sick, but it was one I knew I had to make to maintain my sanity. My family hated the fact that I was leaving again, and for good reason. Fayez, my older brother, warned me that this time I would be disowned. He launched threats that might have made anyone else reconsider, but I knew my parents would never disown me—not now, not after they'd witnessed the worst of me and still held me in their loving arms and helped me heal. I also knew I could fly home and see my mom anytime, and with the rest of my siblings still in Michigan, she would be well taken care of.

Back in New York, I got a job at a small salon on Fifth Street and set it up so that we could stay with Jamie for a couple of weeks, until we found a place of our own. I was in love, and hungry for a new start in New York without drugs. Jan and I moved into a huge but somehow inexpensive loft at the South Street Seaport, a sublet that Ty (who was separated from Lana by this time) had given up because he couldn't afford it. It was an old, gorgeous space with wide plank floors, cast-iron columns, windows overlooking the East River, two bathrooms side by side, one of them with a Jacuzzi, and a chef's open kitchen. We loved it and felt like we'd won the lottery until we realized, after a couple of weeks, that everything in the place smelled like fish because all the commercial spaces downstairs were part of the Fulton Street fish market. No matter what I tried to get the fish smell out of our clothes, nothing worked.

Still, I was seeing clients, staying straight, and making good money, and Jan was doing different retail jobs and acclimating to the city. We were happy, and after eight months together were preparing for our first Christmas in our new home.

Lana lived in the neighborhood, and one day she stopped by my job to say hello. She knew (from Anita) about Jan, and told me she just wanted to be friends, which I thought would be fine. Eventually I introduced her to Jan, and they hit it off and even ganged up on me a bit until we all settled in. There was a strange edge to Lana, and I would catch her eyeballing Jan and, with a tinge of jealousy and admiration, overcompensating to be nice to her. This wasn't Lana—she was usually more straightforward than that—but I let it slide and just felt glad everyone was getting along.

Jan and I bought a Christmas tree from a sidewalk vendor, and I dragged it home and up to the loft to decorate. The smell of pine and spiced wine permeated the loft as we put ornaments and lights on the branches. When we were finished we held each other, admiring our work. I felt happier than I had ever remembered. I loved our relationship, loved being loved by her, and having a life together in New York. It was like nothing I'd ever experienced before, and for the first time, I had a glimpse of the possibility of a life beyond drugs.

We talked about having friends over for Christmas day dinner and decided we would invite Lana and her boyfriend. I spent all day cooking a small turkey and the trimmings, while Jan set a beautiful table and made the apartment picture perfect.

Lana showed up on time, but alone.

"Where's Jim?" Jan asked.

"He wasn't feeling well, I hope that's okay?" Lana said apologetically.

"Of course, it's fine!" I answered, looking at Jan to make sure.

That should have been my cue to send her back home, but of course, I couldn't. The evening was awkward at best—but I didn't realize just *how* awkward until Lana and I were in the kitchen, alone, with her standing so close to me that I could smell her: Lana, the woman I'd practically killed myself over after our breakup. As I got out tin foil to wrap up the turkey, she gave me one of those intense looks that only an old lover can give.

"Can I help?" she reached for the foil and brushed my hand.

"No, I got it." Nervously, I turned away, quickly busying myself with smoothing foil over the leftover pieces of drumstick, ribcage, and breast meat. Then, to get her to leave sooner, I offered her a ride home. (It was snowing, and I had a car, after all.) She accepted.

We said nothing to each other in the car until I pulled up in front of her building. Then she looked at me again in that way. I started to try to say good-bye and thanks for coming, but she put her hand on my arm and continued to look at me. "Rayya," she said. "You must know this already, but if you don't, I have to tell you. I have always loved you. Always. Not leaving Ty for you was one of the hardest decisions I ever had to make, and I wish I'd done it differently." She stared at me while I looked vacantly straight over the steering wheel and out the window trying to keep my eyes on the large snowflakes that were falling on the windshield, unable to conjure up any words and trying not to cry. She reached over and grabbed my face and turned it toward hers.

"Anyway, I want you to know, staying with Ty had nothing to do with how I felt about you, my loyalties have always been fucked up, and I'm sorry I hurt you."

"I can't do this with you right now Lana," I pulled my head back around. "Please, I need to get home." I waited in silence for her to get out of the car, but my determination was weakening.

Why, I wondered, *would she tell me these things now, when it doesn't matter anymore?* I'm proud to say I got out of there before anything could happen—before she could kiss me, before I could get tangled up in her web of seduction. But I was shaken to the core, and I didn't want to go home like this. I drove down to Houston Street and took a left going east. I was looking at people crossing the street carrying gifts. I took a left up Avenue B and came to a stop at Second Street. I knew this intersection so well because this was the corner I used to stand on when I was hustling. I squinted to see if there was anyone out that I recognized. I slowly made a left on Second Street and looked closer, around the building that used to be, and still was, Lucky 7. There was Snake, my old friend and a dealer. I pulled over, got out of the car, and wished him Merry Christmas. We talked about where I'd been and why I hadn't been around the 'hood. He told me that I looked good and couldn't believe that I owned a car. He told me that he got his son a Walkman for Christmas and how he couldn't wait to get off work that night so he could go home and celebrate with his family. We shot the shit for about ten minutes. Then I copped a bag of dope, a dime of coke, and a set of works.

And there I was, driving to my apartment after being clean for months, the thrill of having this New York dope and coke in my hand was so uncontainable I felt like I would puke and crap myself at the same time.

My heart pounded as I entered the loft. Jan was in the Jacuzzi taking a hot bath, which provided the perfect opportunity. My mind was telling me no, to stop this insanity before I could regret it, but my body was desperately going through the motions. I quietly went to the kitchen and got a spoon, then went into the half bath that shared a wall with where Jan was and locked the door behind me. Dry heaves took hold of me as I loaded up the syringe, all the while calling to Jan through the door, "I'll be in the tub soon, baby, just have to go to the bathroom first."

As I emptied the syringe into my vein, there was a brief and horrible moment when I knew I had overloaded it. It was like nothing I'd felt before. The last time I'd OD'd was in the shooting gallery in Detroit, over a year ago. I didn't feel it coming on; it had just happened and then I was out. But this time, standing in front of the mirror looking at myself, I knew that I was going down, and there was nothing I could do to stop it.

I took the spoon that I'd bent with the little piece of cigarette filter in it, the needle that still had traces of my blood floating in the chamber, and tossed them behind the toilet. I tucked the leftover drugs in the fifth pocket of my jeans. And then I watched my face and body slump down and away from the mirror. A surge came through me as my insides turned out, and I threw up in the toilet. That's all I remember.

★

I heard a voice crying, sounding far away. "What am I gonna tell your mom?" Jan pleaded. "Please don't die, please don't die, what am I gonna tell your mom?!"

The voice got louder, and then louder, until it seemed to suck me back into my body.

I drifted off again. When I woke up, I was lying on the floor with a few ambulance guys kneeling over me, one of them holding those heart paddles. "She's back," he announced.

"Merry Christmas," said another.

Jan was at my side, crying and holding my face as I lay on the floor outside the bathroom, the door broken off its hinges.

The EMS guy's face lifted away from mine as he handed the paddles to his partner, who had a huge smile on his face. I noticed there were some cops there walking around as well. I tried to sit up, but they gently held me down. I felt fine—good, actually— though I didn't know why I was on the floor, and I certainly didn't know why everyone was making such a fuss. Jan kissed me on my head and cradled me, telling me everything was going to be fine. *Why wouldn't it?* I thought, and I wanted everyone to leave so I could be with her; I felt so much love for her right then. But the men were asking me questions about how this could've happened. "Did you choke on your vomit, miss?" one asked. "Sometimes that happens."

Just then, one of the officers came out of the bathroom holding the spoon and syringe. And then I remembered, and I knew what I was doing here. *Oh, shit,* I thought.

The mood shifted instantly, from cheerful to hateful. Jan stared at me in confusion and shock, while the officers called me every name in the book for being a junkie bitch who was wasting my life and their Christmas. They handcuffed me, threw me in the ambulance, and took me to the hospital.

I was handcuffed to a bed for a twelve-hour watch where they gave me Narcon, which made me puke and shit until all the drugs were out of my system. Then they booked me and took me to the tombs.

And that was the beginning of the end of the lovely and beautiful thing I had with Jan. We had to lie to everyone about what happened, because we didn't want to get thrown out of the loft and I didn't want to get fired from my job. Meanwhile, Jan was so traumatized by the incident that she started having panic attacks every time she came home and I wasn't there, thinking I was passed out or dead somewhere in the loft. Soon she had to start taking antianxiety medication.

At Christopher Banner, the Fifth Street salon that I worked in, my business was booming and I was building a loyal clientele that had money to spend on good hair. It was a small neighborhood place in the East Village, with four superb stylists. We knew everything about one another and it became increasingly difficult to hide the fact that I was having problems. I'd snuck dope and coke and gotten high a couple of times since the Christmas incident, but had only snorted the drugs. I wasn't prepared to face the consequences of losing Jan if I got caught again. Also, through my clients who were musicians, I auditioned for a lead singing position for a band called Fluffer. I didn't get the job, and I knew I wasn't the right fit, but they hooked me up with a producer who was looking at different artists to record. His name was John Eaton and he worked out of Daddy's House/Bad Boy Studios, which was Puffy's place on Forty-fourth Street. I laid some vocal tracks down for him on a demo he was working on. It was slow and sexy and sounded a bit like Portishead. It had been a while since I'd been in a professional studio and things had changed quite a bit. Everything was recorded on a small laptop computer and I didn't really understand how it all worked, but I did the best I could and he seemed really excited about it, as was I.

On the day before Thanksgiving of 1993, my sister called. My mother was in the hospital again; this time, she wasn't going to make it.

I had known this was coming, but I couldn't have prepared for this level of loss. I went home a wreck.

My mother hadn't spoken coherently or moved in a day or two and was almost in a comatose state. But when I reached her bedside and took her hand and said, "Mom, I'm here," she miraculously opened her eyes, turned her head to face me, and said, "I knew you would come *habibty*." Then she drifted back into a state of unconsciousness.

I sat with her for hours, dripping water into her mouth with a spoon, putting Vaseline on her dry, scabbed lips, telling her I loved her. I listened as she occasionally cried out unconsciously for her own mother, who'd died years before. Finally, I went to my sister's to get some rest. At five in the morning—November 25, 1993, Thanksgiving day—she slipped away.

Jan stayed behind in New York while I was with my family. I couldn't think straight at the hospital, at the funeral, at the family functions and meetings afterward. It was one big nightmare, and even now, I can wrap my head only around parts of it.

Before I went back to New York, I cleaned out my mom's medicine cabinet. I took all the liquid morphine, syringes, and pain meds, ingested what I could, in my old bedroom in my parents' house, and brought the rest back with me.

One week after I got back to New York, I had a complete emotional and physical breakdown doubled over in mental anguish. I was using, I couldn't work, my mom was gone, and I was fucked up and angry. Soon enough, I was fired from my job and John stopped answering my phone calls at the studio.

Jan was beyond devastated, yet somehow kept it together. She held me for hours at a time, rocking me, stroking my hair, telling me everything would be okay. I'm not sure I would have made it without her. Maybe suicide.

Finally, she begged me to detox. So I did: I entered a detox/rehab program at United Hospital in Port Chester, New York, thanks to Medicaid. After three weeks there, I was so shaky they decided I needed additional care, and I was admitted into their dual-diagnosis ward—a locked psych ward. The doctors there were great. They recognized that I wasn't just a drug addict, but also greatly depressed, and rightfully so. After a few weeks there, I went home with a new drug called Paxil, which was supposed to balance my depression.

But I wasn't fixed. I was shattered and didn't know how to fix it—myself, or *us,* Jan and me. She tiptoed around trying not to upset me or stress me out, and, of course, that stressed me out more than anything.

We loved each other; that part was easy. I was crazy about her. But it wasn't enough to keep me off the drugs. And after a while it wasn't enough to stop her from looking outside our relationship for comfort and safety.

I moved so many times in those last couple of years of our relationship, and of my own swan song to drugs: from the halfway house to my parents' house to Jamie's to the loft in South Street Seaport to, finally, our own apartment in the East Village (to get away from the memories, not to mention the god-awful fish smell). I'd OD'd once and been arrested at least twice, went to two seven-day detox centers and a thirty-day rehab program. Eventually, I went back on a low dose of methadone, thinking it might help, then detoxed from it once again. Jan was supportive, hoping every rehab was going to do it and that she'd have me back the way I was in the beginning. It never worked, but I had good stretches when things seemed to be going okay. It was easy to go into a rehab or detox and rest. But to stay clean on my own, afterward, in the real world . . . that was excruciating.

And the tide was turning in New York. Rudy Giuliani was mayor and cracking down on crime. Most of the clubs that I'd once practically lived in had now been turned into expensive condominiums. Operation Pressure Point (an antinarcotics program developed in the early 1980s) was now being implemented to such a degree that *everyone* was being arrested, addicts and dealers alike.

Plainclothes police officers roamed the streets looking like junkies to entrap dealers. Cops were posted on every street corner in the twenty-block radius of the Alphabets. The jails became overcrowded because there weren't enough judges or bailiffs on duty to process all the cases that were hauled in. The streets seemed angrier and more frenetic, because gentrification, once an idea, was now a sad reality. Rents were going up, and stabilization was slowly crumbling. All the big dope houses were slowly getting dismantled, and the dealers, once big-time honchos, were moving from spot to spot trying to avoid the unforgiving narc squads.

I kept a close eye on where the cop spots were relocating and moved my clients to a space that I rented from an antique store that was also a hair salon across the street from our apartment. My clients were incredible. They consisted of regular moms from the East Village, artists and musicians, hipsters and clubbers, fashionistas, dancers, record producers, actors, and business people: all really hip, and so supportive and loyal. They tried other people while I was out of it, but most them wanted to come back to me and constantly called for appointments. When that lease ran out, I moved my business up and into our place. I had a plumber rig a shampoo sink and chair in our kitchen, and I bought two used hair chairs to set up a cutting and color studio in the living room. I loved working from home, making my own hours, making quick cash, and of course having the freedom to get high occasionally while Jan was at a full-time job. I struggled to keep my head up, juggling the immediate world around me.

Just as my dreams of being a musician were dying, Kory stepped up and gave me something to look forward to. His music career was in full bloom, and he was recording his fourth Warrior Soul Album called *Chill Pill* for Geffen Records. He asked me to play keyboards on a few tracks, which I was more than happy to do. The recording sessions took place at Don Fury's studio at 18 Spring Street, and were mixed at Platinum Island. A couple of tracks were also done at the legendary Electric Lady—the Jimi Hendrix studio on Eighth Street in the West Village. I received special thanks for my work in the credits. It was an honor to be part of that record and very emotional for me to weave some of my melodies into the music that had once saved my life.

TWENTY-TWO

JAN WENT TO visit her family for a long weekend, and while she was away I thought I'd get my junkie friends to help me clean the place. I wanted it to sparkle when she got home. We took the apartment apart to give everything a thorough cleaning, but after a couple of days of continuous using and not a moment of scrubbing, they bailed on me. I almost OD'd again, but a homeless woman who had stopped over to sell me a bag of works managed to keep my heart going by walking me around my apartment and slapping me out of it.

I let her crash in our brand-new bed, and she fell asleep with a lit cigarette, burned a huge hole in the mattress, and almost fried the place to the ground. The next night, Jan came back from her trip, as scheduled, and buzzed the door downstairs, as she'd forgotten her keys.

I was not ready. I was out of my mind, plus the place was completely trashed. First I panicked. Then I wedged a ladder against our apartment door. Finally, I retreated to the bedroom to pretend I was asleep, as the buzzer continued to blare.

Eventually, one of the neighbors let Jan into the building. Soon she was pounding on our door, a few feet away from me. I lay in bed, eyes wide open, frozen, afraid to let her in because of what she would find, yet feeling horrible that she was out in the hallway with her luggage, crying.

After what seemed like hours of her banging on the door, Jan called the police. It was the middle of the night by then; the police climbed the fire escape and shone huge flashlights through the window into my bedroom until I finally got out of bed, moved the ladder, and opened the door. The look on Jan's face said it all. She was done.

Within days, she'd found a sweet young gay boy to move in and "help us with the rent." And shortly after that, she asked me to move out. I did. I squatted at an apartment on Fourteenth Street and Avenue B with a former guitar player from Kory's band. But I continued to cut hair from the other apartment, because the lease was in my name and I wasn't about to lose my means of making money. My customers didn't care if I was messed up or off schedule; they just wanted me to do their hair. I was only allowed to be there during business hours, though; Jan wouldn't have it any other way. She gave me a window of time during the day, and I stuck to the schedule.

One afternoon while I was there working, Jan scratched her cornea while trying to blow out her own bangs. She was in a lot of pain, so I took her to the eye infirmary and, because she didn't have insurance, I lied and said she was me, and used my Medicaid to get her help. People had always mistaken us for sisters and I used that to our advantage.

She was so grateful, and also so freaked out by the whole thing, that she asked me to stay with her afterward. Back at the apartment, she passed out in our bed from the pain pills and the ordeal. I sat on the floor at the end of the bed and shot my drugs. I loved Jan and wanted to be there for her, and this was the only way I could stay present and not run out on her to get a fix.

The following night, I needed to go out for more heroin so I could do the half gram of coke that was burning a hole in my pocket. Jan begged me not to leave, but I told her I was going out for air and I'd be right back. She knew better, though. She also knew there was nothing she could do to stop me. She cried some silent tears, which I pretended not to notice.

I walked to a cop spot at Thirteenth Street and Avenue B that I knew had been good the past few days. They called this dope Action, because the dude who usually sold it had seen a lot of action in Vietnam, but the boys working for Action that night were really young—no older than their midteens. I didn't recognize them, but I decided that was no big deal; there were always new kids working for a dope spot. I asked for a three-dollar short on three bags of dope—three bags for twenty-seven dollars.

The young Latino boy held out his hand for the money. "Hurry," he said. "Five-o's been through a lot tonight." He indicated his partner down the block.

"Where's the dope?" I said, looking at him.

"He got it over there." The kid pointed to another young boy, a good ten yards away on his bike.

I knew this wasn't how Action worked the spot. Suspicious, I said, without reaching into my pocket for the money, "Well, go get it."

"What're you worried about?" the kid said. "We always out here."

Funny, as I'd never seen them before. "I ain't worried," I said. "I just wanna see the dope." I had a bad feeling by now.

In fact, standing there, I thought better of this whole thing. "You know what, papa?" I said. "It's cool. Just forget it." I turned to walk away.

"Hey yo, wait," he called after me. "I'll bring 'um to you. Hold on, ma."

I ignored him and picked up my pace, trying to get to the corner where there was a bit more traffic. I was about twenty yards away when the footsteps rolled up behind me, fast and powerful. *Shit,* I thought.

I heard a *swoosh*, and then a loud *crack* as something hit my right ankle. I couldn't tell if it was the crack of the bat against my bone or the sound of my ankle breaking. My platform shoe teetered out from under me, my leg buckled, and I fell to the ground.

I gripped my broken ankle as all three boys descended on me.

"What the fuck?!" I yelled, but as I looked up, the sole of a sneaker came hard at my face, slamming into me.

I curled into a ball on the cement. "Wait!" I gurgled, and tried to reach toward my pocket, "I'll give you the money!"

"Shut the fuck up, you fucking junkie," one of the them spat, and then the kicks rained on my face, my stomach, my ribs, until finally I just covered my head and face and took the beating.

The boys enjoyed the brutality of every moment, backing away to see me writhing in pain, slapping each other around and jumping up and down high-fiving before coming back to go at me again. When they finally stopped, I tried to pull myself up, but I couldn't. I couldn't move in any way.

I screamed. The pain in my foot, which was dangling like a wilted flower on a stem, was unbearable. My nose was bleeding heavily, and blood spurted out of my eye. My lip felt huge, like a ripe tomato. As I tried to raise my head, one of the boys came at me one last time and kicked me down for good.

Out of some undamaged corner of my eye, I squinted to see a taxi slowing at the corner and the driver rolling down his window. I managed to raise my arm. "*Help!*" I screamed, with all the voice I could muster. "Please help me! My leg is broken!"

The taxi driver hesitated, leaning out his window to get a better look.

The boys waved him on. "She ain't hurt, she's high," one of them yelled. The driver sped away.

I watched the taillights of my last hope fade in the distance. Then I put my head back down in a puddle of my own blood and passed out.

★

I awoke to a paramedic putting me in a neck brace; her voice was kind and soothing. "If you have any needles or drugs on you, please tell me," she said.

I couldn't answer her; I could only see the flashing lights of the ambulance and the chaos around me.

"I'm here to help you, don't worry," she said. "If you have anything, I'll get rid of it, okay? Don't worry."

I blinked hard, willing her to know that I did have illegal para-phernalia, and that I was grateful to her.

They rushed me to Bellevue Hospital, where I was listed in critical condition, my ankle broken in three places. They wanted to operate and put pins into my leg, but I wasn't coherent enough to sign off on the surgery. Hours later, after they got hold of Jan, she came into Bellevue emergency, complete with patched eye, and was there by my side when I woke up. I wouldn't let them do the surgery because I still wasn't lucid enough to understand what the doctor was saying, so they set my leg and put a temporary cast on it to see if it would heal without the surgery.

I was released into Jan's care within a couple of days, but could hardly see or speak, the damage to my face was so bad. Jan's apart-ment was on the fourth floor of a walk-up, so the ambulatory service guys carried me up on a gurney.

The pain medication from the hospital had helped with the dope sickness, but without it, I was going through heavy with-drawal. After a day of this, I called the ambulate service, complaining of pain, and asked them to take me back to the hospi-tal. They gave me more painkillers, and then, on the way home, I asked the guys to stop at a dope spot, where I hobbled, on crutches, into an abandoned building and scored drugs to last me a few days. They then had to carry me up the four flights of stairs back into the apartment. I think they felt sorry for me due to my circumstances and, knowing my condition, turned a blind eye and allowed me to cop.

★

After a week or so, I was able to get down the stairs myself, and on the crutches would slowly hobble around the streets to cop. And once the swelling of my eyes came down a bit and I could see, I started cutting hair again. My clients called it my broken-ankle phase, like Picasso's blue period.

Soon, predictably, Jan didn't want me staying at the apartment, so I checked myself into another rehab center, and then another one right after that. I was away for a good three months, during which I got straight again, had my ankle heal perfectly without the surgery, and spent another Christmas and New Year's in an institution. Jan came to visit for family days, and we had counseling. I moved back in with her in February, sober and on more antidepressants.

But I couldn't hold on. I slipped, and kept slipping, and finally slipped away, back into drug oblivion.

Just as I had once called Kurt's father to take care of that situation, Jan called her father to take care of me. He came out to New York, and, with his old-school Italian mentality, in his calm and scary voice, said, "Ya got one day to move out. Or I'll fuckin' kill ya."

So I did.

One thing led to another; things went from bad to worse to just bad again. I couch surfed for a while, taking advantage of everyone who tried to help me, including my clients, something I once thought I'd never do. I reached another rock bottom, even lower than the ones before—like a trapdoor that spit me into a dirty crawl space in an old house. I stole clients' recording equipment, under the pretense of using their studio. I went to Brooklyn with some strange dude, knowing full well he expected sex, but left before putting out. I lived at the St. Marks Hotel with a cute, sweet guy named Mike who took very good care of me, and I in turn had sex with him (something I thought I'd never want to do). One night, I copped this kick-ass dope called "bag in a bag," then went to wait for my favorite cocaine bodega to open so I could get my goods. As I stood on the corner, a frail, skinny kid walked up and asked me where he could get some good dope. He was filthy, with long, stringy brown hair, and he was shaking and nervous, wiping his runny nose on his tattered flannel shirtsleeve.

Victor, a rip-off artist, who had absolutely no scruples, came up and tried to sell this kid a couple of bags of beat dope. (He used old bags from real heroin and refilled them with baking soda, then taped them back up and sold them—so they contained only traces of heroin in the white powder.) I'd seen Victor rip off so many people; he didn't follow the usual street code, which was a) that you tried to help any junkie who just got out of jail, and b) that you never ripped off a dope-sick junkie, since you never knew when it would happen to you. Still, usually I wouldn't have gotten involved, especially with one pocket full of dope and the other full of money to buy coke. But the kid looked desperate, and Victor was a piranha, so I muttered, "Dude, don't buy that. It's beat."

"Fuck you, bitch!" Victor screamed at me as he moved in on the guy. "You just can't afford it!"

"Man, I'm just waitin' for the bodega," I said, calmly. "I already got mine." I stepped back and shrugged, then pulled out a wad of money to prove my point.

"Bag-in-a-bag's dope is really good today," I whispered to the kid. "It's on Eighth and C." I couldn't leave well enough alone—I added, "That's what I copped."

His eyes pierced through me, a look I didn't understand. Did he think I was scamming him? He turned away, then pulled out a twenty, handed it to Victor, took two bags of beat dope, and walked away, turning the corner at a fast clip.

I stood for a second. "He's a fucking cop!" I yelled suddenly to Victor, as the realization spread through me, followed quickly by panic. I knew from experience that when you're sick and an obvious junkie tells you a particular dope is beat, you don't buy it—especially when there's really good dope just down the street.

I began to walk faster—as fast as I could without breaking into a run. But it was too late. I was screwed.

As I tried to hustle away, Pressure Point screeched toward me with cars from every direction. Plainclothes officers jumped out, waving the gold shields and badges that hung around their necks. I was thrown up against a wall before I could say *dumb ass*.

Attempted sale of a controlled substance is a class "D" felony: these were the charges. They thought I was working with Victor, and his bags did have traces of dope, plus I was holding real dope. I was in serious trouble this time, and no slap on the wrist was gonna cut it. Soon enough, I was in the tombs again, kicking as I waited for my arraignment.

When the C.O. (corrections officer) called my name to go up, she smirked as she looked at my paperwork. "You got two-t'-four Roberts, eh?"

"What?" I said. "What's that mean?"

"Judge Roberts," she said. "He don't hand down less than two-t'-four."

I didn't know if she meant months or years (it was years, by the way), but I was so dope sick by the time I saw the judge that I didn't really care. I tried feebly to explain that I wasn't dealing drugs, but after reviewing my rap sheet, he concluded that I was lying. I was arraigned and sent to Riker's Island to await trial.

I'd been to Rikers Island in the eighties, but only held for a couple of days, because they'd run out of room in central booking. This was completely different, I knew. I'd be staying at Rikers for a while. And if the charges stuck after my court date, then I'd be sent upstate to serve my time.

TWENTY-THREE

I WAS SCARED to death as I rode the corrections bus through the Lower East Side toward the Williamsburg Bridge. I looked out through the crisscross bars on the windows and watched as the city I loved and lived in faded out of sight, and the barbed-wire fences appeared. I was a plain old scrawny junkie, and the other prisoners on the Rikers bus had no problem reminding me of that fact. After writhing on the hard cement floors at central booking for those first couple of days, I'm sure I smelled like a bum's sweaty balls on a hot August day. They called out names at me—loser, junkie, little white fucking junkie bitch. It seemed I was again going to be the target and brunt of other's jokes, the way I had been on the school bus back in junior high. Sick and strung out, I first had to find a way to survive in jail without having the other inmates prey on me. I'd shed all my weight again and was in no shape to defend myself. It's funny how ass backward jail is to real life in that way: In prison, the heavier or fatter you are, the *more* respect you get.

★

Detoxing under any condition was no fun, but here, without the possibility of getting anything to ease the pain, I'd have to kick like a dog and shit my brains out and turn senseless inside out puking, with horrible shooting pains that felt like knives being plunged into my legs. I would sweat and have stomach cramps that would travel up and down my spine and settle under my ribs, making me want to rip my skin off. I needed to get something to get me through detox, and locked up, that's easier said than done. I wasn't on the methadone program anymore, so I wasn't entitled to it in prison.

We were handcuffed and shackled together as we got off the bus. Then I was pulled and pushed along, my legs like rubber beneath me. Herded into a huge holding cell, we were unleashed and then given those paper gowns that you get in cheap clinics. It took hours for them to process everyone, and by the end, I was a decaying, putrid little sweat pile, a bag of bones impersonating a human being. I had collapsed physically both before and after they strip searched me and sprayed me down with disinfectant (which they do to everyone coming in).

I was given a medical checkup, a gyno exam, and chest X-rays. Then, instead of putting me in the general population, they sent me to the psychiatric ward. They didn't know what was wrong with me, because I shrieked and cried while they were trying to process me. I told the officers I was dope sick, but they ignored me and just assumed I was insane.

The psych ward at Rikers was no joke.

It was a dorm, with certifiably insane convicts running around, crazier than you can imagine. You don't get your own cell, just a bed in the middle of a huge room with lots of other beds. The smell of old, dried piss mixed with bleach made me dry heave instantly. I lay in my cot, curled up in a ball, drifting in and out of consciousness and praying for daylight. I had no right to ask God for anything, but still, I begged: *Please, God, if you get me out of this last one, I'll be done forever.*

I spent all the next morning crying in the cubicle of a psychiatrist who no doubt had heard it all. By the end of our session, I was sure she'd put me on the methadone detox program. Instead, she said, "You're four days in now. You should be fine in a day or two."

I screamed and called her every name in the book including a cunt stain and a whore, for making me go through this pain. I wanted to kill her. But I also knew she was right. Going back on methadone would just be one more thing to get off eventually.

She moved me out of the psych ward and into the main population. I was assigned to a house (a large dorm with separate cells) and placed with murderers, thieves, and prostitutes, and other drug addicts all awaiting sentencing.

I dragged my ass outside that day for "recreation"—a place you didn't go unless you were looking for trouble or were hanging with a posse. But I needed some kind of elixir that would help me transition into this place without more physical pain, and I thought if I could find it anywhere it would be out there. In the yard, a large group of Latinas with slicked-back hair were gathered and milling around, spitting and swearing. Their clothes were starched and pressed and they all wore perfectly white sneakers and red bandanas. I knew who they were, and I knew they were the ones

I had to see. The Latin Queens were infamous and well known for getting anything and everything into Rikers Island; I'd heard them talked about on the street. That they'd trade sex or gold to some corrections officers to get the dope in.

I walked up to the biggest, meanest looking one, who was talking in Spanish to the rest of them. I tried to look tough and cool, but I was scared shitless. "I wanna join the Latin Queens," I said.

They all laughed.

"I ain't Spanish, but I ain't white neither," I said.

One of the other girls turned to me with a look of disgust. "Get the fuck outta' here, Blanca, 'fore I stick you," she said.

I immediately slunk away, trying not to attract any more attention, and quietly hid in a corner of the yard, looking around for options and trying to think of other solutions for my problem. At least I had a pack and a half of Marlboro reds left (cigarettes are a hot commodity in jail), so I thought maybe I'd be able to trade someone for drugs. When they called everyone to get their medication, I made my way to the line where the girls were getting methadone.

I spotted a fat, ugly bull dagger with a butt in her mouth that looked like it had seen its last days as a smokeable cigarette. With a fierce craving for a little bit of anything that could calm the quake of this dreadful sickness, I walked up and asked her if she would make a trade: cigarettes for methadone.

She wanted a whole pack of Marlboro reds. With little or no alternative, I agreed, and off I went to get the smokes. When I returned, she took them and walked away, never explaining to me how she was going to get me the methadone. My eyes followed her as she walked up to the window to get dosed. She put the cup up to her mouth and drank; all my hopes of getting "well" disappeared, and I raged at her as she came back my way. "You fucking ripped me off?" I snarled under my breath.

"I want my cigarettes back!"

She raised her hand to my mouth to shut me up, and then put her mouth on mine, lips wide open. Before I could move away, she spit in my mouth.

Disgusted, I was about to spit (and gag) when I tasted that sweet and bitter medicinal orange that I knew was methadone. Closing my eyes, I forced myself to swallow. "There you go, babe," she said, and she kissed me, tonguing me heavily. "Just to make it look good, chica," she whispered, afterward.

I was shocked, but also grateful. "Thanks," I managed, while swearing to myself that next time, it *had* to be someone cute.

Unlike state prison, where you have to wear an orange jumper, at Rikers Island you get to keep your own clothes while waiting to be sentenced. Inmates were not usually allowed to wear their own shoes; they were issued department footwear, which they call "Dekks," "Air Guilliani's," or "Kung Fu Slippers." When the prison ran out of sizes, which was more often than not, they let you keep your own shoes, providing they were not dangerous and had the laces taken out of them. They had run out of size tens, so I was able to keep my boots.

In house number fifteen, where they put me, the cells were not barred but had solid metal doors, with little glass windows looking out onto the rest of the dwelling. The doors were usually unlocked, and we were allowed to go to the main area, inside the double-tiered horseshoe of individual cells, to hang out and watch TV, play cards, or pick fights. No one was allowed to be in anyone else's cell at any given time, and to make sure of this, the doors locked magnetically and electronically for ten minutes every few hours, for a head count.

A few days into my stay, I was in my cell—the safest place for me—lying on my cot, still trying to adjust and get acclimated to the place while my body slowly recovered. I was enjoying the lasting effects of the methadone, when I heard the door to my cell open.

I sprung up, my eyes wide, to see a huge black chick standing at the end of my cot, eyeballing me. I had nowhere to go, as she stood between me and the door. "What do you want?" I asked.

"What size 'r those boots?" she said, with a nasty scowl.

"Ten. What's it to you?" I growled back. I was sick of being sick, and tired of being everyone's prey—the weak, skinny, dirty junkie everyone made fun of the minute I walked out of my cell. I was tired of being last in the food line, and getting my bread taken off of my tray. I'd fucking had it.

"I think them *Harley Davidson* boots'll fit me," she said.

"Yeah? Think again," I snapped.

"I ain't got to think again, bitch. I'm from Harlem, and if I want them boots, I'll take 'em right off your feet."

She came at me fast. And all I saw was red. It was like my leather jacket all over again, but this time, I wasn't taking it.

I bent my legs back and let out a yell and a kick all at the same time. "I'm from fucking Detroit, bitch, and you ain't takin' nothin' from me," I screamed, and I kicked her in the chest as hard as I could as she bent toward me, unleashing years and years of anger and frustration, adrenaline and fear, disappointments and failures.

I could've kicked myself all the way to China, breaking down the walls and through the barriers of Rikers Island. But I didn't need to. Suddenly the woman was gone from my view, and as I heard the thud, I realized she'd sailed back, hit the door, and fallen to the floor. I knew this was my window of opportunity, so I sprang up and ran out past her, yelling for a C.O.

The C.O.s came quickly as I stood in the main area screaming, crying, and shaking. They went into my cell and helped her up, then reprimanded her for being there in the first place. She was furious and swore to get even with me, but I saw the fear in her eyes. Deep down, I knew I would be safe in this house from that moment on.

The women that ruled the house nicknamed me Harley Loco after that because those Harley Davidson boots were my trademark, and of course I was crazy. No one wanted to fuck with a crazy person in jail, because you never knew what he or she would do. So no one messed with me after that.

The following day there was an announcement over the loudspeaker to line up if we wanted to go to the beauty parlor. Since I was feeling a little better from the methadone, I thought I'd check it out.

"A beauty parlor at Rikers Island?" I said to this little Puerto Rican femme who was doing one of the bull-daggers' laundry.

"How you think I get this perm?" she snorted, with a Rosie Perez twang in her voice.

I lined up and waited behind Shorty, who had the most perfect fade of a haircut I'd ever seen. The line proceeded out of the cell block and down the long, cream-colored hallway, until I smelled the chemicals—that horrible, rotten-egg-and-onion smell of a perm that I'd have recognized anywhere, along with the scent of burning hairspray, as some irons (curling, straightening) sat on their hotplates, while others exploded plumes of smoke and sizzled some of the women's hair. These once raunchy odors had never smelled so good to me.

Inside the big mirrored room were a handful of old hairdressing chairs and a few dome-top dryers. I was shocked to see all the gear—albeit rusted and spent looking—necessary to run an actual salon. In fact, the room was like some crazy, old-school salon in Harlem or Detroit, with all kinds of big black and Puerto Rican mammas yelling at each other as they ran around in various states of hair disarray.

I took it all in for a moment, overjoyed, though when I caught a glimpse of myself in the mirror, I gasped. I needed some grooming, to say the least, but to trust anyone there to cut my hair would be like throwing myself to the wolves. No way was that gonna happen.

I walked up to the older man wearing a uniform. "May I use these scissors?" I asked.

He looked me over, but gently. "You need to wait in line for someone to cut your hair," he said softly, drawling with what didn't seem like a typical New York accent (and all the while keeping a close eye on the rest of the room). He was a large, dapper, older African American, the kind of man you'd imagine playing a horn in a jazz club in Chicago many years ago. He had big, droopy red eyes, which reminded me of a Great Dane. His name was Mr. Night, it said so on his name tag.

"I'd rather cut it myself," I replied.

He looked at me, then held up his finger, as if to say *just a minute.* Then he began to walk around, making sure no one cut themselves or anyone else. It took him so long to finish his visual rounds that I almost thought he'd taken a nap. But when he returned, he looked me up and down once more, taking in the enormity of my request.

"And . . . do you have a New York State license, miss?" he asked.

"Yes sir, I do," I replied.

"Shut up!" he sang, really loud.

I smiled. "No, really," I said. "I've been an art director for years." I was trying not to attract too much attention, because in jail, being an artist doesn't put you in very good standing.

"Yep, and I'm *Vidal Sassoon*," he teased.

"I've done work with them, too," I responded.

He waited to see if I had anything else to add, then let out a long sigh.

"Seriously," I said. "Can I use them?" I didn't feel well enough to argue or fill him in on my rock-star hair career, so I just looked up at him pathetically.

After waiting for a bit, probably hoping I'd go away, he smiled, revealing a crooked snaggletooth, which exposed a sweet underbite.

"Go ahead," he said finally, and he handed me a pair of dull scissors and a half chewed-up comb.

I grabbed a cape and covered myself with it, then sprayed my hair with a water bottle and went to work. The scissors were so blunt it was like trying to cut my hair with a butter knife, but I chopped and chewed away at it, while Mr. Night watched. By the time I set the scissors down, my hair was a completely different style—clean and cool—and I had everyone's attention.

I stood up, shaking off the remnants.

"That looks *good!*" Mr. Night drawled.

"Thanks for lettin' me hook it up," I said.

He waited a long time to respond. I didn't want to be rude and walk away, so I just stood there while he walked over to check a long haircut that someone had just gotten, and, after fixing a couple of layers on it, walked back rolling his eyes and shaking his head. Finally he looked at me again. "How long you in for?" he asked.

I shrugged. "Not sure. Not long, I hope."

"How long till your court date, then?"

"A couple of weeks at least."

I wasn't sure where he was going with this, why all the sudden interest. And then I found out.

"You wanna job, miss?" he asked.

"Here?" I said almost too quickly, with a nervous laugh.

"No, on fucking Fifth Avenue," he said, the growl in his voice bellowing to the end of the room (where things had quieted down), and then he laughed and coughed at the same time.

I looked at him, and then around the room, not sure what to say. I thought he was fucking with me. There was a scary-looking butch holding a pair of clippers that she'd turned off so she could hear our whole conversation. She was obviously the leader of this squad, because when she went back to work on her customer, the place started buzzing again.

"I don't think so," I said, finally. "I can't quite do a fade, you know?"

"You don't hafta," he said. "A lot of white and Spanish girls round here need hair doing. Plenty of other cuts to be done."

I still didn't answer. I really wasn't sure I wanted to get involved with all this.

"Twelve dollars a week in your commissary," he said, "and you get out of your cell block every day, and we have *good* coffee."

Twelve dollars a week was ludicrous, when on the outside I charged ten times that for one haircut, but getting out of my cell block every day was priceless. "I'll take it," I said. "When do I start?"

"Right now," he said.

He set me up with dull scissors, a weather-beaten blow-dryer, a new comb, and some half-eaten hairbrushes. As I took it all, I realized that maybe through this I could score something else, and I'd better get a handle on it while I was well enough.

The first chick to sit in my chair was a hot, tough-looking Latina femme named Jasmine who was carrying a dated, tattered, *Mademoiselle* magazine. She had earmarked a page with a haircut that I'd taught assistants how to do about ten years back. "Can you do this?" she asked, daring and confrontational, knowing everyone would be watching.

"With my eyes closed," I mumbled.

"What?"

"Yeah," I said. "I think I can manage that."

I shampooed her, giving her a scalp massage that almost made her close her eyes. I then walked her over to the chair, combed her hair out, and ran my fingers through her wet curls, feeling the flow and movement of her hair. Once again, with scissors in hand, I entered the zone and disappeared into my world of magical hair. A place where I was most comfortable and knew I could do no wrong. I started to cut. I was used to scissors so sharp they would split a hair if it fell on the blade, and these were the polar opposite. But I'd also cut Lana's hair into a shag with a pair of bushwhackers, and it had come out perfect. If it had a blade, I could make it perform to my liking.

There's one thing most women have in common, whether they're at Rikers Island or on Rodeo Drive: They all want to look beautiful and feel glamorous. Whether they'd been brutal, or brutalized in their lives, they all want to connect, look good, and be loved. When clients sit in my chair with wet hair, they're vulnerable. The mystique that a veil of hair creates is stripped away for that short time, and their insecurities are glaring back at them in the mirror. It's my job, like that of a therapist or a plastic surgeon, to absorb and help dissolve any negative perceptions, giving them emotional support while using my tools to beautify them and reassure them that all will be well after the cape comes off. I had the magic wand that could transform them into their fantasy and help them express themselves, and the "beauty" of it was, it was never permanent, so as their lifestyles changed, so could their hair. Just like when I found my groove in Detroit, cutting hair for the club kids, which then led me to the music scene, this was a place that I needed to work my magic so I could fit in. Cutting hair resulted in an immediate change, and shifted the way people saw themselves, and in turn looked at me. I'd never questioned my God-given talent for doing hair, that always came easy for me, and I hustled it to my advantage. I'd always known this, but never realized it as extensively as that day when I finished cutting Jasmine's hair and blew her out.

Mr. Night and the chicks all hawked me, and at the end, Mr. Night walked up, took a close look at Jasmine's new haircut, and roared, "Elias, you're gonna make a lot of girls *very* happy."

I would've never imagined that I would be doing hair in the beauty parlor at Rikers Island all those years ago when I was a young stylist looking to make my mark in the world of fashion. Haircutting had been what brought me to New York. My talent for it had been my best and only friend on many occasions. It allowed me to make money so I could pursue a music career, and gave me all the human interaction and client connections that I needed for every other facet of my life and future. Even in prison, hairdressing had given me a way to distinguish myself and shine.

I shrugged. "If you say so," I said, because this was easy. I could do this in my sleep.

Everyone watched as Jasmine gave me a huge smile while patting her hair as if it were her pet dog. Then she got up, placed two cigarettes at my station, and sashayed away.

Two other chicks got in line, and more after them. By the end of that day, I not only had cigarettes to last me, but also a Valium and a Klonopin to help with my current condition.

Girls waited for me daily, and I never again had to kiss a bull-dagger for drugs at Rikers. I got what I wanted, and to my heart's content: cigarettes, Valium, Xanax, and any treats that weren't served in the cafeteria, like cake and candy (gold to a junkie).

All the cute femmes wanted a Rayya Special so they could feel sexy while doing time. I also learned how to cut a kick-ass fade from watching a girl named Lefty—one of the meanest bull dykes on the island.

Lefty ranked at the top of the food chain at Rikers, and cut a fade better than any I'd seen coming out of the barbershop on East Houston Street. I'm not sure what she'd done on the outside to earn so much respect and credibility, but this chick was a quiet hard ass, and so butch that if you ran into her on the street you'd never know she was a dyke, you'd just think she was a badass thug of a dude.

Lefty had a dilemma though, a very sexy girlfriend named Violet, who wanted hair like Cindy Crawford's, which Lefty didn't have a clue how to cut. I saw her practice on a couple of other girls and fuck up their hair, but they were too scared to bitch, so they kept their mouths shut while eyeballing the haircuts stepping out of my chair.

Lefty had never spoken to me, but she always had her eye on me, trying to figure me out. She would glance over once in a while and grunt or snort when a girl raved about her hair as she was leaving my station. I never knew if the snort was a compliment or if it was done with disdain, so I ignored it and tried to avoid eye contact with her. (It's like the principle you use with a wild animal: If you look them straight in the eye, it means that you're challenging them, and that was *not* what I wanted to do with Lefty.) But one afternoon, I heard her call my name. I wasn't sure if she was talking to me, but I looked up, acknowledging that I'd heard her.

"Harley, come over here," she said.

Instantly, I was nervous. Worried I'd somehow done something to disrespect her, I stood perfectly still.

"Com'*ere* 'n let me *talk* to you, Loco," she said.

I walked over slowly, terrified.

"You need anything?" Lefty asked, when I finally arrived.

"Uh—like what?" I stuttered.

"Anything. Whateva'." She looked around straightening her workstation—anywhere but at me.

"Nah, I'm good," I said, finally. "But thanks." There was a long silence, and I didn't know whether to stay put or walk away. I looked at the floor, keeping my eyes fixed on the little piles of hair scattered all over it.

Finally, Lefty broke the silence. "Violet wants a shag," she blurted out. She was obviously uncomfortable, maybe even a bit confrontational; I doubted she was used to admitting any kind of weakness.

I stood silently, waiting for my cue. I was in a precarious position, because offering to cut Violet's hair could have insulted Lefty. Finally I spoke. "I'm sure it'd look great on her."

"You got time, ma?" she said. "You see how busy I am."

For a moment, I saw a vulnerable side to her—one that if crossed, could no doubt turn mighty ferocious. Lefty was certainly busy, but my line was always full as well.

"Yeah, no problem," I said. "I know you're slammed."

"Thanks for lookin' out," she said.

"No prob."

"Do it *real* nice yo."

I nodded and walked away.

Violet came in a little later, and I made sure I cleared my schedule for her. It was obvious how excited she was, as she'd brought a little cheering squad with her. Lefty kept busy while I cut Violet's hair, but still made time to walk by a couple of times and pretend to scrutinize my work, then declare it passable. After I finished blowing it out, I respectfully walked over to Lefty and asked her if she wanted to check it out. It was standard salon etiquette, but this earned so many brownie points that even Lefty could hardly contain a smile.

"That's alright, Harley," she said. "I'm sure it's fine."

And that was it. I now was right there with Lefty at the top of the heap at Rikers. The Latin Queens didn't look at me with disgust anymore, because their girlfriends raved about my haircutting talent, and when their girlfriends were happy, so were they. One of the girls offered to do my laundry. (I declined with humility; I just didn't feel right about it.) And no one took bread off my food tray anymore, though I sometimes gave it away to the new girls who seemed weak and scared. I felt good about it, too, because that's about as friendly as one gets in jail.

★

My court date was fast approaching, and I became more and more nervous. I'd established my position at Rikers, but upstate was a whole different dog-and-pony show. I talked to some of the girls who were repeat offenders, and they said that Rikers was a walk in the park in comparison to state prison. It was more violent and angry, and I really didn't know how I was going to manage. I'd kicked heroin while I was in jail and gradually stopped the other drugs, and I couldn't fathom a two- to four-year prison sentence at this point. I didn't think of myself as a criminal, but neither did many of the women I'd encountered. They were drug addicts like me who had lost their way in life and ended up here.

I'd acquired little things while I was there for those weeks—a couple of new T-shirts, some new sneakers, and a lot of candy—so the night before my court date, I piled everything together and told one of the girls that if I didn't come back, she should dispense them to the others. I showered that night and then laid out my clothes, because the bus from Rikers to the Manhattan court left very early. I was looking and feeling much better than the day I'd shown up in front of Judge Roberts a few weeks earlier.

I loved the city early in the morning; even as I sat in the bus looking out of barred windows, a shot of adrenaline ran through me as we crossed the Queensborough Bridge and headed down Second Avenue. We were driving toward the same tombs I'd visited so many times, but for the first time I was clearheaded. I was able to take it all in, and it wasn't pretty.

There were about twenty of us there, and they put us all in a holding cell to await sentencing. It was the first time I'd noticed that the color of the cell walls was blue. My state-appointed nebbish of a lawyer came and pulled me out of the main holding cell and into another one, so we could talk before my hearing.

After asking me exactly nothing about what had happened, he advised me to plead guilty, and strike a deal hoping to have the charges reduced, so I could do the least amount of time and let Judge Roberts sentence me to what he deemed fair. *What a load of bullshit*, I thought. *A quick close for him—no effort, and certainly no heart*. I wasn't guilty of this particular crime. I might have been guilty of many other things, many other times, but this time, this felony, I did not commit.

As he explained my plea and what I was to say in front of the judge, a sturdy woman in a gray suit walked in and asked if she could have a word with me. My lawyer departed. And Kathy Brooks stuck out her hand and introduced herself to me.

TWENTY-FOUR

KATHY BROOKS'S HAIR was blond and gray with a perm that was partially grown out, and she had a calloused exterior, unsmiling as she looked through the thick folder in her hand. My first take was that she was there to gloat. My second was that she was part of a tag team to convince me to plead guilty. But when she finally looked up and her eyes met mine, they were a watery blue that exuded so much kindness that I was disarmed.

"I'm here to help you, if you'd like," she said.

I was so used to being dehumanized, and had also spent so much time dehumanizing myself, that I'd forgotten there were people out there like her. "How?" I finally said.

"Are you a criminal, Rayya?"

I shook my head. "No."

"Are you a drug addict?"

"Yes." The moment the word came out of my mouth, I broke

301

down in tears. She had finally said what I had known for a long time: I was a drug addict.

"Do you want to get sober?" she asked.

"Yes." I wiped my nose on my sleeve.

"Are you sure?" She pulled a pack of tissues out of her bag, laid them on the table, and continued to watch me. I nodded and kept crying, unable to stop. I didn't care that a woman I'd never met was observing me. I was worn out, my rough exterior melting away.

When my tears finally slowed, she spoke. She was from a women's outreach program called Crossroads, she told me, which was an outpatient rehabilitation center for women who were incarcerated. They researched the women, looking deep into their histories, then tried to help the ones who truly wanted help. She had studied my case and knew about my drug history and all the jail time I'd done in the past. She was aware of the many rehab and detox centers I'd been to, the institutions and psych wards I'd checked myself into to try to stop the madness of the drugs that had taken over my life.

Incredibly, she listed all the jobs and career titles I'd had—and noted the fact that I'd traveled and taught others and was well respected within my field. When she started to list all the positives, I started to cry again. No one had ever done this for me.

"You've got to be able to take in the good stuff, too," she said, but I didn't feel worthy. I was a class A fuckup who didn't deserve anything nice being said about me.

But she was not there to condemn or judge me, she said. She was there to advocate for me. If I made a commitment to the outpatient program for one year, she thought I had a good chance of reducing the felony charge to a misdemeanor and getting out. She promised that if I finished and graduated from this program, I would be a free woman.

I would've agreed to anything at that moment in order not to have to go back to Rikers or to state prison. I didn't have anywhere to live, and there was no way they would release me without a place to stay, so Ms. Brooks made a few phone calls and found a place for me. It was called WPA (Women's Prison Association), and they agreed to house me for six months to give me a chance to get on my feet while attending the daily outpatient program. I was skeptical of a place called the Women's Prison Association, but had no choice at this point.

My attorney came back in, and Ms. Brooks told him what we were going to do. After looking through the files with her, he agreed.

We went in front of Judge Roberts, and after Ms. Brooks, who was now my lawyer, stated my case, the judge agreed, too. I was mandated to Crossroads for a one-year outpatient treatment program, to live at WPA for the first six months.

On the way out of the courtroom, I couldn't stop thanking Ms. Brooks for what she'd done. "That's my job," she said, completely matter-of-factly. She championed women on a daily basis, giving them a chance at a new life. For her, this was just another day.

But for me, it was a divine mercy.

A court-appointed officer left with me to escort me to the WPA. As we walked through Chinatown, he stopped at a food cart and bought me some fried rice and an egg roll. "Enjoy, Elias," he said, as we sat down on a bench in a park downtown to eat. The food tasted like a king's feast.

When we finished, we got into a taxi. "Where's WPA?" I asked, assuming that I was headed to Harlem or the far reaches of Brooklyn, Queens, or Long Island.

"Second Avenue and Seventh Street," he said to the driver and me at the same time.

My mouth fell open. "What? But that's my old address!"

"No, Elias," he said. "That's where WPA is."

I was confused: I still thought he must have it wrong. But sure enough, when we pulled up in front of the brownstone that was the Women's Prison Association, it was not only in the East Village—the place I most loved—but also literally right next door to my old building.

I was stunned. How, I thought—after living here for years—did I not know that this building was the Women's Prison Association? And how did I get so lucky?

When I walked into the WPA with the officer, I was amazed at how nice it was on the inside. A woman sat at the desk, signing inmates in and out. She smiled at me while I waited in the front room until a counselor came to show me around.

Including me, there were twelve of us living in the four-story building, which had wood staircases and hardwood floors. On the main floor was a huge cafeteria-style room with tables and a television. (There was a restaurant-type kitchen in the back.) The second floor had two large bedrooms—each bigger than most one-bedroom apartments I'd seen in New York—with three beds each. There was a bathroom with a few stalls and a shower. We continued up to the third floor, which is where I would be sharing a room with two other women. I was shocked at how much space I had and how clean and lovely the room was. Out the barred window, I looked directly onto Second Avenue. There was Kiev, one of my favorite Polish diners. I shook my head in happy disbelief.

The place was like a big dorm, except all twelve women who lived there were mandated by the court, otherwise looking to serve a prison sentence. I was the only one from the neighborhood (and I'm guessing the rest of them would've rather ended up in the Bronx or Harlem or Brooklyn or Queens . . . somewhere closer to home). We had a big, bossy house mamma, who also ran some group therapy—or, in this place called "airing our differences" (and there were many). A few staff counselors came in daily, along with a rotating staff of sober counselor wannabes, all of whom manned the front desk and made sure everything ran smoothly 24/7. We had to sign in and out and were accountable for every moment of every day; if one of us strayed, the rest of us were responsible for setting that person straight or telling a counselor. Drug tests were given randomly. If you failed, you went back to jail.

We were expected to make our beds and keep the place clean; there was a sheet of weekly rotating chores that none of us was able to dodge. As the new arrival, I was the lowest man on the totem pole, and next to my name was written "third floor bathroom." I kept to myself that night, watching everyone click around the dinner table. There was joking around and what looked like friendships, but I knew how these things went: everyone preyed on the weak, and people tested you to see how you'd fit in and what you had. I had nothing—just relief at being out of my five-by-eight cell and back in my old 'hood, eating chicken, rice, and beans that one of the girls had cooked. It tasted so good I could hardly contain myself.

In the morning I walked with the other girls to the Crossroads office, on Nineteenth Street, and after thanking Kathy Brooks again, I spoke to a counselor and was introduced to the women there. I would be there five days a week from ten in the morning till four in the afternoon. I would participate in multiple group therapies, have lunch there, then private counseling, and more group therapy, all courtesy of the state.

It was hardly my first time in rehab, so I knew what to expect and what was expected of me. In the past I had wanted to do well, and I *did*—I put forth a great effort—but I hated every bit of it. It takes hard, hard work to get well. But the results are worth it. I had the drive this time, and after six months I was ready to move out. I still had to do one year in the outpatient program, but I was free to live wherever I wanted.

Jan and I had been friendly again; after a month at WPA you got passes to leave on weekends, and I'd had lunch with her a few times. I always assured her I was doing well, and at one point I had professed my love for her. She had looked at me with love and pity and told me she was seeing a guy and was happy. Now, still seeing the guy but wanting to help, she introduced me to an older woman she knew who let me move into an unoccupied storefront in her brownstone in Carroll Gardens, Brooklyn.

It was a large, dirty space that hadn't been used for anything but storage, with a metal garage door that was rusted shut over the windows. The heat didn't work—and this was February in New York—but the woman let me stay there for free, and I needed free. A friend from AA helped me clean out a corner of it and put in a bed, a dresser, and a little space heater. I was still on welfare and doing haircuts at my clients' apartments for extra cash.

I kept going to my outpatient program, and soon I was able to move into an SRO (single room occupancy) on Third Street and Second Avenue, which was no bigger than a Rikers Island cell, but with a window looking out on Third Street. It was on the Hell's Angels block in the East Village, close to everything important— so, perfect for the time being. I shared a bathroom with the legendary Quentin Crisp, the author of a book about manners (who, interestingly, never put down the toilet seat or flushed). Though I was still in love with Jan and she loved someone else, I was doing okay: dating a bit, and making money. Life was filled with drama and excitement even though I was sober. I was finishing my Crossroads program, going to AA meetings, and enjoying all of it. I felt carefree for the first time in my life. And I loved the freedom of not being on drugs. New York felt crisp and fresh, and I found that I still had a breath of a dream left. I spent most of my downtime with other newly recovering friends, going to the movies quite a lot, one of the three Ms that got us through early sobriety: movies, meetings, and masturbation. I was also able to travel home for a weekend without being chained to methadone or dope, and sincerely reconnect with friends like Anita and Barry. My future felt bright.

TWENTY-FIVE

JAN FOUND OUT through friends that I was dating Tate—a woman I'd met in Detroit who she also knew—and went out of her mind with jealousy. She came over one morning and stood outside my window, calling up to me. I let her up and into my room, and she asked me if I really was seeing this woman. When I said yes, she started crying and proceeded to rip off my clothes and make love to me.

I knew I should stop her, but I thought I would never have her again—never smell her, or touch her beautiful face and body—and I was swooning with love and happiness. A few hours later, after feeding on each other's fear and angst, we decided to keep this a secret. We had no trust in this thing that was us, and we didn't want to lose our other anchors.

Still, we started a full-blown affair. I was juggling Jan and Tate.

Tate took me to California for my birthday. I'd never been to L.A. or San Francisco, and I was thrilled to be there. But naturally, in Los Angeles, we went out to a couple of girl bars, and as I watched Tate have some drinks and let loose—the soft tingle of alcohol looking better and better—I got more and more uptight and awkward. I hadn't been in this situation before, because my other friends knew how extreme my addiction was and kept their partying to a minimum around me. I made it through the night—practically carrying Tate to the car and up to our room at the Mondrian Hotel—but after getting her into bed, I realized how close I'd come to losing myself. I was still on legal probation and would be for three years. I was still looking for something to take me out of myself, and I didn't trust myself even around alcohol at this point. In the morning, I told Tate how close I'd come to drinking and asked if she could chill around me, and she agreed.

When I got back to New York, I spent a weekend with Jan, and we proclaimed our love once again. We promised each other that we would tell our companions the truth soon enough, so we could finally be together again. I was happy and giddy; I couldn't believe this was really happening, after all we'd been through. But as soon as the wonderful weekend ended, she left for a week with her boyfriend.

I should have been able to take it. I know it now, just as I knew it then. But the knowledge of what I *should* have done, *should* have felt, of the way I *should* have acted, had never gotten me much of anywhere. Instead, I felt a bone-crushing agony. With nothing in my system to dull the pain, the thought of Jan with this guy, after we'd just been together, was too much to bear.

I went out "for some air." Before I knew it, I was on my old block copping my favorite numbing solution, coke and heroin, the perfect speedball.

The only good part of this story, and that's an overstatement, is that I intended to get wasted just for the weekend and somehow I managed that, taking my last shot late Sunday night and starting fresh on Monday. I told my probation officer I was sick and put off my drug test for another week, knowing that if I drank enough water, the chemicals would wash out of my system. Meanwhile, I kept going to meetings and didn't share my slip-up with anyone. I even celebrated one year clean and spoke on my supposed anniversary at the East Village meeting, where people knew me and were proud of and happy for me.

I believed that I was fine, that it wasn't a big deal, so I never mentioned it to anyone. But the ache grew inside me, and I felt more and more like a fraud. It ate me up, knowing that I'd given in to the drugs and then lied about it. I was agitated, tense, and angry with myself and with everyone else. I kept seeing Jan in spite of feeling hurt around her all the time. It was the Lana syndrome all over again, and it was swallowing me up like the drugs once had.

My close friends and Tate could see that something was wrong, but I told everyone I was fine. Meanwhile, Tate moved from Detroit to New York, into an apartment on Bleecker Street, leaving her job and her family so she could be with me.

The affair with Jan was becoming increasingly painful, but as usual I couldn't stop myself. I was in love with someone who was with someone else, and I was seeing someone who was in love with me. I'd finished my program at Crossroads and now was on straight-up probation, having to go in once a month and drug test by pissing in a cup. All the chaos was sending me over the edge;

the only relief I felt was once a month, when I now allowed myself to go on a bender.

Somehow—probably the fear of going back to jail—I kept it under control. I would use right after I saw my probation officer, so that by the end of the month I was clean again for my next test. Tate suspected, so I finally told her what was going on. She wasn't shocked or disappointed, but actually relieved to know that she wasn't crazy—at least until I turned back into a mean junkie who used her and her money and destroyed anything that stood between me and my next fix.

Since I was managing my addiction, I was able to get a job at Recine's, one of New York City's hottest salons, written up in *Vogue* magazine. It was chic there to be a little fucked up, though of course no one knew just how fucked up I really was. I started making great money, and cutting the hair of some very big name models and actors; on my bender weekends, I'd slip into the bathroom downstairs in the employee's lounge and shoot speedballs, still managing my clients and work mode.

Soon enough, I was blowing off Tate more and more, unless I wanted to get high with her. I spent much clean time with Jan, so she never knew what was happening, and we were still "a secret." Finally, Tate had enough of my bullshit and moved back to Michigan to the cushy life she'd left behind—but not before she reached out to Jan, told her how fucked up I was, then slept with a friend of mine. Jan disappeared, and I couldn't blame her. I wanted to disappear, too. But as hard as I tried, I couldn't.

My probation officer stopped drug testing me, which was probably the worst thing that could've happened. I was completely alone, and my world had caved in.

I contemplated suicide, but I didn't know how to do it. I couldn't bear the thought of hanging myself, slitting my wrists, or shooting myself. It all seemed too scary and violent.

So I did what I knew best. I bought enough cocaine and heroin to kill a large buffalo and took it home.

That night, alone in my room, I tied on the tourniquet. Then, before I slipped in the magical cocktail that would allow me to escape one last time, I thought about my life.

For as long as I could remember, I had tried to do everything I could in order to feel something other than pain, insecurity, and humiliation, as well as wanting to do something to distinguish myself. I had always felt I was unique, and that I'd be one of the "chosen" ones—someone who could hone my talents and be accepted and admired and loved. But now, I realized, the legend existed only in my head. I was a regular girl, or worse; I was a junkie and a fuckup. And this was it, the end of the line; my beliefs and dreams were gone, and I saw only black in my future. Blackness and pain and suffering.

★

I tapped around for a vein (hoping to find one that still worked), got a register, and shot it all into my arm. After a second, I felt myself slipping into the bliss of ever after. *This is it*, I thought, *I don't have to do this anymore.*

TWENTY-SIX

KATIE COURIC'S VOICE was blaring sound bites over the air, and my ears hurt. Everything hurt. I must be in hell.

My eyes were resistant, but I managed to open them. And there I was, Katie's voice getting louder and louder, until I couldn't deny the truth. I had survived another overdose. Alone in my same little room, I was alive and breathing, heart beating and veins pulsating in the aftermath.

I looked around. Bloody, dirty needles littered the floor and the nightstand; blood spatters, from cleaning my syringes, adorned the walls like gruesome artwork. Dirty laundry, cigarette butts spilling out of ashtrays, half-empty beer bottles, a coffee mug with mold growing inside it, the remnants of some uneaten food rotting in a baggie . . . there it all was, just as I'd left it, the sun, forcing its way through the shade I'd closed tight the night before, shining bright light on all of it.

It *was* hell. Just not the hell I'd expected.

People talk about that moment of clarity for drug addicts. I sat there, in the pile of dirt and sweat I'd woken up in, and I cried. Unable to get up, unable even to turn off the hideous TV, I cried and cried, out of fear for myself and sadness at the mess I'd made of my life. There were no police, parents, rehabs, shrinks, friends, or lovers to tell me what was wrong with me. There was only a voice inside my head, first low and weak, but quickly gathering strength and conviction till it rumbled through me as powerfully as the call for heroin had the evening before. It said: *Rayya, you don't need to do this anymore. You can be free.*

To be fair, I had heard this voice before; in fact, it had saved my ass on many occasions. It had come to me in jail, and in rehab, and on the street when I'd been in tight spots, among other places. But this voice had always sounded nervous in the past: hyper and chaotic, just the way *I'd* always been. Now, though, it was clear as day, as clear as a bell. As clear as if I were sitting next to the tower of the Blue Mosque in Istanbul, where the voice coming out of there drowns out every other call for prayer in the whole city.

I could be free. The edge on life that I'd been looking for all along could be mine now: my work, my goal, my pride, and my dream. It seemed easy and obvious and like the only conceivable choice. All I had to do was be clean, that *was* the edge.

I rolled out of bed, feeling physically awful but mentally sound. I popped a Vicodin to take the edge off what I knew was going to be my final, monster kick. I would give myself seven days of Vicodin, and then I was done. No more inpatient detox. No more rehab, ever. It was now up to *me*.

I got out a garbage bag and started to clean. I cleaned my place until it was spotless, scrubbing the walls and floors and sink till they shone— as much as they could in that place, anyway. Then I showered and got dressed and went back to my East Village meeting, but this time, I was different: I *wanted* to be there, I raised my hand and said, "I'm Rayya Elias, I'm a drug addict and I have one day back." There was a huge applause, which made me break down and cry. People welcomed me back, extending themselves to me as they had previously, never once doubting my intention. But now, I didn't doubt them, either. This time, after seven years of trying to get sober, at the age of thirty-seven, I knew I would stay sober. I knew I could do it.

★

Once again I called my sister, Maya, and asked her to put me up for a while so I could get back on my feet. She said yes, and I moved to Detroit, clean and sober.

Anita called me one morning and told me that Lana—still far and away the greatest love of my life—had breast cancer. I was devastated. I asked Anita to ask her if I could visit her, and soon the answer came back: yes.

I continued going to New York once a month while living in Detroit, to work for some die-hard clients who were willing to maneuver their schedules and have me cut their hair in their homes. I crashed on my friend's couch in Tribeca, then made my rounds for a few days, hit my favorite meetings, then went back home. So the next time I was there, I went to see Lana. It was the same building I'd dropped her at on that Christmas night six years earlier, and the first time I'd seen her since then.

I buzzed and was let in. Her place was on the third floor. I couldn't believe how nervous I was. I put my hand up to my mouth and breathed into it to check and make sure my breath was fresh. I checked the wrapping on the dozen roses I'd brought to make sure it was perfect.

When she opened the door I was shocked. She looked terrible. She was too thin, yet puffy from all the medication—much the way my mom looked in the last few years of her life. I was depressed and frightened at the sight of her, but I also wanted to be there for her: We immediately hugged and held each other for a few moments.

"I brought these for you," I said, holding out the yellow roses. She was weak, but cracked a smile. I helped her back to the couch and sat with her.

"Can I do something for you?" I asked.

"You are, Rayya, just by being here." Her eyes were loving, and I could see that I was more frightened than she was. She'd already had a partial mastectomy but the cancer was spreading. She had no one except for her old hippy boyfriend, a wake-and-bake type who could hardly take care of himself, much less her. I was honored to be there and wanted to be present for every occasion whether good or bad. I knew that I'd be visiting often and would do whatever I could to help her. Being of service to her was my only motive and my biggest mission.

After that, I visited her every time I went to the city. She loved *All My Children*, just as my mom had, and loved ice cream (just like me), so I'd bring a pint of Ben and Jerry's Chunky Monkey over and we'd watch the soap together, and then we'd talk about life. One by one we healed all the old wounds. It felt cleansing and fantastic.

Eventually, of course, I moved back to New York, and then into the neighborhood that had taken me down. It wasn't my first choice, for obvious reasons, but after I looked at about twenty apartments in different areas of the city and they all sucked, I found the perfect place smack-dab in the heart of the 'hood that had chewed me up and spit me out. So I took it, a bright, sunny one-bedroom on the third floor of a small building on Eighth Street and Avenue C. There was a garden across the street, and my favorite mom-and-pop bakery on the corner that, along with managing to stay in business during the transformation and gentrification of the neighborhood, boasted the best *avena* (Puerto Rican oatmeal), egg sandwiches, pulled pork, and rice and beans you could ever hope for.

I loved the familiarity of the area, and I was finally well and present enough to enjoy it. And though the neighborhood was still a bit iffy, I could see that great strides had been taken to clean it up. Instead of bombed-out buildings, vandalized cars, and dope houses, now there were restaurants and bars and neighborhood gardens. As much as I had hated Rudy Giuliani's regime for pushing out all the artists, I couldn't help but appreciate the fact that it had also pushed out the drug dealers and criminals. Tompkins Square Park: taken over by riot squads not that many years ago, the place I called home when I was homeless, was now a playground for NYU students, Yuppies pushing baby carriages, (which still scares me), and, best of all, the Tompkins Square dog run. The empty lot that usually allowed the bag-in-a-bag drug dealers to thrive was now slated to become the site for a new police station (which made me uncomfortable given my history). There was a swanky Italian restaurant open in the space that had been the Lucky 7 building, and it was harder to get a reservation for a table than it had been to cop a bag of dope a few years earlier. The neighborhood felt safe and clean, and I was glad to return. I felt that we had hit the depths of hell together, me and the Lower East Side, and now it was coming back, just like me.

Lana was very ill by now—close to death. I took her in for chemotherapy treatments, but it was pretty obvious that she was dying. I felt helpless as they poked and prodded her, burnt her scalp with radiation, and generally sucked the spark out of her. It took strength and emotional perseverance on my part to continue showing up, but I felt like it was a debt I needed to pay, since the experience reminded me of my mother's illness and I felt I hadn't really been there for her, on any level (I'd been too fucked up). I was there for Lana, and proud of it. During that difficult time, we became like sisters.

She needed a bone marrow transplant. The night before the procedure, I showed up in her hospital suite with a movie and two pints of Chunky Monkey (which was the only thing she could stomach by then). After coaxing her to eat some, I put on the movie and lay on the couch.

"Rayya, will you come here and sit with me?" she asked, her voice very weak by then.

"Of course." I scooted a big chair close to her bed, sat down and looked at her for direction. She held her hand out for me to hold, so I did.

"Thank you," she whispered, and she fell asleep with my hand in hers, looking comfortable and at peace. After a while, I kissed her on the forehead and left, planning to return the next day, after work, in time to watch her wake up from the anesthesia.

But during work, I received a phone call from our friend Karen, who was there at the hospital. Lana's heart had arrested during the procedure. She was dead. I was in disbelief, I'd just been with her and it seemed that the doctors were hopeful. But she was gone, and that was it.

I spent the next couple of days in a fog of disbelief. After her funeral, I felt the fog morphing into depression. I was living in New York, not dating anyone, trying to make new friends. I was going to meetings and plucking away at life on a daily basis. But it was never easy for me when things weren't chaotic. I felt alternately depressed and restless.

My sister had invited me to tag along to the Middle East for summer vacation, and given my state of mind plus the fact that I hadn't been there since I was fourteen, I decided I'd go. I made plans to go to Paris for a week to visit a friend, and then meet my family in Lebanon for a month. I arrived in Beirut one week after Israeli prime minister Benjamin Netanyahu's defeat in the June 1999 elections.

Prime Minister Netanyahu blew up the power plant in Beirut. Things were in massive chaos, and there was no electricity or air-conditioning in the July heat. What's more, as I began to visit with my extended family outside Beirut, I realized how socially inept I was, especially when I wasn't in my own environment. My family members knew nothing about me. They didn't know I was gay, or a drug addict in recovery. Around them I was ashamed of who I was, and I found myself withdrawing and trying to fit into the confines of their social setting. The elaborate and dressy dinner parties that I remembered as a child were now casual, understated meals, with probing questions from relatives who I hardly knew.

"Why aren't you married?" people would ask. It always came down to this particular point for them to judge whether my happiness was at stake. My answer was always the same: "Because I don't want to take care of a man, I like being alone."

"You didn't want children?" some would pry further. "It's hard enough taking care of myself" I would say, "but I don't like kids anyways, only dogs." The looks I would get, though slightly different depending on whether it was a man or a woman asking the question, were usually peculiar, like something they couldn't wrap their heads around—a subject they'd have to ponder and process. Some would look at me like I was totally untrustworthy, or give me a pathetic, patronizing smile that made them look like they were sick to their stomachs. Only once in a while would I get a woman who would nod her head in agreement, eyes wide, and give me a conspiratorial smile. The relatives from my mom's side, who had lived in the affluent Hamra district of Beirut many years ago when we visited, had been pushed out to much less desirable neighborhoods. My cousins, who had once been modern, liberal, and open, had become conservative and fearful of life. During the Lebanese civil war, they'd been stuck living in their stairwell for three months, putting their lives on the line every time they went out for bread. I, on the other hand, had created my own imprisonment, and had single-handedly taken myself to the depths of misery. I had been to jail and to institutions, and even nearly dead a few times. I felt guilty for my emotional problems, since they were nothing compared to what these people had unwillingly gone through for the past twenty-five years.

★

But back home, I felt disconnected again. Lana was dead, which left a hole in my heart and my schedule, and the fear of being in New York without a purpose was registering. The reality of life and the emptiness of my daily routine left me searching. I poured my energy into my hair studio, which was in my apartment once again. My clients were happy to come and have their hair done, and referred their friends. My business was growing and the money was good. I was also secretly writing songs and playing a little bit of acoustic guitar. I didn't have any expectations for myself, nor did I feel like any of my prior dreams of becoming a rock star or a successful musician could ever come true: I just loved to escape through the music, and I used it anytime I felt uncomfortable or unfulfilled. It was my alternative to drugs. I also actively helped my friend Shelley Maple, who owned a small alternative record label called Jet Set, just so I could stay in the mix of the music business. We would go and see new bands that she was interested in signing or I'd style some of the bands for an album cover or video. Life just seemed to cruise by day in and day out, without any real drama or chaos. Had I known then what I know now, maybe I would've enjoyed it more. The calm and smooth ride of life, without all of the peaks and valleys, is a goal I constantly strive for now. But back then, it felt unnatural.

In the fall of 1999, I had a night that was a turning point and sealed the deal for me. I was confronted by all my demons, weaknesses, strengths, and spirituality, and there was no turning back. There I was again, on the Lower East Side with Shelley, watching some new band that I didn't really care about, and I found myself agitated. I didn't know why—I wasn't drinking like everyone else, but that was normal, and there was nothing different about that evening—but as the night went on, I became even more irritable and wanted to leave. Shelley kept asking if I was okay. "Of course I am," I snapped. "Why wouldn't I be?"

"You seem a little off," she said, looking at me. She knew me all too well, as she'd watched me struggle those last couple of years before I got sober.

"I'm just tired," I said. I couldn't stand the scrutiny or the bar any longer, so I split.

I started walking the same route as always to go back to Avenue C and Eighth Street. But this time, when I hit Avenue C, I kept going. I knew why, but I didn't want to believe it.

I told myself I wanted to walk off the feelings of agitation and discontent, that I wanted to walk around the projects for old time's sake, maybe to see if there were still people in the neighborhood who I recognized. *Of course I wasn't considering getting high, I wouldn't cop at this point,* I told myself. *No way I would even* think *about getting high! That wasn't even an option.* I fed myself these lies all the way down the block, wanting to believe them—right up until I saw Flaco, one of the drug dealers I used to cop from, standing on the corner, and I instantly knew I was full of shit. I wanted dope. I wanted a bag of dope more than just about anything. I wanted that warm, comfortable, secure feeling I had only ever gotten from drugs, even if only for a moment. I was angry that I had thrown away my dreams, and that *I* wasn't the one who was on stage performing for a possible record deal. Torn between the necessity to maintain this life that I'd worked so hard to achieve and the desire to escape from it, I walked up to Flaco.

"Hey, what's up yo!" I said.

"Holy shit, mommy!" he said, raising his eyebrows. "Look atchu! You look good. You got big."

On the street, it's the same as in jail: the bigger you are, the more respect you get, because it's obvious you're not using drugs.

Still, it wasn't what I wanted to hear. "Ah, you're killin' me with that shit, Flaco," I said.

"No, really, mommy! You look real good. You been locked up?"

"Nah. Just haven't been around. You got anything?"

He stood and looked me up and down for what seemed like an eternity. Finally he said, "Rays. You know I always had your back, right?"

I nodded. "Yeah, man. So let me get one and one."

He looked around, motioned to his partner across the street, and then kicked at the pavement. "I don't think so, mommy. Not tonight."

I was stunned. "What the fuck man, why not?" I said. "Let me get one C and one D. Come on. I got the cash."

But he shook his head. "I said no, ma. Walk away." He looked extremely uncomfortable. "If you still want it tomorrow," he added, "you know I'll be here."

I couldn't believe he wouldn't serve me. I was furious, which made me want the drugs even more. "Fuckin' ay, Flaco!" I said. "C'mon! Do me a solid."

"That's the point baby, I *am,*" he said. "Now bounce."

I squinted, glaring at him. "Yo, fuck you, man. I'll just go down the block."

He shrugged, "They don't know you. And you're lookin' like five-o right now."

I stomped away in disbelief, cussing him out. He thought that I looked like a cop? I stormed up Avenue D, certain that when I showed those boys my old track marks they would sell me whatever I wanted. It was insulting to have a drug dealer refuse to serve me, and I was more angry and determined now. I crossed the street and walked up a couple of blocks to find some young boys grouped together. When I started to approach, a couple of them quickly walked away. *What the hell?* I thought, but I kept calm and approached the one who'd stayed. "Give me one and one," I said.

The kid looked at me like I was crazy. For a moment I thought the lingo for coke and dope had changed on the street.

"C and D?" I said.

He continued to look puzzled, "I don't know what you're talkin' about" he said, and there was an angry edge to his voice.

"Look man," I said, exasperated now. "I got track marks. I ain't a cop." I started pulling up my sleeves to look for the track marks that had haunted my arms for so many years. But even they had faded just enough and couldn't be seen in the darkness of the night.

One of the other boys came up quickly now. "Yo, put that shit away," he said.

I shook my head. "No, really, I got tracks, see? Right here."

"I don't wanna see shit!" he spat. "Now fucking move out, before I kick your ass."

I pulled down my sleeve, remembering the time I had been beat up, almost to death. I scampered down the street, hating Flaco and those new boys, unable to think of where I could find another dope spot. Couldn't they tell I wasn't a cop? "They're so fucking stupid," I muttered. Stupid and *young*.

As I walked, I heard a van roll up beside me, and when I looked over, I realized it was an undercover police van. It slowed to a crawl, and then the window rolled down.

"Hey Elias," someone said.

I looked over my shoulder. An undercover cop whose narc squad had busted me several times in the past was hanging out the window. "What are you doing out here this time of night?" he asked.

I stood still a second. Then said, "Just going home, officer."

"I hope so." He motioned with his fingers that he had both his eyes on me. Then he yelled, "Go home, Elias!"

"Yes sir," I replied.

"I don't want to see you out here again."

"Yes sir," I said again.

They watched me turn the corner. Then they sped away in the van.

My heart beat so hard that my chest ached as I raced down the street. I stopped for a moment and leaned against a building on Seventh Street just to catch my breath. *What the fuck just happened to me, was I crazy?* I thought. And as strong as the feelings to use were a few moments before, the realization that I'd almost given up everything I'd worked so hard for hit me like a ferocious beast. I collected myself and continued walking down the block. I passed another group of boys who were obviously dealing drugs, and they called out to me trying to serve me, "What you need, baby? We got C and D, C and D, c'mon!"

"I'm good," I said, feeling the warmth and wetness of my tears and the fierce need to get to the safety of home, "I'm good." I'd had a weak moment of absolute insanity, but that was it, it was over. I kept walking, hardly able to breathe, and completely nauseated, but I did it, and then I was there.

I walked in the door. I was sweating and freaked out.

I collapsed in the bathroom, crying and trembling at the thought of what had almost just happened. I lay on the floor, feeling the coolness of the tile on my face, and then knelt and threw up in the toilet. When my stomach was empty, I lay back down on the floor for a while, until I calmed down.

Then, slowly, I pulled myself up. I turned on the water, then stripped and threw my clothes in the hamper. I climbed into the tub and let the hot water wash over me. When I was good and waterlogged, I got out, dried off, and went to bed. Since I was a kid, the thought of God had always confused me. Now, it all finally made sense, God was just a collective of something bigger than me, that could take the hit for me when I couldn't take it for myself. In one moment of weakness, I had almost slipped down the steps to my old life again, but collectively, Flaco, those boys, and that cop had helped me, just long enough for me to help myself. The gratitude that I felt for the divine intervention that enabled me to reach the safety of my bed that night is overwhelming to this day. This was the end and the beginning, the beginning and the end. Even though I didn't get high that night, I felt hungover from the intensity and pain of that experience, thinking of what could have happened, and all that had come before, but I'm one of the lucky ones, I've never gotten the urge to use since that night. I've realized that the edge of living without substance is razor sharp and cuts deeper than everything else. The experience is more radical than any high I've ever known. Yes, life can sometimes be dull and mundane, but most of the time, it's more interesting and exciting than anything I experienced when I simply plunged into it without thinking.

EPILOGUE

RAYYA ELIAS HAS been clean since August 8, 1997. She currently resides in New York City and Little York, New Jersey. She's a writer, musician, hairdresser, filmmaker, and also sells real estate to make some extra scratch.

ACKNOWLEDGMENTS

THIS BOOK IS the story of my life. I have re-created all situations and conversations to the best of my ability. My life was so chaotic that I've had to edit some timelines so they would help the narrative flow. It was hard for me to remember everything in its exact order, so please forgive me. Some characters' names have been changed to protect their privacy—those whose names were not changed generously agreed to let me use their real ones. One of my favorite sayings has always been "the truth has legs, it always stands." This is my truth, and it may not be pretty, but I own it.

★

First and foremost, I'd like to thank my mom and dad for putting up with all my crap for so many years. Their patience is a true testament of their love and loyalty. They taught me a sense of family and gave me an anchor called home. I don't feel as though I'll ever deserve the kindness they showed me. I miss them.

My sister Maya saved my life more times than I can count. She was on my side when everyone else had given up on me, and for that I am eternally grateful; I love you so much. I want to thank her husband, Farid (one of the kindest men I've ever known), for never judging me and always making me feel like I was one of his own. Her three kids are my dearest family. My nephew Sami Jano—for taking the music to the next level, you're a constant inspiration to me. You're my personal art department and my ideas guy. My niece Nyla Jano—talented designer and bright-eyed little pup, I want to constantly cuddle you. My nephew James Jano (I will forever call you Jimi)—an amazing drummer; my great thinker, humble, fair, and kind. All three of you live under my skin. When I see myself through your eyes, I look really good.

The rest of my family—Somay (your depth humbles me), Fares, Bassam, Maggie, Thomas, Keyla, Jacob, Anthony, and Frankie—I love you.

I want to thank Tiny (who is now gone) and Ricky, whose fuzzy little face kept me sane while I was working on this book. Sometimes the only words I would speak all day were "come," "sit," "stay," or "let's go for a walk."

My dear friends who have shown me moral support throughout the years, my heart is full of gratitude to you. GiGi Madl—for your love and encouragement throughout my creative endeavors. For giving me time and space to put my thoughts together in short stories all those years ago. Also for teaching me how to sell real estate in New York City—we rocked some great deals together.

A very special thanks to my oldest friend, the unforgettable Kory Clarke.

Anita Schwartz (my dearest Anita)—for always staying, even when I didn't deserve it.

Shawn Felker—thank you for helping me keep my sanity in real estate so I could afford to work on this book for three and a half years. Barb Morrison—for being my football buddy and my amazing music producer (even if you do hate the Giants). It was love from the moment you nicknamed me Pickle.

Stacey Weinberg—for always treating me (and making me feel) like a rock star. Lisa Ross—for your loyalty, love, support, and gorgeous artwork. Steve Loeb—for all the music equipment from Green Street Studios and the great caviar and love. Barry Harper and Irene Onikle—don't know if I'd be here without you. Jo Gould, Shelley Maple, and Tod Ashley—for being so kind to me near the end.

Last but certainly not least, I thank you, Elizabeth Gilbert, my dear friend, for seeing *me* through all of my character flaws and defects. For loving me and recognizing my potential. You are a rare gem and there will never be enough words to express the love and gratitude that I have for you. I am humbled by your generosity. You gave me not only a place to write, but a place I call home. And finally, Jusband, you know who you are, the best parts of my family into one cool papa dude. MLY so much.

Thank you to my early readers, who braved the first few drafts and always seemed excited, even though you were probably bored to death. You guys have encouraged me and believed in me from the beginning: Chriss Coats, Sammy Biro, Shelley Maple, Inge De Taeye, Sherrisse Alvarez, Tod Ashley, and Carey Lovelace (for your wonderful feedback). And of course you, Lizzy.

I'd like to thank Cathi Hanauer for helping me edit this into a manageable manuscript.

On a different note, I'd like to thank Sarah Chalfant for believing in me, standing behind me, and giving me a forever home at Wylie. Jin Auh for making sure I was taken care of in New York with all of my questions, and the rest of the Wylie team for their hard work.

Thank you Paul Slovak (for your support), and for picking up the pieces, and Clare Ferraro and the rest of the team at Viking for finding a place for this book.

I'm especially grateful for Amber Qureshi, my editor, for understanding me and being so passionate about this book. "She just gets it."

Thanks Kyle Davis for sorting me out.

Thank you Lindsay Prevette for getting onboard.

To Alexandra Pringle of Bloomsbury UK, thank you for connecting with my story; this makes me so happy.

A special thanks to my clients over the past years—Shelby, Lori, Kara, Colleen, Kim and Rob, Matt, Roemer, and many more. Your love and support has allowed me to chase my dreams, and there's nothing better than that.

Thank you Janet Waddell for always keeping a chair empty for me to use.

Thank you to Pattie Canova, who told me I should write (she's a psychic).

For helping me with my past film endeavors, I'd like to thank Steve Gallagher (*Filmmaker* magazine), Roger Bordeaux, Simon MacArthur, Kris Kazor, Lucy Sexton, Lori E. Seid, Sue Ann

Horan, Lauren Ayles, and Tracey McKnight (you've always been in my corner). Thank you to all the crew members and actors that made the films possible.

Lastly, and very important, I have to thank the city of New York for being there for me. You're in my blood and I couldn't have become the Rayya who I now love without you. You have given, taken, compromised, and given back everything I'd always hoped for. You are my greatest lover, my dearest friend, my most respected enemy, and you will always be my muse.

A special thanks to all of the anonymous people that have passed through my life, whether in jail, on the streets, in detox and rehabs, therapists (especially Sonya), and social workers. The rooms are the best gig in town; I'm blessed to be on the other side.

MUSIC LINKS

THERE ARE SIX tracks of my own music that I like to think of as a
soundtrack to this book. They can be downloaded at my website,
www.rayyaelias.com.

I found the recording of the last song, "Nothing Matters,"
in an archive from a studio session with my band circa 1985/86,
so please forgive the sound quality, as it will surely differ from
the others. The five other tracks are from different times in
my life, all very near and dear to me. I started writing these
songs slowly, when I got sober. Then in 2002, a friend and
incredible music producer, Barb Morrison, helped me bring
them to life.

Music has always been my favorite means of communication in
life; it has helped me to breathe, and it has allowed me to connect
to the rest of the world. I hope you enjoy these songs as much as
I've cherished making them.

"Fever" (Rayya Elias, produced by Barb Morrison, additional production Charles Nieland; engineered by Tommy Mokas)

"Miss You" (Rayya Elias, produced by Barb Morrison, additional production Charles Nieland; engineered by Tommy Mokas)

"Loaded Gun" (Rayya Elias, produced by Barb Morrison, additional production Charles Nieland; engineered by Tommy Mokas)

"Star" (Elias/Morrison/Nieland, produced by Barb Morrison, additional production Charles Nieland; engineered by Tommy Mokas)

"Myself Without You" (Rayya Elias, produced by Barb Morrison, additional production Charles Nieland; engineered by Tommy Mokas)

"Nothing Matters" (Rayya Elias 1985–86)

All drums except "Nothing Matters" by James Jano.

Extra keyboards and effects on "Myself Without You" by Sami Jano

All songs except "Nothing Matters" mixed at Casa Nova Studios.